Business Ethics

A Global & Managerial Perspective

Business Ethics:

A Global & Managerial Perspective

David J. Fritzsche
Penn State Great Valley

McGraw-Hill
Irwin

Boston   Burr Ridge, IL   Dubuque, IA   Madison, WI   New York
San Francisco   St. Louis   Bangkok   Bogotá   Caracas   Kuala Lumpur
Lisbon   London   Madrid   Mexico City   Milan   Montreal   New Delhi
Santiago   Seoul   Singapore   Sydney   Taipei   Toronto

The *McGraw·Hill* Companies

 **McGraw-Hill Irwin**

BUSINESS ETHICS: A GLOBAL AND MANAGERIAL PERSPECTIVE
Published by McGraw-Hill/Irwin, a business unit of The McGraw-Hill Companies, Inc.,
1221 Avenue of the Americas, New York, NY, 10020. Copyright © 2005, 1997 by The
McGraw-Hill Companies, Inc. All rights reserved. No part of this publication may be
reproduced or distributed in any form or by any means, or stored in a database or retrieval
system, without the prior written consent of The McGraw-Hill Companies, Inc., including,
but not limited to, in any network or other electronic storage or transmission, or broadcast
for distance learning.

Some ancillaries, including electronic and print components, may not be available to
customers outside the United States.

This book is printed on acid-free paper.

1 2 3 4 5 6 7 8 9 0 DOC/DOC 0 9 8 7 6 5 4

ISBN 0-07-249690-8

Vice president and editor-in-chief: *Robin J. Zwettler*
Editorial director: *John E. Biernat*
Senior sponsoring editor: *Andy Winston*
Editorial assistant: *Emily Yim*
Marketing manager: *Lisa Nicks*
Project manager: *Kristin Puscas*
Production supervisor: *Gina Hangos*
Designer: *Mary E. Kazak*
Photo research coordinator: *Kathy Shive*
Supplement producer: *Lynn M. Bluhm*
Senior digital content specialist: *Brian Nacik*
Cover design: *Jenny El-Shamy*
Typeface: *10/12 Times New Roman*
Compositor: *Carlisle Communications, Ltd.*
Printer: *R. R. Donnelley*

Library of Congress Cataloging-in-Publication Data

Fritzsche, David J.
    Business ethics : a global and managerial perspective / David J. Fritzsche.--2nd ed.
       p. cm.
    Includes bibliographical references and index.
    ISBN 0-07-249690-8 (alk. paper)
    1. Business ethics. I. Title.
  HF5387.F75 2005
  174'.4--dc22   2003068850

www.mhhe.com

To My Wife, Nan, and
To My Daughters, Sonja and Tanya.

Business Ethics: A Global and Managerial Perspective

Preface

Business Ethics: A Global and Managerial Perspective was written to help the business student and/or business practitioner acquire the tools needed to evaluate the ethical dimension of business decisions. It is not meant to serve as a documentary on the latest transgressions by business. The business press does that job quite nicely. The material in the book was carefully selected to provide a balanced coverage of five major types of ethical issues faced by business practitioners. Examples span a broad time frame set in a number of different countries. Numerous examples of both ethical and unethical behavior are included. Material from the business press can be used effectively to supplement the text examples. As this edition went to press, stories on Enron, Tyco, WorldCom, and others would be of interest. Their outcomes are still to be written. Positive stories such as Maulden Mills should also be included.

This book grew out of a series of published and unpublished manuscripts on business ethics that the author has written over the past 20 years. It includes new material not presented elsewhere and some conceptual development. It should be of interest to the professor who wants to incorporate ethics into business and society courses and business policy/strategy courses. The text is also suitable for management development courses covering business ethics or as one of the texts for a business ethics course. For those who do not use text, this book can serve as a valuable supplement to a readings packet.

Business Ethics: A Global and Managerial Perspective was written because the current offerings on business ethics omit several important areas with which students and practitioners should become familiar. They need to understand the multitude of influences managers encounter when making decisions containing an ethical dimension. This develops an awareness of the different forces driving decisions. Chapter Four, which focuses on the ethical dimension of decisions, describes the decision process via a model that incorporates most elements found in ethics models extant in the literature. An understanding of the decision process should provide insight into opportunities that exist for influencing the ethical dimension of a decision.

There is a rapidly growing body of empirical literature that documents ethical reality in the business world. Students and practitioners need to learn how things actually work, not just how they should work. Chapter Five reviews the empirical business ethics literature. In an attempt to make the chapter readable and interesting without distorting the findings, much of the research jargon has been filtered out. A summary is provided.

Only a few books on business ethics contain some type of decision support model. Chapter Six of this book contains the most comprehensive model to date and provides a checklist to follow when evaluating the ethical dimension of decision alternatives. The model does not provide answers but rather a series of logical steps for the decision maker to follow to generate answers.

This book emphasizes the integrative social contracts approach to business ethics. At this time, it appears to offer the best fit between theory and practice. However, for those who prefer another approach, the integrative social contracts dimension can be de-emphasized. Chapter Three contains a compact treatment of consequentialist and nonconsequentialist ethical principles. These principles are offered as guidelines that may be used for developing community norms. One could easily focus on them as primary ethical principles by omitting the latter section discussing integrative social contracts.

Suggestions for Use

Students would likely get more from *Business Ethics: A Global and Managerial Perspective* when it is used as a module in a course. The chapters build on each other; thus, results should be better when the chapters are used consecutively rather than integrated with other material in a course. The only exception may be a business ethics course in which several sources might be used concurrently to develop more depth.

This book would make a valuable supplement to the main text used for business and society courses as well as for business policy/strategy courses. When used in a business and society course, it could be introduced following the material on the business environment and corporate social responsibility. This placement would make the material available for use in the remainder of the course.

For a policy/strategy course, *Business Ethics: A Global and Managerial Perspective* would work well if used after the basic mission, goals, and strategy groundwork have been introduced. It also fits nicely after culture has been covered. It is best to cover the ethics material before beginning case analysis so that students can incorporate the ethical dimension into their analysis. If one is using a simulation, the ethics material should be covered early in the simulation experience for the same reasons.

In business ethics courses, this textbook likely will be paired with other ethics texts. Here, it may be advisable to integrate the chapters with the other material. Alternatively, one can use this textbook with a casebook that contains substantive cases or a series of readings. This book would be covered first followed by case analysis using the approach suggested in the casebook. A variant of this procedure would be to assign actual companies instead of cases. Student teams could research the ethical problems the firms have experienced and provide recommendations on how they might have been solved and on how future problems could be prevented. The results could be shared via class presentations.

When used in an executive development course, *Business Ethics: A Global and Managerial Perspective* should provide all that is needed for a short, concise course on business ethics. The cases can be used as good discussion vehicles augmented by actual executive war stories.

Structure of the Book

This book is structured to provide a logical flow. It begins with a description of what business ethics entails. It then explains why business ethics is important, describes criteria to use in making a decision, discusses the process used in making a decision, examines what has been discovered concerning ethics in the business world, provides a guide for making a decision, and offers some examples of firms' decisions that can be considered successful and not successful. In the latter cases, the guide is used to analyze the decisions in question.

Chapter One opens with examples of actual ethical problems faced by specific businesses and then turns to developing a typology of ethical issues faced by the business world. Chapter Two focuses on the importance of ethics in business with an emphasis on the role of trust. Chapter Three discusses moral standards that can be used to evaluate the ethical dimension of decisions and integrated social contracts theory. Based on the research and subsequent theory development, Chapter Four presents a model of the decision process with an emphasis on the ethical dimension. Chapter Five summarizes what has been learned about business ethics through empirical research. Chapter Six offers a decision support model designed to assist managers in evaluating the ethical dimension of decision alternatives. Finally, Chapter Seven describes the ethical experiences of several companies, some exemplary and others wanting.

There are twenty original short cases at the end of the book; twelve of them are set in countries outside the United States. The cases cover a variety of ethical issues. Some describe blatantly unethical behavior, whereas others describe situations that are in the murky gray area.

The cases can be used on a selective basis with each chapter or after the seven chapters have been covered and students have become familiar with the tools needed to evaluate the ethical dimension of decision alternatives. The cases also may be assigned to teams tasked with researching the cases and presenting them to the class. Information for some cases will be much easier to find than for others. Allowances must be made for this when evaluating the research output of a team.

Nearly all of the examples and cases in this text are taken from actual business experiences. Extensive citations are provided at the end of each chapter so the reader can easily locate the sources for a more extensive examination or for checking for developments since the publication of this book. A number of the examples are from outside the United States. Since all business is now becoming international business, students and practitioners need to extend their thinking beyond their own borders.

Business Ethics: A Global and Managerial Perspective is accompanied by an *Instructor's Manual* that contains teaching notes and suggested answers for the twenty short cases at the end of the book, as well as suggested answers for the discussion questions at the end of each chapter.

Acknowledgments

The author is indebted to all who labored in this area. This book is based on theory and research developed by a myriad of individuals over the years, many of whom are cited. Others who contributed indirectly through earlier work may have escaped recognition. Apologies are in order for all unrecognized contributions and for omissions.

The author would also like to acknowledge the valuable contributions of the members of the International Association for Business and Society and the Social Issues in Management Division of the Academy of Management via presentations and personal and public discussions. The helpful comments of the following reviewers, whose contributions significantly strengthened the manuscript, are also much appreciated:

Brad Brown
University of Virginia

Gordon Clanton
San Diego State University

Diane Dodd-McCue
University of Virginia

Dr. Kenneth G. Ferguson
East Carolina University

Maria George
University of Missouri–St. Louis

John P. Loveland
New Mexico State University

Mary D. Maury
St. John's University

David P. Schmidt
Fairfield University

John F. Steiner
*California State University,
   Los Angeles*

Jim Weber
Duquesne University

Finally, I would like to thank my wife Nan who provided much moral support as well as invaluable technical support during the final phases of the manuscript preparation. Responsibility for any errors or omissions in content or documentation rests solely with the author. As Harry Truman said, "The buck stops here." Corrections from readers are most welcome.

David J. Fritzsche

Business Ethics

A Global & Managerial Perspective

Business Ethics

A Global & Managerial Perspective

Chapter 1

Business Ethics: A Global Framework

Business involves economic relationships among many groups of people known as stakeholders: customers, employees, stockholders, suppliers, competitors, governments, and communities. Today's manager must consider all of the firm's stakeholders, not just the firm's stockholders. These stakeholders are likely to be located in multiple countries rather than in a single country as has been the case for most of history. Customers, suppliers, competitors, employees, and even stockholders frequently hail from around the globe. Globalization of the business environment has created an increasingly complex set of relationships for the modern business manager.

The complexity increases when stakeholders have conflicting claims, which is often the case. For example, the question of whether to continue production in an existing plant or to contract the work out to a firm in another country involves numerous stakeholders. Stockholders are looking for the greatest return on their investment. Local employees want to keep their jobs. Prospective employees in the foreign country want to obtain jobs. The local community wants to protect its tax base, and the government is concerned with the welfare of its citizens. The foreign community wants to enhance its tax base, and so forth. Regardless of the decision a manager makes, some stakeholders will gain at others' expense.

In this book, we will examine ethical issues within these complex business relationships—those issues that involve moral relationships among people. Some problems do not involve moral relationships and thus do not contain ethical dimensions. For example, the decision to introduce a new product in the Eastern region of the United States or in the European Union prior to full national or world distribution is not likely to raise an ethical issue. However, many decisions do raise ethical concerns. Some decision makers quietly go about their business adhering to high ethical standards. Others do not and occasionally make headlines: for example, Enron, Tyco, and Worldcom.

1

The following five cases provide examples of actual ethical issues addressed by major firms. Consider several questions as you read each case:

1. How would you describe the ethical issue?
2. What conditions created the issue?
3. How would you have handled the ethical dilemma?
4. In your opinion, how well did the firm handle the dilemma?
5. What could be done to prevent the issue from recurring?

Actual Experiences

French Frigates Sold to Taiwan

Thompson-CSF, a large state-owned French defense contractor, began negotiations in 1988 in a bid to sell six new 3,500-ton frigates to Taiwan for about $2.8 billion.[1] The French Foreign Ministry initially opposed the sale, believing it would harm relations between France and the Chinese government. France's prime minister, Roland Dumas, personally opposed the sale.[2]

Dumas was a Resistance fighter during World War II. After the war, he became a lawyer and moved up the political ranks to become a member of President Francois Mitterand's inner circle and served as his foreign minister during the years 1984 to 1995. Following his service as foreign minister, he was appointed to head the highest court in the land.[3]

Christine Deviers-Joncour, a former model, became Dumas's mistress in the late 1980s. They appeared together in many fashionable spots inside and outside of the country even though they were both married to others at the time.[4] In 1989 Dumas suggested that Elf Aquitaine, the largest company in France, hire Deviers-Joncour as a "public relations consultant" (quotation marks in original).[5] Elf Aquitaine was a state-owned French oil company started by Charles de Gaulle after World War II.

In 1990 Alfred Sirven, Elf's director of general affairs and number two man, offered the company's services as an agent to assist Thompson-CSF with its frigate sale by using Elf's extensive network of contacts.[6] After reaching an agreement with Thompson-CSF, Sirven initiated contacts with the Chinese and assigned Deviers-Joncour to lobby Dumas. Deviers-Joncour was on a retainer of Fr 50,000 per month (approximately U.S. $8,300), and she was provided with a credit card on which she charged about Fr 200,000 a month (approximately $33,000).[7] These expenses were covered by a slush fund that Sirven controlled.

Dumas began to benefit from this relationship. Deviers-Joncour gave him a dozen antique Greek statues worth Fr 274,000 and a pair of hand-crafted boots from Berluti worth Fr 11,000.[8] Elf funded a tony $2.8 million apartment on the Left Bank for their meetings and covered meals worth up to $42,000 a month at Le Pichet on the Seine.[9]

Dumas's resistance to the frigate sale waned, and in 1991 he dropped his objections. Elf's "influence" in China also began to yield results as China's objections diminished, and in August 1991 the sale went through.[10] For her part Deviers-Joncour received Fr 14 million in 1991 and Fr 45 million in 1992 via a Swiss bank account. Total "retro-commissions" (quotation marks in original), as kickbacks are known in France, amounted to $500 million or about one-quarter of the purchase price of the frigates according to Dumas.[11]

In 1996 French magistrate Eva Joly initiated an investigation of Elf Aquitaine during Loik Le Floc-Prigent's tenure as chief executive from 1989 to 1993. In what became known as "L'affaire Elf" (quotation marks in original), she discovered a series of payoffs via Swiss bank accounts to political figures in Africa, France, and Germany.[12] As the investigation was getting closer to Sirven in 1997, he withdrew Fr 150 million from a series of bank accounts and fled the country.[13]

Sirven was caught and brought back to France in 2001. In May of that year, Dumas, Deviers-Joncour, Le Floch-Prigent, and Sirven were convicted on corruption charges. All were levied significant fines and given prison terms.[14] Details of the scandal were provided in an autobiography that Deviers-Joncour wrote entitled *La Putain de la Republique* (*The Whore of the Republic*).[15] This case may have been only the tip of the iceberg because prior to being returned to France, Sirven bragged that he knew enough dirt to "bring down the republic 20 times over."[16] In 1999 Elf Aquitaine was privatized and taken over by Totalfina, a French-Belgian oil group.

Tylenol Tampering

On Thursday, September 30, 1982, reports first began to filter into the headquarters of Johnson & Johnson that people had died in Chicago after taking Extra-Strength Tylenol capsules laced with cyanide.[17] The product, manufactured by McNeil Consumer Products Company, a subsidiary of Johnson & Johnson, held 35 percent of the analgesic market and accounted for approximately 7 percent of Johnson & Johnson's total sales and 15 to 20 percent of its profits.

An initial investigation by management disclosed that cyanide is used in testing the quality of raw materials at the production site, a fact Johnson & Johnson first denied due to an internal communication glitch, but then announced to the press the following morning. By the end of the first day, management was convinced that the cyanide contamination did not occur at its Fort Washington, Pennsylvania, plant. However, it could not take a chance, so it recalled all 93,000 bottles produced in the lot from which the poisonings occurred. All advertising for Tylenol was suspended.

The following morning, management learned that a sixth victim of the poisoning had taken a capsule from a bottle that was manufactured in a lot at its Round Rock, Texas, plant. This supported the belief that the tampering had taken place in Chicago and not at a Johnson & Johnson plant. It would have been almost impossible to contaminate Tylenol at both plants.

Johnson & Johnson Chairman and Chief Executive Officer James E. Burke decided to take personal charge of the company's response to the Tylenol crisis. On Monday, October 4, he traveled to Washington to meet with the FBI and the FDA. He was considering recalling all Extra-Strength Tylenol capsules but was advised against such action by both agencies. "The FBI didn't want us to do it," explained Burke, "because it would say to whomever did this, 'Hey, I'm winning, I can bring a major corporation to its knees.' And the FDA argued it might cause more public anxiety than it would relieve."[18] However, the next day, after a strychnine poisoning involving Tylenol in California, the FDA agreed with Burke that all Tylenol capsules had to be recalled.

The recall involved 32 million bottles of Tylenol capsules worth over $100 million in retail sales. The recall was initiated with advertisements to consumers offering to exchange capsules for tablets. Thousands of letters were sent to the trade magazines, and statements were made to the media in an effort to recover all outstanding Tylenol capsules. Burke appeared on major national television programs, including the "Phil Donahue Show," and Johnson & Johnson allowed Mike Wallace to film a meeting of the firm's strategy group for use on "60 Minutes."[19]

The Johnson & Johnson case differs from the other cases in this chapter in that the poison was added to the product after it had left the firm. Johnson & Johnson had no contact with the person who contaminated the product. However, Tylenol was still associated with Johnson & Johnson. The firm was caught in a position where a dangerous product with the company's brand name on it was being sold.

Sears Auto Repair

In February 1990, Sears, Roebuck & Co. changed its compensation program for its service advisers as part of a major reorganization program designed to trim costs and boost revenue.[20] Service advisers work with customers to determine what repairs should be made to their cars. The advisers' compensation under the new program was based entirely upon the total cost of repairs that customers authorized. The program set sales quotas on certain auto parts, which service advisers were expected to meet. Customer complaints began to rise.[21]

The growing number of consumer complaints prompted the California Department of Consumer Affairs to launch a year-long undercover investigation into the billing practices at 33 Sears automotive service centers in southern and central California.[22] The investigating agents were overcharged nearly 90 percent of the time with the average excess charge being $223. The Department accused Sears of violating state laws by engaging in fraud, making false and misleading statements, willfully departing from accepted trade practices, and using misleading advertising.[23] It proposed that the state revoke the company's license to operate automotive service centers in the state.

Sears immediately denied the state's allegations and said it would appeal any delicensing action.[24] However, 10 days later, Chairman Edward A. Brennan announced that he was taking personal responsibility for the troubles at the firm's auto service unit, and the firm was discontinuing the compensation program that led to the problems. He also disclosed that New Jersey and Florida were investigating billing practices at Sears auto service centers. Sears decided to send the attorneys general of every state a copy of its new auto repair policies. In addition, Sears took out a one-page ad in major newspapers throughout the country, explaining its position to its customers. The ad is shown in Figure 1.1.

General Motors versus Volkswagen AG

In the early 1980s, J. Ignacio Lopez de Arriortua attracted the attention of General Motors Europe by significantly improving efficiency at the General Motors (GM) plant in Zaragosa, Spain.[25] The Spanish engineer's reputation for cost cutting became somewhat of a legend as he made significant reductions in procurement costs at GM Europe. When John Smith was promoted to the presidency of GM after heading GM Europe, he discovered that Ford Motor Company spent $795 less in labor per car than GM spent.[26] Smith turned to Lopez to get costs under control. Lopez arrived in Detroit during April 1992 to begin his cost-cutting magic in North America.

Lopez immediately set out to duplicate his success in Europe. He put extreme pressure on suppliers to reduce costs, and he began making significant alterations in production and purchasing operations. Symbolically, he directed all managers, including Smith, to wear their watches on their right wrist until the company returned to profitability.

On February 15, 1993, *Der Spiegel,* a German newsweekly, carried a story that Lopez was being courted by Ferdinand Piech, the new chairman of Volkswagen AG (VW).[27] VW was experiencing the same high-cost problems as GM. Smith, fearing that VW might lure Lopez away, decided to promote Lopez to group vice president, which made him one of the top dozen executives at GM. Piech then sweetened his offer to Lopez by promising him a seat on VW's managing board and the head of VW manufacturing operations worldwide. On March 9, 1993, Lopez signed a contract to become purchasing chief for Volkswagen AG.[28] GM's Smith countered on March 11 by offering to promote Lopez to executive vice president and to make him head of GM North America.[29] Lopez stuck by his decision. The following day, Smith and two other GM executives met with Lopez and told him they were willing to consider building a new assembly plant in his native Spain. The plant, which was a pet project of Lopez, would test Plateau Six, the name Lopez assigned to a project designed to assemble automobiles using 10 hours of labor, half the time required by Toyota. The following day, March 13, Lopez told Smith that he had decided to stay with GM. However, on Monday, March 15, two hours before a news conference

FIGURE 1.1 An Open Letter from Sears

Source: Courtesy of Sears, Robuck and Co.

An Open Letter to Sears Customers:

You may have heard recent allegations that some Sears Auto Centers in California and New Jersey have sold customers parts and services they didn't need. We take such charges very seriously, because they strike at the core of our company—our reputation for trust and integrity.

We are confident that our Auto Center customer satisfaction rate is among the highest in the industry. But after an extensive review, we have concluded that our incentive compensation and goal-setting program inadvertently created an environment in which mistakes have occurred. We are moving quickly and aggressively to eliminate that environment.

To guard against such things happening in the future, we're taking significant

- We have eliminated incentive compensation and goal-setting systems for automotive service advisors—the folks who diagnose problems and recommend repairs to you. We have replaced these practices with a new non-commission program designed to achieve even higher levels of customer satisfaction. Rewards will now be based on customer satisfaction.
- We're augmenting our own quality control efforts by retaining an independent organization to conduct ongoing, unannounced "shopping audits" of our automotive services to ensure that company policies are being met.
- We have written to all state attorneys general, inviting them to compare our auto repair standards and practices with those of their states in order to determine whether differences exist.
- And we are helping to organize and fund a joint industry-consumer-government effort to review current auto repair practices and recommend uniform industry standards.

We're taking these actions so you'll continue to come to Sears with complete confidence. However, one thing we will never change is our commitment to customer safety. Our policy of preventive maintenance—recommending replacement of worn parts *before* they fail—has been criticized by the California Bureau of Automotive Repair as constituting unneeded repairs. We don't see it that way. We recommend preventive maintenance because that's what our customers want, and because it makes for safer cars on the road. In fact, 75 percent of the consumers we talked to in a nationwide survey last weekend told us that auto repair centers should recommend replacement parts for preventive maintenance. As always, no work will *ever* be performed without your approval.

We understand that when your car needs service, you look for, above all, someone you can trust. And when trust is at stake, we can't merely *react*, we must *overreact*.

We at Sears are totally committed to maintaining your confidence.
You have my word on it.

Ed Brennan
Chairman and Chief Executive Officer
Sears, Roebuck and Co.

© Sears, Roebuck and Co. 1992

announcing Lopez's new position, a friend of Lopez delivered a letter of resignation to Smith. Lopez went with VW and took seven associates with him. GM claims Lopez saved GM $1 billion during the 10 months he was with them.

On March 22, GM executive vice president and general counsel, Harry Pearce, sent Lopez a letter reminding him of the GM policy on proprietary information. He asked Lopez to confirm that he had not taken ". . . any documents [copies or originals] or any information stored in any data processing or electronic medium, obtained . . ." while employed at GM.[30] Pearce further stated that if Lopez did have any such materials, he should itemize the documents and then return all materials plus any copies to Pearce. Lopez responded in early April that he did not take nor was he in possession of any confidential documents belonging to GM or its Adam Opel AG subsidiary.

Shortly after Lopez left, Opel found that a series of documents was missing.[31] At least some of the documents were among those requested by Lopez and his associates prior to their departure. Lopez received one of the documents, GM's "Epos List," a detailed list of the parts, prices, and suppliers involved in GM's European operations, in December 1992.[32] GM charged Lopez and his associates with taking confidential GM documents with them. Investigations were begun by the U.S. Justice Department and the public prosecutor's office in Darmstadt, Germany. GM contended that Lopez was negotiating a deal with VW at the same time he was attending top-level strategy meetings held at GM subsidiary Adam Opel AG, VW's arch-rival.[33] A member of VW's management board confirmed that he met with Lopez in Germany on January 15, February 14, and on March 9, the day Lopez signed the contract. He denied requesting any GM documents.

The day after signing the contract with VW, Lopez attended a personnel policy meeting at Adam Opel's headquarters in Ruesselsheim. Opel officials stated that Lopez never mentioned that he was leaving GM. However, he asked for a group of Opel documents to be mailed to him at his brother-in-law's address in Spain.[34] Lopez claimed these documents were personal papers from his office in Ruesselsheim, not GM secrets.[35] Lopez stated that when he took the VW job, he had the company immediately ship the boxes to VW headquarters in Wolfsburg, Germany.[36] Lopez admitted that GM documents were contained in the boxes. He stated that they were erroneously included in the boxes of personal papers that GM employees packed for him. He also admitted supervising the shredding of the papers at the VW guest house, Rothehof, after GM asked for their return.[37]

GM claimed that during February, Lopez's right-hand man, Jose Manuel Gutierrez, asked for and received 10 to 12 binders of materials.[38] Gutierrez went to VW with Lopez. *Der Spiegel* published written and oral testimony from 22 GM employees who claimed that Lopez and his associates had received large numbers of confidential documents on future products, parts prices, and machinery costs prior to leaving the company.[39] The magazine also claimed that a dozen VW trainees were instructed to enter GM/Opel data into VW computers at the end of March.[40]

In mid-July, German prosecutors found four boxes of GM documents in a Wiesbaden apartment that was rented by two of Lopez's associates who followed him to VW.[41] The contents were reported to include secret minicar plans that Adam Opel was developing.[42] Three of the four boxes were identified as having been packed and originally sent to Spain at the request of Lopez.[43]

Las Vegas Review-Journal

The Las Vegas Review-Journal was founded in Las Vegas, Nevada, in 1905. The *Review-Journal* is the largest newspaper in Nevada, with a daily circulation of approximately 145,000 and a Sunday circulation of approximately 205,000.[44] It is also the largest of the 52 daily newspapers owned by the Donrey Media Group of Fort Smith, Arkansas.

Mary Hausch joined the *Las Vegas Review-Journal* as a reporter on October 4, 1971.[45] She was promoted to assistant city editor in 1975 and to city editor in 1976, the highest position ever held by a woman at the *Review-Journal*. In 1978 she became managing editor. In 1980, Hausch started filling in for editor Don Digilio when he was away from the office. She received a written commendation for her work as acting editor after Digilio left the company. During this time, Hausch also attended the prestigious American Press Institute (API) course for executive editors.

In August 1988, editor Tom Keevil, who succeeded Don Digilio, died. Hausch inquired about the vacant position and was advised to apply for it. She submitted a written application on August 26, 1988. However, she was never interviewed, even though she inquired about an interview. On September 7, 1988, Hausch was told that she would not be appointed editor. According to Hausch, Donrey Media Group President Fred W. Smith told Hausch that she was not promoted because her husband was an elected official and she had not "paid her dues."[46] Instead, she was promoted to associate editor, a position Hausch contends was newly created and one that is not normally used in the newspaper industry for the second-in-command of news departments.

Sherman Frederick, the general manager of the *Alamogordo Daily News*, a Donrey paper in Alamogordo, New Mexico, was appointed editor.[47] At that time, the *Alamogordo Daily News* had a circulation of approximately 9,000 compared to the *Review-Journal*'s circulation of approximately 145,000. Hausch contends that Frederick had less management experience and fewer professional credentials than she did. Interestingly, Frederick had been hired by Hausch as a reporting intern for the *Review-Journal* a number of years earlier.

In her new position as associate editor, Hausch found her management responsibilities slowly being taken away from her.[48] She lost her involvement in personnel matters such as employee selection, evaluation, and review. Frederick removed her from the editorial decision-making process, and she no longer was allowed to schedule editorial board guests. Her budget responsibilities were diminished, and other employees began to be given credit for her work. Syndicated feature selection and purchasing responsibilities were given to other staff members. Hausch had been actively involved in an earlier redesign of the newspaper, but she was excluded from the current redesign activity. In March 1989, she was informed that she was no longer welcome at department-head meetings.

In March 1989, Hausch filed a discrimination charge with the Nevada Equal Rights Commission.[49] Her job responsibilities continued to erode. She was becoming more and more isolated both personally and professionally. Hausch had received above-average to superior performance ratings from 1978 to 1987. In 1989 her performance rating fell. Despite never being late nor missing a day of work, Hausch was marked down for attendance. Another employee, who had missed approximately two weeks of work, was given a higher attendance rating. On September 4, 1990, Hausch filed a second charge with the Nevada Equal Rights Commission and with the U.S. Equal Employment Opportunity Commission, claiming that she had been the victim of unlawful retaliation for filing the first discrimination charge. The isolation continued.

On November 20, 1990, David Osborn, general manager of the *Review-Journal,* told Hausch that she could no longer work at the paper because she had filed the charge of discrimination based on retaliation. He placed her on suspension with pay and told her to vacate her office immediately, turn in her keys and employee badge, take her personal effects, and not return to *Review-Journal* property without his permission. On February 4, 1991, Osborn fired Hausch for "loss of trust." The position of associate editor was not filled.

On April 19, 1991, the Nevada Equal Rights Commission completed its investigation into Hausch's charges. It ". . . determined that there was Probable Cause to believe that the charge is true . . ."[50] It referred the case to the U.S. Equal Employment Opportunity Commission (EEOC) for further processing. On February 12, 1993, the EEOC issued its findings in the form of a Determination.

The EEOC found that Hausch was better qualified than Frederick but was wrongly denied promotion to editor due to discrimination based on her sex.[51] The Determination stated that ". . . the person who was the decision maker, the General Manager, stated he would not hire a 'God damn woman.' " The EEOC further found that Hausch was retaliated against after she filed her first complaint. She was given an unfair performance rating and her responsibilities were reduced. Finally, when Hausch filed charges of retaliation, she was suspended from her position and subsequently fired.

Types of Issues

You have just read specific examples of ethical problems faced by firms and the different approaches they have taken to resolve the issues, some more successfully than others. We now look at the types of ethical issues a firm may experience. Table 1.1 summarizes the findings of four studies that examined ethical issues encountered by business executives. The first two studies, conducted more than 15 years apart and summarized in column one, sampled readers of the *Harvard Business Review* and thus contained responses from managers in all business disciplines.[52] The respondents were asked to cite the unethical practice in their industry that they would most like to see eliminated.

The study of marketing managers asked respondents to list the job situation that posed the most difficult ethical or moral problem for them.[53] The study focusing on marketing researchers posed the same question.[54] In all four studies, the responses may not represent the most frequent ethical issues facing management, but they do represent very troubling issues. For each study, the issues are listed in order of frequency of response.

The ethical issues in Table 1.1 can be classified into five general categories of ethical problems: bribery, coercion, deception, theft, and unfair discrimination. These five categories include the most troubling and/or reprehensible business practices cited by managers in four different empirical studies. They will provide the structure around which to organize our discussion of ethics.

Bribery

A bribe is used to manipulate people by buying influence. Bribery has been defined as "the offering, giving, receiving, or soliciting of something of value for the purpose of influencing the action of an official in the discharge of his or her public or legal duties."[55] The item of value may be direct payments of money or property. It may also be in the form of a kickback after a deal has been completed. Manuel Velasquez refers to a commercial bribe as a "consideration given to an employee by a person outside the firm with the understanding that when the employee transacts business for his or her own firm, the employee will deal favorably with that person or with that person's firm."[56]

Bribes create a conflict of interest between the person receiving the bribe and his or her organization. This person has a fiduciary responsibility to the organization.* The bribe creates a private interest that is likely to be in conflict with the organization's interest. Bribery is most often used to gain

---

*A person with a fiduciary responsibility holds a position of trust with another, in this case with the organization. The fiduciary must exercise all rights and powers associated with the organization for the benefit of the organization.

TABLE 1.1ᵃ   Ethical Issues Faced by Business Executives

Harvard Business Review Readers	Marketing Managers	Marketing Researchers
Gifts; gratuities, bribes; call girls	Bribery	Research integrity
Price discrimination; unfair pricing	Fairness	Treating outside clients fairly
Dishonest advertising	Honesty	Research confidentiality
Misc. unfair competitive practices	Price	Marketing mix and social issues
Cheating customers; unfair credit practices; overselling	Product	Personnel issues
Price collusion by competitors	Personnel	Treating respondents fairly
Dishonesty in making and keeping contracts	Confidentiality	Treating others in company fairly
Unfairness to employees; prejudice in hiring	Advertising	Interviewer dishonesty
Other	Manipulation of data	Gifts, bribes, and entertainment
	Purchasing	Treating suppliers fairly
	Other issues	Legal issues
		Misuse of funds
		Other

ᵃThis table was taken from David J. Fritzsche, "Marketing/Business Ethics: A Review of the Empirical Research," *Business & Professional Ethics Journal* 6, no. 4 (1987), p. 68.

sales, to enter new markets, or to change or avoid public policy. We are not referring to "grease" payments made to customs agents to process goods at ports of entry. Grease payments are a form of tip for performing services that are customarily paid for in certain countries.

While the use of call girls and cash payments are easy to spot as bribes, the intent of gifts can at times be much more difficult to determine. A gift may be given as a common courtesy for an occasion, or it may be meant to influence business decisions at some future point in time. The key questions seem to be intent and the expected response. If the gift is given with the intent of influencing behavior, it is a bribe. If the gift actually influences behavior, whether or not the influence was intended, the gift functions as a bribe. If the gift has no influence on future behavior, it does not function as a bribe. However, lack of influence is sometimes hard to prove.

From the information available in the case of the sale of French frigates to Taiwan, Elf Aquitaine via Sirven appeared to have provided funds to influence the sale on behalf of Thompson-CSF. Both the French foreign minister and Chinese officials were recipients of funds totaling approximately one-fourth of the purchase price of the frigates. The French foreign minister was influenced by lavish gifts funneled to him by his mistress in the form of artworks, apparel, and fancy entertainment. His opposition to the sale was converted to at least neutrality, resulting in the sale of the frigates.

Coercion

Coercion controls people by force or threat. It is defined as "compulsion; constraint; compelling by force or arms or threat. . . . It may be actual, direct, or positive, as where physical force is used to compel action against one's will, or implied, legal or constructive, as where one party is constrained by subjugation to another to do what his free will would refuse."[57] The force is often the threat of the use of power upon the disadvantaged party. Coercion may involve the threat of blocking a promotion, the loss of a job, or blackballing an individual in the industry. It may be forcing a person to act in a manner that is against the person's personal beliefs. Coercion is used to compel an individual to act in a way that is against her or his will. Coercion may also be used against firms—for example, forcing a retailer to handle specific products in order to obtain other desired products.

The Tylenol tampering case discussed previously appears to be an example of coercion. Tylenol was contaminated with the intent of harming the company by damaging its reputation and forcing it to incur great expense in dealing with the problem. The exact motive and the individual(s) responsible for the act are not known. It should be noted that there were several subsequent copycat contaminations performed to harm a particular individual.

Extortion may be considered a special form of coercion. Velasquez defines extortion:

> . . . an employee is engaged in commercial extortion if the employee demands consideration from persons outside the firm as a condition for dealing favorably with those persons when the employee transacts business for his or her firm.[58]

Extortion may involve some type of threat that is "bought off" via the payment. Intentional threats are most often used to ensure continued operation in a market, to stave off threatening competition, or to prevent some type of other harm from befalling the firm.

Deception

Deception manipulates people and firms by misleading them. Deception is "the act of deceiving; intentional misleading by falsehood spoken or acted. . . . Knowingly and willingly making a false statement or representation, expressed or implied, pertaining to a present or past existing fact."[59] This dishonest behavior is one of the most common ethical transgressions. Deception includes distorting or falsifying research or accounting data, creating misleading advertising, and misrepresenting a product. It also is involved in fake expense reports, fudged performance appraisals, and misrepresented financial positions. Deception ranges from the small innocuous lie, which may cause little or no harm, to significant schemes to deceive, which may cause major economic or physical harm, including death.

The Sears auto repair case is a classic example of deception. Since most people have a very limited understanding of the mechanical workings of their automobiles, they must put their trust in auto service managers when seeking repairs. The service advisers at Sears were given economic incentives to bolster repair sales. Thus, they prescribed numerous repairs that were not actually needed. Customers were misled into authorizing more work than was actually required to fix their automobiles.

Theft

Theft is the taking of something that does not belong to you. Joseph Nolan and Jacqueline Nolan-Haley define it as "the act of stealing. The taking of property without the owner's consent."[60] This does not apply to property that is lost due to competitive forces when play is according to the economic rules of the culture. However, if property is lost through a change in the rules, the loss may be considered theft if it meets one of the following conditions:

1. It was not possible to take action that would comply with the new rules.
2. It was not possible to foresee the development of the new rules in time to comply with them prior to the loss.

Theft, too, covers a wide variety of ethical transgressions. The property may be physical or conceptual. Theft occurs in insider trading when one uses privileged information as one's own. It also occurs when products are counterfeited, or one engages in price gouging. Theft occurs when a firm's proprietary information is used to further another firm's ends. This information may be obtained via unauthorized use of company computers and programs.

Price collusion results in theft because collusion keeps prices higher than normal and thus takes from buyers' money that should not need to be paid to complete an exchange. Dishonesty in making and keeping contracts also results in theft. The party who is wronged loses something of value that is taken without consent. Cheating or overselling customers likewise takes something of value without the owner's consent, as does unfair pricing.

When Volkswagen hired Lopez, it got Lopez, a few of Lopez's colleagues, *plus* a number of important General Motors' papers. The papers contained sensitive information that was protected by General Motors's policy on proprietary information, a policy with which Lopez had to be familiar. Whether Piech or others at VW knew of the paper transfer, Lopez appears to be guilty of theft. Some of his colleagues who went with him to VW could also be guilty because they would have known about the policy.

Unfair Discrimination

Unfair discrimination is defined as "unfair treatment or denial of normal privileges to persons because of their race, age, sex, nationality or religion. . . . A failure to treat all persons equally when no reasonable distinction can be found between those favored and those not favored."[61] We refer to this as unfair discrimination in contrast to discrimination based upon relevant criteria that is perfectly acceptable behavior to most people. Individuals are hired based upon their qualifications, and people are compensated on the basis of their relative contributions to the organization. Unfair discrimination occurs when one individual or class is favored over another on the basis of nonrelevant criteria. The key is the criteria utilized. Are the criteria relevant to the requirements of the job or function? Velasquez cites three basic elements that must be present for unfair discrimination in employment to occur:

1. . . . it is a decision against one or more employees (or prospective employees) that is *not based on individual merit* . . .
2. . . . the decision derives solely or in part from racial or sexual prejudice, from false stereotypes, or from some other kind of *morally unjustified attitude* . . .
3. . . . the decision (or set of decisions) has a *harmful or negative impact* upon the interests of the employees . . .[62]

Unfair discrimination is present when an individual is denied a job, promotion, or other benefit based upon the individual's race, sex, or religion. These criteria have no relevance to such decisions.

In the *Las Vegas Review-Journal* case, all three of Velasquez's elements appear to be met. First, Hausch had more management experience at a much larger newspaper than Frederick. She also had more professional credentials, such as the American Press Institute schooling. Second, the promotion decision appears to be based solely on sex, as indicated by the comment of the general manager cited by the U.S. EEOC. Third, the decision was very damaging to a very successful career. Mary Hausch began working as a journalism lecturer at the University of Nevada, Las Vegas, after she was fired. Taking this position resulted in a significant decline in income and prestige compared to the editorship of the *Review-Journal*.

What's Ahead

This chapter provides an introduction to the study of business ethics. We have discussed the types of issues businesses encounter and have presented several examples of firms dealing with ethical issues. The following six chapters will provide insight into ethical theory and practice. We take an international approach because neither business nor ethics respects political boundaries.

Chapter 2 discusses the importance of ethics in business decisions. Issues covered include the importance of ethics in business relations, the distorting effect of unethical behavior on the allocation of goods and services in our economic system, the public policy implications of unethical actions, and the impact ethical relationships have on maintaining and furthering the customer base.

In Chapter 3 the normative ethical principles of philosophy are introduced. We will focus on the principles of egoism, utilitarianism, rights, and justice as they relate to business decisions. We will then place the principles in context using one of the newest developments in business ethics philosophy, integrative social contracts theory.

Chapter 4 discusses a process model of decision making. The model is based on management and ethical theory along with the empirical research discussed in Chapter 5. The model describes the process the decision maker goes through when considering decision alternatives that possess ethical dimensions.

Chapter 5 contains a review of the empirical research in business ethics. This stream of research began with Raymond Baumhart in the early 1960s and has mushroomed in the last few years. This chapter will bring you up to date.

Chapter 6 focuses on guides that can be used to enhance the ethical aspects of decision making. It discusses the stages in the decision process where ethical aspects of the decision can be influenced. This chapter also covers a variation on a model developed by Gerald Cavanagh and others to guide decision makers considering the ethical dimension of a decision.

Chapter 7 contains a series of cases dealing with a variety of ethical issues. The discussion of the cases uses the modified Cavanagh model, the value-based process model of decision making, and other material presented in this book.

Following the seven chapters, Appendix A and B contain two statements of rights. The United States Bill of Rights is reproduced in Appendix A. Appendix B contains the not-often-seen United Nations Universal Declaration of Human Rights. Both are worth more than a few minutes of study.

Finally, you will find 20 cases that you can use to develop your understanding of the concepts in this book. Many of the cases deal with situations outside the United States.

There is a good deal of ethical analysis throughout this book. In many places, judgments are made based on ethical principles. Some readers may disagree with specific judgments presented, which is their right. However, such disagreement should be based on accepted ethical principles that can be used to defend the reader's position.

Discussion Questions

1. Who bears more responsibility for the frigate sale payments, Thompson-CSF, Elf Aquitaine, or the French foreign minister? What should have prevented this from happening? Who was harmed? Who was helped?
2. Why do you think the individuals laced Tylenol with poison? What were they trying to accomplish?
3. Did Sears's top management play any role in the decision by their service managers to recommend unneeded repairs?
4. Do you think VW hired Lopez with the expectation that he would bring along GM secrets? What responsibility did he have to GM?
5. Because Hausch had risen above any former female employee at the *Review-Journal,* do you think she should have been satisfied remaining as managing editor? Why or why not?
6. For which of the above firms would you rather work? Why?
7. Do you think the ethical issues listed in this chapter—bribery, coercion, deception, theft, and unfair discrimination—are considered unethical in all developed countries? Are they considered unethical in developing countries? In underdeveloped countries?
8. Which of the cases discussed is the most disturbing to you? Why?
9. What differences do you see in the cultures of the companies discussed? Does this influence the ethical nature of their behavior?

End Notes

1. "Murder Allegations against French Firm Latest Twist in Elf Scandal," *Agance France-Presse,* November 28, 2000.
2. John Lichfield, "Mr. Honesty and His £ 1,100 Shoes," *The Independent* (London), March 15, 1998, p. 16.
3. Pierre-Antoine Souchard, "Former French Foreign Minister to Appeal Conviction in Elf Scandal," The Associated Press, November 4, 2002.
4. David Ignatius, "A Very French Pastry," *The Washington Post,* August 2, 1998, p. C05.
5. Lichfield, "Mr. Honesty and His £ 1,100 Shoes."
6. "Murder Allegations against French Firm."
7. Ignatius, "A Very French Pastry."
8. Alan Freeman, "The Hero, the Mistress, the Scandal, the Fallout Court Convicts Dumas as France Adandons Its Laissez-Faire Attitudes toward Corruption," *The Globe and Mail,* May 31, 2001, p. A1.
9. Ignatius, "A Very French Pastry."
10. Ibid.
11. Keith B. Richburg, "France Faces Dizzying Dose of Corruption; Politics and Business No Longer Go Hand in Hand in New 'Investigative Culture,' " *Washington Post Foreign Service,* March 25, 2001, p. A24.

1. You fly into a country in Southeast Asia and begin to work your way through customs. You are scheduled for a meeting with an important customer in an hour. You notice that all of the people ahead of you who "tip" the inspector are processed rather quickly, but people who do not provide a "tip" seem to get stuck in line. When you reach the inspection station, do you "tip" the inspector? Why or why not?

2. The next day you go down to the seaport to check on a shipment you had sent ahead to arrive when you got here. You ask customs how long it will take to process your shipment because you need it in the next couple of days. You are told it will take 10 days but are led to believe that it could be processed much quicker if you provide a monetary incentive. Would you pay customs to speed up the processing of your shipment? Why or why not?

3. While in the country, you hope to make a significant sale to the coun-try's government. When you visit the contracting officer, you are told that there are three other competitors vying for the contract. You soon learn that the officer will not award the contract based upon the lowest bid or even upon the product's performance. The decision will be made based upon how much the officer personally gains from the contract. You are told what the three other competitors are offering and you are asked if you can top that. Their bids include up to 10 percent of the purchase price being set aside for the contracting officer. This is a large contract that would certainly help your career with your firm. Would you submit a bid that would top the competitors' contributions to the officer? Why or why not?

What are the similarities in these three decisions?

What are the differences?

Were you comfortable making each decision? Why or why not?

12. Pierre-Antoine Souchard, "Former French Foreign Minister to Appeal Conviction in Elf Scandal," The Associated Press, November 4, 2002.

13. Freeman, "The Hero."

14. Souchard, "Former French Foreign Minister."

15. Freeman, "The Hero."

16. Ibid.

17. Thomas Moore, "The Fight to Save Tylenol," Fortune 106, no. 11 (1982), pp. 44–49.

18. Ibid.

19. Mitchell Leon, "Tylenol Fights Back," Public Relations Journal 39, no. 3 (1983), pp. 10–14.

20. Gregory A. Patterson, "Sears's Brennan Accepts Blame for Auto Flap," The Wall Street Journal, June 23, 1992, pp. B1, B10.

21. Tung Yin, "Sears Is Accused of Billing Fraud at Auto Centers," *The Wall Street Journal* 126, no. 115 (June 12, 1992), pp. B1, B5.
22. Ibid.
23. Ibid.
24. Ibid.
25. Paul Ingrassia and Douglas Lavin, "Lopez Reverses Plan to Quit GM for Volkswagen," *The Wall Street Journal* 221, no. 50 (March 15, 1993), pp. A3, A5.
26. Ibid.
27. Paul Ingrassia, "April Fool's Day Comes Early at GM, but It's No Joke," *The Wall Street Journal* 221, no. 51 (March 16, 1993), pp. A1, A10.
28. Audrey Choi, "VW's Chronology of Lopez Overtures Could Benefit GM," *The Wall Street Journal* 129, no. 18 (July 27, 1993), p. A5.
29. Ingrassia, "April Fool's Day Comes Early."
30. Audrey Choi, "Lopez Concedes He Supervised Shredding Data," *The Wall Street Journal* 129, no. 40 (August 26, 1993), p. A4.
31. Audrey Choi, "GM Offers Chronology to Show Lopez Got Documents after Signing with VW," *The Wall Street Journal* 129, no. 21 (July 30, 1993), p. A3.
32. Ibid.
33. Choi, "VW's Chronology of Lopez."
34. Choi, "GM Offers Chronology."
35. "Chiefs of GM and VW to Hold Talks as 'Car War' Escalates in Germany," *The Wall Street Journal* 129, no. 22 (August 2, 1993), p. A5.
36. Choi, "Lopez Concedes."
37. Ibid.
38. Choi, "GM Offers Chronology."
39. Audrey Choi and Joseph B. White, "VW Receives Setback in Efforts to Blunt Charges against Lopez," *The Wall Street Journal* 129, no. 14 (July 21, 1993), p. A11.
40. Patrick Moser, "GM, VW Legal Battle Reaches New Heights," *The Christian Science Monitor* 85, no. 189 (August 25, 1993), p. 9.
41. Choi, "VW's Chronology of Lopez."
42. Moser, "GM, VW Legal Battle."
43. "Boxes of GM Papers Tied to Shipments for Lopez," *The Wall Street Journal* 129, no. 30 (August 12, 1993), p. A4.
44. *Mary E. Hausch* vs. *Donrey of Nevada, Inc.,* Order CV-S-93-432-PMP from the U.S. District Court, District of Nevada on September 20, 1993.
45. *Mary E. Hausch* vs. *Donrey of Nevada, Inc.,* Complaint CV-S-93-432-PMP filed in the U.S. District Court, District of Nevada on May 11, 1993.
46. Ibid.
47. M. L. Stein, "Former Editor Files $10 Million Sexual Discrimination Suit," *Editor & Publisher* 126, no. 21 (May 22, 1993), p. 36.
48. *Hausch* vs. *Donrey,* Complaint. May 11, 1993
49. Nevada Equal Rights Commission, #0323-89-120L.

50. Letter to Ms. Mary Hausch, dated April 19, 1991, from Delia E. Martinez, executive director, Nevada Equal Rights Commission.

51. Determination issued by the U.S. Equal Employment Opportunity Commission, dated February 12, 1993, in regards to charges numbers 34B890368 and 34B910061.

52. Raymond C. Baumhart, SJ, "How Ethical Are Businessmen?" *Harvard Business Review* 39, no. 4 (July–August 1961), pp. 6–19, 156–176; and Steven N. Brenner and Earl A. Molander, "Is the Ethics of Business Changing?" *Harvard Business Review* 55, no. 1 (January–February 1977), pp. 57–71.

53. Lawrence B. Chonko and Shelby D. Hunt, "Ethics and Marketing Management: An Empirical Examination," *Journal of Business Research* 13, no. 4 (1985), pp. 339–359.

54. Shelby D. Hunt, Lawrence B. Chonko, and James B. Wilcox, "Ethical Problems of Marketing Researchers," *Journal of Marketing Research* 21, no. 3 (August 1984), pp. 309–324.

55. Joseph R. Nolan and Jacqueline M. Nolan-Haley, *Black's Law Dictionary* (St. Paul, MN: West Publishing Company, 1990).

56. Manuel G. Velasquez, *Business Ethics: Concepts and Cases* (Englewood Cliffs, NJ: Prentice Hall, 1992).

57. Nolan and Nolan-Haley, *Black's Law Dictionary.*

58. Velasquez, *Business Ethics: Concepts and Cases.*

59. Nolan and Nolan-Haley, *Black's Law Dictionary.*

60. Ibid.

61. Ibid.

62. Velasquez, *Business Ethics: Concepts and Cases.*

Chapter  2

The Importance of Ethics in Business

Ethical behavior is essential for long-term business success. This is true from both a macro and a micro perspective. The macro argument considers the importance of ethics within the economic system. Unethical behavior distorts the market system, which leads to an inefficient allocation of resources. The micro argument addresses the importance of ethics to the individual firm. Unethical behavior leads to decreased long-run performance. We begin with the macro argument.

The Macro Perspective

A growing number of countries rely on the market system to allocate goods and services. They believe that while not perfect, the market system is a more efficient and effective way of allocating a country's resources than any command system* yet devised. Some conditions required for the market system to work effectively include:

1. The right to own and control private property.
2. Freedom of choice in buying and selling goods and services.
3. The availability of accurate information concerning those goods and services.

Ownership of private property is necessary for exchange to take place. Freedom of choice in exchange allows the forces of competition to police the market. Accurate information enables buyers to locate desirable goods and services in the marketplace so that they can exercise their freedom of choice.

*An economic system in which a central authority allocates the country's resources.

Private property is essential for exchange. Ownership of private property implies protection of property from exchange without one's consent. If you are selling a bicycle that I would like to have, I must give you something I own in exchange for the bicycle. That something may be in the form of another good, for example, a CD player, or it may be in the form of money, a surrogate for other goods. You must agree to accept what I have offered to give you before I may take possession of your bicycle. If you do not agree and I take the bicycle, I am guilty of theft: I have taken your private property without your consent. If you and other bicycle sellers know that your bicycles will be stolen, you will stop selling bicycles. Thus, the market for bicycles breaks down due to the refusal of suppliers to provide products and services for which they will not be compensated. For the market system to work, you must have the right to own private property, and your property right must be respected.

Freedom of choice in exchange implies that you may buy any CD player you desire if you have the money to pay for it. The retailer that you choose will sell the player if the model is in stock. In order to select both model and retailer, you need accurate information. You can decide which CD player you like best only if you can determine what models are offered and the various features available on each model. Information on reliability is also helpful. Product information is usually provided by manufacturers, retailers, and wholesalers, but it may also be provided by third parties and publications such as *Consumer Reports.* Other key pieces of information include price and the location of retailers. When you purchase a specific CD player, you are voting to allocate resources to the production of the player you purchased. This is true whether you purchase the CD player with dollars, marks, pesos, yen, or other currency. You have decided that the player is worth at least the amount of money you had to pay for it.

Your purchase of a CD player is one of millions of purchases that determine what is made and sold within your country. Each buyer votes with her or his money each time a purchase is made. Resources are allocated to products and services that people want to buy and are taken away from products and services that are not wanted. If you are satisfied with the CD player you purchased, the allocation was successful. If you are disappointed with the product, the market is not working properly. You were misinformed and voted for the wrong product.

The total set of goods and services available in a country using the market system is allocated to people based on their individual purchases. Each person buys the goods and services that he or she believes will best satisfy his or her individual needs. In the aggregate, the goods and services are allocated in the most effective manner possible, that is, according to perceived value by the individual buyers. An item that is valued at less than its price stays on the shelf. An item valued at equal to or greater than its price is purchased. Thus, the market allocation of goods and services causes resources to move to their most valued use. This is true as long as there is a close correlation between perceived value at the time of purchase and during actual use.

Problems occur when either buyers or sellers are not free to exchange, or when information concerning the good or service is incorrect. The market system cannot work properly, so people buy products and services that provide less satisfaction than would be gained from alternative purchases. Because the market system allocates resources based on sales volume, more of the goods and services that provide less satisfaction are produced, and fewer of the goods and services that provide more satisfaction are produced. Thus, total satisfaction is less with this suboptimal allocation than it would be with other allocations.

Effect of Unethical Behavior from a Macro Perspective

Bribery

Bribery reduces freedom of choice by altering the conditions under which a decision is made. A bribe is used to make one choice more attractive to a decision maker. The greater appeal is created by enhancing the personal gain associated with the choice by the addition of an unearned payment in the form of goods, services, or money. While the decision maker gains by selecting the alternative with the bribe, the choice itself is usually less attractive and generally provides less total satisfaction. Otherwise, why would a bribe be paid? The bribe thus results in allocating more resources to a less-desirable alternative. Often, the overall cost of the alternative proves to be more expensive because the cost of the bribe has to be recovered.

Coercive Acts

Coercive acts—threats or force that prevents a seller from dealing with certain customers, buyers from purchasing from certain sellers, or buyers from buying certain products or service—decrease effective competition. This usually results in higher prices being paid and possibly poorer products and/or services being provided than would occur if more competition had been present. The higher price decreases the demand for the goods or services below that which would occur at competitive prices. Thus, fewer resources will be allocated to producing the goods or services than would be the case if competition had not been constrained by coercion. Buyer satisfaction with the products and/or services may also likely be lower due to inferior performance.

Deceptive Information

Deceptive information creates false impressions and leads buyers to select goods and services that provide less satisfaction than those that would have been purchased using accurate information. Deceptive information may also lead to deliveries at times other than promised, which can create costly disruptions in production runs, resulting in higher cost output.

Buyers must pay more and thus buy less than would be purchased if deliveries had been on time. False delivery promises to consumers can also increase the cost of using products or services. Misinformation squanders money that could be used for other purchases. Delivering products and services that differ from those promised also distorts the system because resources are allocated to the delivered items and not to those wanted.

Theft

Theft significantly increases the cost of providing products and/or services. Losses due to theft of any type must be made up via larger profit margins on products sold, which increase prices. The artificially increased prices due to theft lower demand and thus result in a misallocation of resources. In extreme cases, theft can result in a product or service exiting from the market.

Unfair Discrimination

Finally, unfair discrimination often results in the purchase of services from less-capable people or the sale of goods and services to people who value them less than those discriminated against. Once again we see a misallocation of resources. Unfair discrimination generally results in a lower level of satisfaction than fair discrimination. Table 2.1 summarizes the macro impact of unethical behavior.

Constraints in the form of bribery, coercion, deception, and unfair discrimination limit the freedom to act, and they may produce inaccurate or deceptive information, resulting in suboptimal shifts in the cost and purchase of goods and services. Theft may lead to an actual breakdown of a market

TABLE 2.1 Macro Effect of Unethical Behavior

Behavior	Impact on Decision Maker	Likely Result of Behavior
Bribery	Unearned personal gain Alteration of decision choice	Increased costs. Reduced product/service quality
Coercion	Fear of harm Alteration of decision choice	Increased costs. Reduced product/service quality
Deception	Alteration of decision choice	Reduced satisfaction
Theft	Loss of resources	Increased costs or elimination of product/service
Unfair Discrimination	Purchase of inferior services Sales level below market	Increased costs. False demand reduction

and, at best, results in artificially high prices. Purchase choices made that do not reflect the free choice of buyers and sellers lead to a misallocation of the country's resources. Constraints on freedom, misinformation, and theft are associated with unethical behavior. Thus, from a macro perspective, ethical behavior is a prerequisite for the market system to function effectively.

The Micro Perspective—Ethics and Trust

From the perspective of the firm, ethics is closely associated with trust. Most people will agree that in order to develop trust, behavior must be ethical. While ethical behavior is not sufficient to gain trust, it is necessary. There is a growing body of literature on the importance of trust in business relationships. We will use this literature to support the importance of ethics in business. Trust is used as an indicator variable for ethics. If trust is important and ethical behavior is necessary to obtain trust, then ethics is as important as trust. Ethical behavior is a necessary component of developing and maintaining trust.

Bernard Barber argues that there are two kinds of trust: ". . . trust as expectations of technically competent performance and trust as expectations of fiduciary responsibility. . . ."[1] Both types of trust apply within and among businesses. People hired to work are expected to be competent. They also represent the interests of the business when they deal with external stakeholders. Much business is done relying on a person's word, a handshake, or the expected honesty and decency of the other party. Trust in the business setting reduces costs, makes life more pleasant, and improves efficiency.[2]

Stewart Macauley found that two norms are widely accepted in business dealings:

1. Commitments are to be honored in almost all situations; one does not welsh on a deal.
2. One ought to produce a good product and stand behind it.[3]

R. Golembiewski and M. McConkie highlight the importance of trust when they state that ". . . perhaps there is no other single variable which so thoroughly influences interpersonal and intergroup behavior."[4] Finally, Kenneth Arrow states, "Virtually every commercial transaction has within itself an element of trust, certainly any transaction conducted over a period of time."[5] We can safely conclude that business would not run smoothly if business people could not trust one another.

Trust is comprised of three fundamental elements: predictability, dependability, and faith.[6] Predictability tends to eliminate surprises that are not usually welcome in the business environment. Dependability provides assurance that one can be counted on to perform as expected. Faith is the belief that one will continue to be predictable and dependable. The need for trust arises when you face some type of risk. Trust in a person or a firm is developed based on experience over time. As one gains positive experience and develops trust in another, the perceived risk of dealing with the party declines. Thus, trust is a risk-reducing mechanism.

LaRue Hosmer defines trust as

> . . . the reliance by one person, group, or firm upon a voluntarily accepted duty on the part of another person, group, or firm to recognize and protect the rights and interests of all others engaged in a joint endeavor or economic exchange.[7]

Trust, based on experience that the other person, group, or firm will honor the duty to protect rights and interests, lowers perceived risk. Let's look at the role trust plays in supplier, customer, and employee relations.

Trust in Supplier Relations

Suppliers, often called vendors, provide a firm with the products and services it needs to conduct business. These include, but are not limited to, raw materials, products, communication services, consulting services, financial services, accounting services, and computer services. Thus, suppliers are important stakeholders of an organization. A business often deals with some of its suppliers over an extended period of time, developing symbiotic relationships. Purchases move from a series of discrete transactions to an ongoing buyer-seller relationship that we will refer to as an exchange relationship. An exchange relationship is based on trust between both parties that each will honor her or his commitments and thus minimize surprise. This significantly reduces the risk involved in the buying process. In addition to economic exchange, the parties ". . . can be expected to derive complex, personal, noneconomic satisfactions and engage in *social* exchange."[8] The feeling of mutual trust that develops promotes cooperation.

Trust increases efficiency in exchange as each party gains faith that the other will act in a predictable and dependable manner. Buyers rely on suppliers to provide products and services of acceptable quality when promised. Early deliveries increase storage costs, and in the case of services, early deliveries may be unusable if required at a later time. Late delivery may halt production, causing skyrocketing costs.

With trust, the buyer gets a dependable source of supply. Purchases should be of acceptable quality and should arrive on time. Time previously spent on frequent checks on quality and delivery can be more productively spent elsewhere. During periods of shortages when supplies become difficult to get, the relationship increases the chances of the needed items being obtained. Suppliers take care of customers with whom they have relationships before they take care of others.

A buyer earns a supplier's trust when good credit standing is maintained and all commitments are honored. A supplier's trust is lost when a buyer engages in "sharp" (questionable) practices such as playing off one supplier against another in an effort to gain a price advantage.[9] Other attempts to chisel on price, including lying and cheating, also destroy trust. A reputation for sharp practices precedes a buyer, making dealing with suppliers difficult and decreasing the value of the buyer to her or his firm. Having a reputation for sharp practices also makes it more difficult to find work elsewhere. Exchange relationships based on trust develop when the supplier is treated as the buyer would expect to be treated. This does not preclude being firm in negotiations, but it does require fairness. The Golden Rule is a useful guide to follow.

Trust in Customer Relations

Suppliers form the other side of the exchange relationship. The supplier's contact with a customer is through its sales force. Honesty is expected and is required to maintain trust. Competence is also a prerequisite of trust. Customers rely on salespeople as sources of information concerning new and existing products and services. Salespeople also must be able to provide information regarding shipping alternatives and arrival dates. An incompetent salesperson who cannot provide the needed information is of no value; trust becomes a moot point. A customer orientation makes the buyer the number-one priority, which increases buyer satisfaction and thus trust. A customer can relate to a likeable salesperson. We tend to trust people we like. Thus, a salesperson earns a customer's trust by being dependable, honest, competent, customer-oriented, and likeable.[10]

Exchange relationships also provide important benefits to suppliers. Relationships provide an enduring customer base. Customers who trust suppliers are more likely to stay with them. Thus, new customers add to the existing customer base rather than replacing customers lost from the base. Sales become more predictable. A stable or growing customer base ensures a constant source of business. Relationships free up time that would be required to develop discrete transactions with existing customers, time that can be spent developing new business. Collection costs are also significantly reduced. Finally, as before, the parties ". . . can be expected to derive complex, personal, noneconomic satisfactions and to engage in *social* exchange."[11]

Trust in Employee Relations

Trust applies to peers as well as to superiors and subordinates. A climate of trust provides improved communications; greater predictability, dependability, and confidence among employees; a reduction in employee turnover; an openness and a willingness to listen and accept criticism nondefensively; and a reduction of friction among employees.[12] Jitendra Mishra and Molly Morrissey report factors that promote trust:

1. Open communications.
2. Giving workers a greater share in the decision making.

3. Sharing of critical information.
4. True sharing of perceptions and feelings.[13]

This list is consistent with a study at General Motors that found five factors that appear to be correlated with trust in one's employer. They include:

1. Perception of open and honest communication both up and down the organizational ladder.
2. Fair and consistent treatment of employee groups.
3. Shared goals and values between workers and supervisors.
4. Autonomy from close supervision, a sign of personal trust in employees.
5. Feedback from and to management regarding employees' performance and responsibilities.[14]

Trust is an important element in the empowerment process. Jay Conger and Rabindra Kanungo define empowerment as ". . . a process of enhancing feelings of self-efficacy among organizational members through the identification of conditions that foster powerlessness and through their removal by both formal organizational practices and informal techniques of providing efficacy information."[15] Self-efficacy is the belief that you have the power to produce an effect. Managerial strategies and techniques that promote self-efficacy include participative management, goal setting, a feedback system, and job enrichment.[16] These are the same factors cited previously that have been found to build trust. E. Neilsen argues that empowerment strategies that provide emotional support and create a supportive, trusting atmosphere can be effective in strengthening self-efficacy beliefs.[17]

Employee empowerment is a prerequisite for the development of quality circles and work teams designed to improve productive efficiency and competitiveness. By management's making work meaningful, employees develop an internal commitment to their job. They determine the best way to get the job done and take ownership in the quality of the results. They are able to see and develop a pride in their accomplishments. This is possible because an atmosphere of trust promotes a sense of self-efficacy, and trust rests on a foundation of ethical behavior.

As stated above, we believe ethics is essential for long-term business success. This belief is supported by the description of the experiences of the following four firms.

The Importance of Society's Perception

Johnson & Johnson Revisited

To illustrate the importance of society's perception of a firm, we will continue with the Tylenol case from Chapter 1. Prior to the crisis, Tylenol held 37 percent of the pain reliever market, making it the market leader. Sales of Tylenol products fell sharply with the recall of the Extra-Strength capsule product. Some estimates put the loss at as much as 80 percent. Johnson & Johnson reported that the voluntary action they took to protect the public during 1982 cost the company $100 million.[18]

The open manner in which the firm handled the crisis appeared to sustain the sense of trust the company had built up over the years. Johnson & Johnson recognized the problem immediately; was proactive in dealing with it, utilizing top-level executive talent; and immediately set to work to find a solution. The combination of the public's perception that the company was putting public safety ahead of financial considerations, along with intelligent marketing, revived Tylenol. Tylenol sales hit a new market high by the end of 1985.[19]

On February 9, 1986, a young woman in Yonkers, New York, was found dead in her bed. The two Extra-Strength Tylenol capsules that she had taken the night before were laced with cyanide. The Tylenol nightmare began anew!

The new poisoning was particularly puzzling because the bottle that contained the capsules had been triple-sealed in response to the earlier poisonings in 1982. Chief Executive Officer James Burke immediately canceled all advertising for Tylenol in capsule form. On February 13, a second contaminated bottle was found in a Yonker's store. This bottle had obviously been tampered with. Johnson & Johnson created a crisis-management team of top executives to respond. During their meeting, Burke concluded that "there is no tamperproof package [and there] is never going to be a tamperproof package."[20] On February 16, the company decided to recall all Tylenol capsule products and to cease selling any over-the-counter products in capsule form.

Tylenol staged a second rapid recovery. Within five months, market share had risen to 90 percent of its previous level. A year after the second poisoning, Johnson & Johnson was again the leading seller of over-the-counter pain relievers.[21] Johnson & Johnson believes a number of factors helped it maintain the public's trust and confidence. In addition to putting public safety first, the firm provided excellent cooperation with the Food and Drug Administration, the Federal Bureau of Investigation, and various state and local authorities. It also maintained open communication with the public via an 800 telephone number, thousands of mailgrams, numerous press conferences, and media interviews. Finally, the capsules that were recalled were replaced without question or charge.[22] The public's trust was maintained by quick, caring action. Open communication was maintained throughout both crises. Customers were treated fairly with product replacement provided at no cost. Thus, no groundswell for public policy action occurred. The only regulation to grow out of the two tampering cases increased the penalties in the federal antitampering laws.[23]

Intel's Pentium Chip

Professor Thomas R. Nicely, a mathematician at Lynchburg College, had been conducting research in computational number theory, an area of pure mathematics, for several years. He was testing computer code written to calculate prime, twin prime, prime triplet, and prime quadruplet numbers for all positive integers up to a very large limit. A number of checks built into the code enabled him to compare his results with certain published numbers.

On June 13, 1994, Nicely discovered that some of his check values disagreed with the published numbers.[24] After extensive testing for the source of the error, he began to isolate the problem during the week of October 22. His tests indicated that the floating point unit (FPU) of the Pentium chip appeared to be the culprit. He contacted his computer manufacturer and then Intel. Neither had an answer to his problem. Further testing on other brands of computers using the Pentium chip replicated the error. On October 30, 1994, Nicely sent the e-mail message shown in Figure 2.1 to a number of individuals and organizations asking them to verify his findings on other Pentium computers.

Author Andrew Schulman received a copy of the message and subsequently sent it to Richard M. Smith, president of Phar Lap Software, for corroboration.[25] After confirming the bug at Phar Lap, Smith e-mailed Nicely's message to Intel and several compiler companies. He also posted it on the Canopus forum of Compuserve, asking for others to confirm the bug in order to see how widespread it was. Ten confirmations came back within 24 hours.

Alex Wolfe, a reporter for *Electronic Engineering Times* magazine, read the message on Compuserve and immediately set to work developing a story that ran in the November 7th issue. Wolfe found that Intel had discovered the problem in midyear and had fixed the problem with what was referred to as a mask change to the Pentium's floating-point unit. Wolfe quoted Steve Smith, a Pentium engineering manager at Intel, as saying "This was a very rare condition that happened once every 9 to 10 billion operand pairs."[26] Intel did not change part-number designations or otherwise mark the updated chips to differentiate them from the flawed chips.

Industry analysts estimated that Intel had shipped at least two million defective chips by the time the problem became public knowledge.[27] Intel and computer manufacturers continued to sell their stocks of defective chips and machines containing the chips. Intel maintained that the average user would never see the error. It did acknowledge that some specialized users working in scientific and engineering areas might be affected by the flaw. It offered to work with such individuals to resolve the problem.

On November 27, 1994, a message was posted on the Internet from Andy Grove, president of Intel.[28] He stated that the Pentium had been more thoroughly tested than any other chip in history, but that it was the most complex chip they had ever built. He stated that Intel continues to test its chips and fix bugs as they are found. He acknowledged: "After almost 25 years in the microprocessor business, I have come to the conclusion that no microprocessor is ever perfect; they just come closer to

FIGURE 2.1 E-mail Message Sent by Professor Nicely

FROM: Dr. Thomas R. Nicely
                 Professor of Mathematics
                 Lynchburg College
                 1501 Lakeside Drive
                 Lynchburg, Virginia 24501-3199

                 Phone: XXX-XXX-XXXX
                 Fax: XXX-XXX-XXXX
                 Internet: XXXXXX@acavax.lynchburg.edu

TO: Whom it may concern

RE: Bug in the Pentium FPU

DATE: 30 October 1994

It appears that there is a bug in the floating point unit (numeric coprocessor) of many, and perhaps all, Pentium processors.

In short, the Pentium FPU is returning erroneous values for certain division operations. For example,

$$1/824633702441.0$$

is calculated incorrectly (all digits beyond the eighth significant digit are in error). This can be verified in compiled code, an ordinary spreadsheet such as Quattro Pro or Excel, or even the Windows calculator (use the scientific mode), by computing

$$(824633702441.0)*(1/824633702441.0),$$

which should equal 1 exactly (within some extremely small rounding error; in general, coprocessor results should contain 19 significant decimal digits). However, the Pentiums tested return

$$0.999999996274709702$$

for this calculation. A similar erroneous value is obtained for x*(1/x) for most values of x in the interval

$$824633702418 <= x <= 824633702449,$$

and throughout any interval obtained by multiplying or dividing the above interval by an integer power of 2 (there are yet other intervals which also produce division errors).

The bug can also be observed by calculating 1/(1/x) for the above values of x. The Pentium FPU will fail to return the original x (in fact, it will often return a value exactly 3072 = 6*0x200 larger).

The bug has been observed on all Pentiums I have tested or had tested to date, including a Dell P90, a Gateway P90, a Micron P60, an Insight P60, and a Packard-Bell P60. It has not been observed on any 486 or earlier system, even those with a PCI bus. If the FPU is locked out (not always possible), the error disappears; but then the Pentium becomes a "586SX", and floating point must run in emulation, slowing down computations by a factor of roughly ten.

I encountered erroneous results which were related to this bug as long ago as June, 1994, but it was not until 19 October 1994 that I felt I had eliminated all other likely sources of error (software logic, compiler, chipset, etc.). I contacted Intel Tech Support regarding this bug on Monday 24 October (call reference number 51270). The contact person later reported that the bug was observed on a 66-MHz system at Intel, but had no further information or explanation, other than the fact that no such bug had been previously reported or observed.

Further information can be obtained by contacting me directly, and by downloading files from the [anonymous.nicely.pentium_bug] directory of the acavax.lynchburg.edu machine via anonymous ftp on Internet (password ANONYMOUS, user ID = Internet ID). These files include a documentation file, a DOS executable image demonstrating the bug, and the source code for the demonstration. The zip file uses PKZIP version 2.04g.

I would be interested in hearing of test results from other Pentiums, and also from 486-DX4s and (if anybody has one yet) the AMD, Cyrix, and NexGen clones of the Pentium.

You may use this information freely as long as you give me attribution by name and employer.

perfection with each stepping."[29] Stepping refers to creating a new set of masks to correct for bugs found to date. Grove indicated that microprocessors normally go through a half dozen or more steppings during their production life.

He went on to talk about the remote possibility of encountering the error as the reason they did not find it sooner. Grove closed with the offer to resolve the problem on an individual basis and asked all users involved in heavy-duty scientific/floating-point calculations to contact Intel via 800 numbers that had been set up for that purpose. He even held out the possibility of replacing chips if necessary.

The Pentium bug would not affect programs that do not perform division. Thus, errors would not occur in word-processing, database, and electronic mail-handling programs. Even in programs that performed division, the largest error in a single division would be 0.006 percent, with most being much smaller, according to Tim Coe, an engineer at Vitesse Semiconductor Corporation.[30] Nevertheless, mounting criticism on the Internet, in the press, and on talk shows put pressure on Intel. A recent "Intel Inside" marketing campaign had created strong consumer name recognition. Consumers began to identify the Pentium as a flawed product.

On December 12, 1994, IBM announced that it was suspending shipment of IBM personal computers containing Pentium microprocessors. G. Richard Thoman, IBM senior vice president and group executive, stated: "We believe no one should have to wonder about the integrity of data calculated on IBM PCs."[31] While Intel had said that on a random basis the likelihood of a customer encountering an error while using a spreadsheet was once in 27,000 years, IBM indicated that its tests showed users of spreadsheet programs recalculating for 15 minutes a day could produce an error every 24 days. This would result in numerous errors per day in a large company. IBM also stated it would replace Pentium chips for any of its customers free of charge.

While Intel had urged all computer manufacturers to refer their customer calls regarding the Pentium to Intel, more manufacturers began to follow IBM's lead of offering Pentium replacements. Prior to the IBM announcement, customer calls concerning the Pentium were declining at Intel. Following the IBM announcement, the company began receiving "tens of thousands" of calls requesting Pentium replacements.[32] In addition, lawsuits were being filed and state officials were readying additional suits charging Intel with violating their unfair-trade-practices laws.[33]

On December 20, 1994, Intel announced that it would replace all flawed Pentium chips with no questions asked. In the news release, Andy Grove stated:

> ... we are today announcing a no-questions-asked return policy on the current version of the Pentium processor. Our previous policy was to talk with users to determine whether their needs required replacement of the processor. To some people, this policy seemed arrogant and uncaring. We

apologize. We were motivated by a belief that replacement is simply unnecessary for most people. We still feel that way, but we are changing our policy because we want there to be no doubt that we stand behind this product.[34]

The announcement was followed up with the ad shown in Figure 2.2 that was run in major newspapers in North America.

Intel reported that its fourth-quarter profit declined 37 percent due to a $475 million pretax charge taken for the replacement of the flawed Pentium chips.[35] The company also said that consumer purchases of Pentium computers had never slowed despite two months of negative publicity.

Beech-Nut Nutrition Corporation

Beech-Nut Corporation, founded in 1891, had grown to be the second-largest baby food company in the United States. The firm built a reputation on products known for their purity, high quality, and natural ingredients.[36] This was ingrained in its corporate culture. Unfortunately, Beech-Nut's baby-food business rarely made a profit; thus, in 1973, Squibb sold the baby-food business to a group headed by Pennsylvania lawyer Frank Nicholas. The group purchased Beech-Nut almost entirely with borrowed funds and did not provide the capital needed to support the firm properly. A market share of 15 percent, compared to the market leader Gerber Products Company's 70 percent share, did not help matters.[37] Losses mounted and by 1978 suppliers were owed millions of dollars.[38]

In 1977, Beech-Nut reached an agreement with Interjuice Trading Corporation, a wholesaler, to buy apple concentrate at a price 20 percent below the going market rate. The deal was a major coup for Beech-Nut, given its deteriorating financial position and the fact that 30 percent of its sales were from products containing apple concentrate. However, as with most deals too good to be true, it was. Rumors were flying that apple juice adulteration was widespread within the industry. The deal with Interjuice raised suspicions among employees of the research and development department that the concentrate was bogus. Unfortunately, at that time, there was no test that could prove that the concentrate was anything but pure apple juice. Still, several employees, including Jerome J. LiCari, director of research and development, urged Beech-Nut to stop buying from Interjuice. Their request was denied primarily due to the shaky financial condition of the firm.

The Nicholas group sold Beech-Nut to Nestlé in 1979.[39] Nestlé invested heavily in Beech-Nut, but the losses continued, reaching $2.5 million in 1981.[40] In 1981, LiCari decided to launch a major effort to improve adulteration testing. He believed that the major product-line restructuring that Beech-Nut was planning would be jeopardized if they continued to buy from Interjuice. By August he had developed very strong evidence that the Interjuice concentrate was fraudulent. He took the evidence to

FIGURE 2.2 Intel Pentium Replacement Advertisement

Source: Reprinted with permission of Intel Corporation.

pentium

To Pentium™ processor-based computer owners and the PC community:

We at Intel wish to sincerely apologize for our handling of the recently publicized Pentium processor flaw.

The Intel Inside® symbol means that your computer has a microprocessor second to none in quality and performance. Thousands of Intel employees work very hard to ensure that this is true. But no microprocessor is ever perfect.

What Intel continues to believe is technically an extremely minor problem has taken on a life of its own. Although Intel firmly stands behind the quality of the current version of the Pentium processor, we recognize that many users have concerns.

We want to resolve these concerns.

Intel will exchange the current version of the Pentium processor for an updated version in which this floating-point divide flaw is corrected for any owner who requests it, free of charge anytime during the life of their computer. Just call 1-800-628-8686.

Sincerely,

Andrew S. Grove
President and
Chief Executive Officer

Craig R. Barrett
Executive Vice President and
Chief Operating Officer

Gordon E. Moore
Chairman of the Board

intel.

John F. Lavery, head of operations, but was rebuffed. He then met with company president, Neils L. Hoyvald. Nothing happened. Later in the year, Lavery suggested to Hoyvald that they change apple concentrate suppliers even though costs would increase. Hoyvald refused, stating that the budget was already too high. Hoyvald had promised Nestlé that Beech-Nut would be profitable in 1982.[41]

In June 1982, a private investigator hired by Processed Apples Institute, Inc., the trade association for companies that process fresh apples, provided Beech-Nut with proof that the apple concentrate they were buying was adulterated. Beech-Nut was asked to join in a lawsuit against Interjuice. It refused, but it immediately canceled its contract with Interjuice. Beech-Nut continued to sell existing supplies of products made with the fake apple concentrate.

After the contract was canceled, Beech-Nut was left with an inventory of $3.5 million in bogus apple-juice products.[42] In order to sell its inventory, Beech-Nut engaged in a variety of questionable acts. When the FDA identified an apple-juice lot as adulterated, Beech-Nut destroyed the lot before the feds could seize it. In August, an official from New York State informed Beech-Nut that a sample they collected contained "little, if any, apple juice."[43] Concerned that the state might seize its entire inventory, the company hired nine trucks and moved the inventory to a New Jersey warehouse. It then proceeded quickly to distribute the inventory to the Caribbean and Puerto Rico. Under mounting pressure, the company issued a national recall of its apple juice in October 1982. Amazingly, Beech-Nut continued to sell mixed juices containing the fake concentrate until March 1983.[44]

The Justice Department opened a criminal investigation into the Beech-Nut case in June 1985.[45] On November 13, 1987, the firm pleaded guilty to 215 felony counts, including intentionally selling adulterated and misbranded juice in 20 states and Puerto Rico, the Virgin Islands, and five foreign countries. The FDA fined Beech-Nut $2 million. On February 17, 1988, Lavery was convicted on 448 counts, and Hoyvald was convicted on 359 counts of violating federal food and drug laws, including conspiracy and mail fraud.[46] They each were sentenced to a year and a day in prison and were fined $100,000 apiece. Their appeal to the Supreme Court was denied in October 1989.[47]

How did Beech-Nut employees rationalize their behavior? They used two arguments:

1. They believed that "everybody's doing it."
2. Even though the juice was adulterated, it was perfectly safe.

The fact was that only 5 percent of the apple juice sold in the industry was adulterated.[48] There was also a question of whether some of the ingredients in the bogus juice could have long-term negative effects.

The consequences of selling the adulterated concentrate were major. Total fines from all jurisdictions were estimated at $25 million plus legal costs.[49] Juice sales fell by 20 percent during 1987, and the company incurred record losses of about $15 million.[50] The company was barred from doing any business with the federal government from December 1986 through 1991.[51] One could not even argue that the decision had a positive cost benefit ratio.

Beech-Nut was sold to Ralston Purina Company in 1989 for about half the value of its annual sales.[52] Food companies were typically selling for two and a half times the value of their annual sales. Beech-Nut was sold again in 1998 to Milnot.[53]

Manville Corporation

The Manville Corporation, founded in 1858, was incorporated as the Johns-Manville Corporation in 1901. The firm grew to become the world's leading asbestos company by the turn of the century. It mined and sold raw asbestos fibers and developed, manufactured, and sold intermediate and finished asbestos products. Some of the many uses to which asbestos had been put in the home and workplace are described in the following excerpt:

> Perhaps no other mineral is so woven into the fabric of American life as is asbestos. Impervious to heat and fibrous—it is the only mineral that can be woven into cloth—asbestos is spun into fireproof clothing and theater curtains, as well as into such household items as noncombustible drapes, rugs, pot holders, and ironing board covers. Mixed into slurry, asbestos is sprayed onto girders and walls to provide new buildings with fireproof insulation. It is used in floor tiles, roofing felts, and in most plasterboards and wallboards. Asbestos is also an ingredient of plaster and stucco and of many paints and putties. This "mineral of a thousand uses"—an obsolete nickname: the present count stands at around 3,000 uses—is probably present in some form or other in every home, school, office building, and factory in this country. Used in brake linings and clutch facings, in mufflers and gaskets, in sealants and caulking, and extensively used in ships, asbestos is also a component of every modern vehicle, including spaceships.[54]

The firm had grown and prospered over the years, paying dividends every year except the war years of 1915–1916 and the depression years of 1933–1934. Manville had been listed in the Dow-Jones Industrial Thirty for many years.

However, major problems of long-standing origin were brewing. In 1898, Manville founder Henry Ward Johns died of dust phthisis pneumonitis, now known as asbestosis. Lawsuits began to be filed in the 1920s on behalf of employees who had died or fallen ill from breathing asbestos fibers. The firm was successful in defending itself, arguing that its employees assumed the risks of employment. They knew or should have known of the dangers of asbestos and thus were contributively negligent.

An early study of the effects of asbestos workers inhaling asbestos fibers was begun in 1929 by Metropolitan Life Insurance Company, Manville's insurance company. The study was conducted at the request of firms representing the asbestos industry. Metropolitan assigned Dr. A. J. Lanza to conduct the study. In 1931, at its conclusion, Dr. Lanza submitted to the firms galley-proof sheets of the report entitled "Effects of Inhalation of Asbestos Dust upon the Lungs of Asbestos Workers."[55]

More than two years passed before Vandiver Brown, head of Manville's legal department, acknowledged receipt of the report that was submitted for publication in the United States Public Health Service Report. After reviewing the report with an outside attorney, Brown sent editorial suggestions to Dr. Lanza and stated:

> I am sure that you understand fully that no one in our organization is
> suggesting for a moment that you alter by one jot or tittle any scientific
> facts or inevitable conclusions revealed or justified by your preliminary
> survey. All we ask is that all of the favorable aspects of the survey be
> included and that none of the unfavorable be unintentionally pictured in
> darker terms than the circumstances justify. I feel confident that we can
> depend upon you and Dr. McConnel to give us a 'break' and mine and
> Mr. Hobart's suggestions are presented in this spirit.[56]

Additional studies were conducted in the 1930s and 1940s, but the results were always squelched.

In a letter to an industry colleague in 1935, Brown stated, "I quite agree that our interests are best served by having asbestosis receive the minimum of publicity."[57] His comment was in regard to a letter received from Anne Rossiter, editor of the industry journal *Asbestos*. Miss Rossiter wrote:

> You may recall that we have written you on several occasions concerning the
> publishing of information, or discussion of, asbestosis and the work which
> has been and is being done, to eliminate or at least reduce it. Always you
> have requested that for obvious reasons, we publish nothing, and naturally
> your wishes have been respected. Possibly by this time, however, the reasons
> for your objection to publicity on this subject have been eliminated, and if so
> we would like very much to review the whole matter in *Asbestos*.[58]

In 1950, Dr. Kenneth W. Smith, chief physician for Manville, issued an internal report showing that only four of 708 workers he studied were free of asbestosis. He diagnosed the damage as permanent and irreversible. Smith recommended that the workers not be told of their condition so that they would not become distressed and shorten their productive time with the company. In 1953, however, Smith requested that caution labels be placed on asbestos. He was overruled by senior management.

Manville and other manufacturers continued to suppress negative information about asbestos and blocked scientific studies in an attempt to control the flow of negative information. In the meantime, people continued to die of asbestosis.

Scholarly journal articles began appearing in the 1950s, linking asbestos to other diseases. A major paper by Dr. I. J. Selikoff of Mt. Sinai Medical Center in New York was read at the 1964 meeting of the American Medical Association. Dr. Selikoff's findings linked asbestos ingestion with thousands of deaths and injuries. He subsequently estimated that more than 100,000 Americans would die of asbestos-related diseases.

Under increasing pressure, Manville agreed to put labels on asbestos products. The labels read: "Inhalation of asbestos in excessive quantities over long periods of time may be harmful." They recommended that users avoid breathing asbestos dust and wear masks when working in places with inadequate ventilation. The firm released the following statement justifying their failure to alert asbestos users earlier:

> During the periods of alleged injurious exposure, medical and scientific authorities, government officials and companies supplying products containing asbestos fiber believed that the dust levels for asbestos recommended by the United States Public Health Service did not constitute a hazard to the health of workers handling asbestos-containing insulation products. Accordingly, the company has maintained that there was no basis for product warnings or special hazard controls until the 1964 publication of results of scientific studies linking pulmonary disease in asbestos insulation workers with asbestos exposure.[59]

Lawsuits against Manville were being filed in increasing numbers by workers and their families. Some victims were beginning to win judgments. In 1977, an attorney representing asbestos victims accidentally discovered the minutes of a 1933 meeting between Raybestos-Manhattan, another asbestos producer, and Manville. At the meeting, the two firms discussed the findings of a health survey Raybestos-Manhattan had commissioned. The study reported a high incidence of asbestosis among its workers and contained a strong warning of the health hazards of exposure to asbestos. Both firms agreed to keep the report secret to avoid lawsuits. Manville had misplaced its copies in the corporate headquarter's move from Chicago to Denver, but Raybestos-Manhattan had its copies in a vault over the years.[60] This information destroyed Manville's argument that it was unaware of the dangers of asbestos until 1964. Record punitive damage awards followed.

The number of lawsuits filed ballooned. At the same time, asbestos sales, the most profitable part of Manville's business, declined. An increasing number of lawsuits were being found for the plaintiff. Manville was able to stall payment by appealing the cases. However, it was becoming clear that the company was in deep trouble.

Prior to the early 1970s, workers had to pursue wrongful injury claims through the state workers' compensation systems. Then state courts began permitting injured asbestos workers to file tort actions against asbestos manufacturers. Jury awards for tort suits were far higher. In addition to the change in legal charges, the legal doctrines of product liability were changing. Until the 1960s, a manufacturer's liability was limited to negligent conduct. A claimant had to prove that a manufacturer was negligent or irresponsible in order to win a suit. The law evolved during the 1960s to the concept of strict liability. Manufacturers could be found liable for damages even though they were not intentionally negligent or blameworthy.

The strict liability doctrine dramatically altered the legal environment in which Manville was operating. The *Beshada* v. *Johns-Manville Products Corp.* case in New Jersey extended the liability of Manville and other asbestos manufacturers for asbestos injuries that were incurred prior to the time it could be proven that the firms were aware of asbestos hazards.[61] The symptoms of asbestos injury may not appear until 30 or 40 years after exposure. Thus, Manville argued that prior to the 1960s, the scientific evidence was not conclusive enough to require manufacturers to warn workers of the hazards of working with asbestos. Their argument was rejected. As a side note, the company changed its name to Manville in 1981.

The changes in the legal environment launched a wave of increasing settlement costs. A new industry developed to litigate asbestos claims. The biweekly publication *Asbestos Litigation Reporter* was launched and new pressure groups formed. They included the White Lung Association, Asbestos Victims of America, and the Asbestos Litigation Group (a coalition of 500 lawyers and thousands of claimants suing Manville).

Even though it was operating profitably, Manville Corporation filed for bankruptcy on August 26, 1982. This voluntarily placed the firm under Chapter 11 of the Bankruptcy Reform Act of 1978. At that time, the firm faced 16,500 asbestos-related injury lawsuits. Settled claims were averaging $40,000. New suits were being filed at the rate of 500 per month. Projections indicated that 36,000 additional suits would be filed by the year 2000, resulting in a minimum of $2 billion in claims (double the company's net worth) with the final figure likely being much greater.[62] Earlier in the year, five lawsuits were settled with punitive damages awarded averaging $616,000 each. Punitive damages are awards in addition to the amount provided to pay for damages suffered by the injured person. The damages are meant to punish a firm for outrageous and willful misconduct.

Chapter 11 protects a firm against its creditors while it develops a reorganization plan to pay its debts. The reorganization plan must be approved by 50 percent of the firm's creditors who hold at least two-thirds of the debt owed by the company. During the time the firm is developing its plan, it is not obligated to make any payments to its creditors. Thus, it can continue to operate using cash from its sales to finance new supplies. In addition to protecting Manville from its creditors, the bankruptcy petition protected Manville from making payments on the lawsuits. This freed up additional funds for current operations. In the meantime, a number of the plaintiffs were dying.

Manville emerged from Chapter 11 on November 28, 1988. The firm had maintained profitable operations through most of the period. During the reorganization, Manville divested its asbestos operations, its most profitable business. It reorganized into three operating groups. Its fiberglass group produced insulation and auto parts. Its forest products group manufactured wine-cooler cartons, grocery sacks, and folding cartons. Its specialty products group consisted of a variety of businesses, including lighting fixtures for stadiums, roofing, filtration minerals, and palladium mines.

The reorganization plan contained two trusts to settle and pay claims. The Personal Injury Settlement Trust was created with $2.5 billion to pay health-damage claims of present and future asbestos victims. The trust was funded with 80 percent of Manville's common stock, making the company's stockholders the biggest losers. The firm was also required to pay $75 million annually into the fund plus 20 percent of its operating profits from 1992, until 2015. The Property Damage Settlement Trust was created with $240 million in cash and insurance proceeds. It was established to pay claims of owners of buildings containing asbestos materials. Both trusts are run by an independent trustee. In addition to the trusts, Manville agreed to pay $700 million to creditors and to create a charitable fund of $5 million for asbestos victims who did not technically qualify for compensation. A further condition of the agreement was that Manville could no longer be sued by asbestos victims. This removed the threat of punitive damage awards.

Manville's top-management team was forced out as part of the reorganization. Eighty percent of the common stock was transferred to the Personal Injury Settlement Trust. Both top management and the Manville stockholders paid dearly for past actions.

Manville has evolved into an international holding company. The company has two principal subsidiaries, Riverwood International Corporation, a packaging systems and paper products company, and Schuller International Incorporated, a fiberglass-based business making building insulation, roofing systems, and mechanical insulation. Manville changed its name to Schuller Corp. in 1996 and changed it back to Johns Manville Corp. in 1997.[63] The company was sold to Berkshire Halfaway, Warren Buffet's holding company, in 2001.[64] It is a totally different company today.

Summary

We have seen that ethics is good business both from a macro and a micro perspective. Ethical behavior supports the market system, and unethical behavior distorts the market. Buyers benefit from ethical behavior that creates the needed trust to support exchange relationships. Sellers also benefit from exchange relationships made possible by trust supported by ethical behavior. There is strong motivation to build trust among employees and management. Trust promotes productivity. Trust requires ethical behavior.

We have presented cases showing how ethical behavior and trust have affected the fortunes of four major companies. Johnson & Johnson took immediate action to solve a problem with its product, a problem it did not create. By acting quickly to protect the interests of its customers, the firm maintained their trust. It was able to survive a major catastrophe, actually two catastrophes, and attain an improved market position.

It took Intel much longer to realize that it had a major problem. Once the magnitude of the problem was realized, Intel took swift action to resolve it. According to Andy Grove,

> . . . we got caught between our mindset, which is a fact-based, analysis-based engineer's mindset, and customers' mindset, which is not so much emotional but accustomed to making their own choice. I think the kernel of the issue we missed was that we presumed to tell somebody what they should or shouldn't worry about, or should or shouldn't do.[65]

Intel was on the brink of losing customer trust. Much more delay in handling the problem could have cost the company dearly. Fortunately, it acted in time.

In contrast, Beech-Nut took the low road. The firm was under significant financial pressure. In an attempt to become profitable, the firm began cheating its customers by passing off bogus apple juice as the real thing. Even after its actions were exposed to the public, the firm continued to sell the fake juice. As a consequence, the firm lost the trust and confidence of its customers and their support. In addition, members of top management were fined and sentenced to time in jail.

Finally, Manville had a long history of unethical actions. It knew of the hazards of asbestos back in the 1930s. In trying to protect its core business, it kept the knowledge secret so that its employees, customers, and the government were unaware of the hazards. It refused to take any action to protect its employees or customers. In contrast to Johnson & Johnson, Manville showed a total disregard for both groups. Even when the evidence became irrefutable, Manville still denied the danger. Such behavior destroyed the trust that had built up between the firm and its customers. The end came when the firm was forced into bankruptcy. Management was sacked, and the stockholders, for all practical purposes, lost their company. The firm also lost its most profitable product. The majority of the assets of the former firm are now controlled by the trusts representing the people who were injured by the firm. The remaining assets form the basis of a much smaller new firm that has been sold to an organization known for its positive behavior.

Of the four firms, two took the ethical route, albeit one was a little slow, and both are highly successful. A third took the unethical road for a relatively short period of time, and its decision makers ended up in jail. The fourth practiced unethical behavior for many years, and the owners and managers ended up losing the company.

Discussion Questions

1. How did Beech-Nut's use of fake apple-juice concentrate alter the market system's allocation of resources?
2. How did Johnson & Johnson's actions promote the effectiveness of the market system in allocating resources?

3. How does trust as expectations of technical competence differ from trust as expectations of fiduciary responsibility?
4. What creates trust between two people or between two businesses?
5. How is trust lost in a business relationship?
6. When did Manville begin to lose the trust of its employees? How did the firm try to maintain the trust?
7. If you were the CEO at Beech-Nut, what would you do to regain the trust of LiCari and his co-workers?
8. How did Manville attempt to regain society's trust?
9. How close did Intel come to losing the trust of its customers?
10. What would the likely result have been if Intel had maintained its original policy of replacing the Pentium only for users doing heavy-duty scientific/floating-point calculations?

End Notes

1. Bernard Barber, *The Logic and Limits of Trust* (New Brunswick, New Jersey: Rutgers University Press, 1983), p. 100.
2. Roland N. McKean, "Economics of Trust, Altruism, and Corporate Responsibility," *Altruism, Morality, and Economic Theory,* Edmund S. Phelps, ed. (New York: Russell Sage Foundation, 1975), p. 29.
3. Stewart Macauley, "Non-contractual Relations in Business: A Preliminary Study," *American Sociological Review* 28 (1963), pp. 55–67.
4. R. T. Golembiewski and M. McConkie, "The Centrality of Interpersonal Trust in Group Processes," *Theories of Group Process,* C. L. Cooper, ed. (New York: John Wiley & Sons, Inc., 1975).
5. Kenneth J. Arrow, "Gifts and Exchanges," *Altruism, Morality, and Economic Theory,* Edmund S. Phelps, ed. (New York: Russell Sage Foundation, 1975), p. 24.
6. John R. Rempel and John G. Homes, "How do I Trust Thee?" *Psychology Today* 20 (February 1986), pp. 28–34.
7. LaRue T. Hosmer, "Trust: The Connecting Link between Organizational Theory and Philosophical Ethics," *Academy of Management Journal* 20, no. 2 (April 1995), pp. 379–403.
8. F. Robert Dwyer, Paul H. Schurr, and Sejo Oh, "Developing Buyer-Seller Relationships," *Journal of Marketing* 51, no. 2 (April 1987), pp. 11–27.
9. William A. Messner, *Profitable Purchasing Management* (New York: AMACOM, 1982), p. 263.
10. John E. Swan, I. Fred Trawick, Jr., David R. Rink, and Jenny J. Roberts, "Measuring Dimensions of Purchaser Trust of Industrial Salespeople," *The Journal of Personal Selling & Sales Management* 8, no. 1 (May 1988), pp. 1–9.
11. Dwyer, Schurr, and Oh, "Developing Buyer-Seller Relationships."
12. Jitendra Mishra and Molly A. Morrissey, "Trust in Employee/Employer Relationships: A Survey of West Michigan Managers," *Public Personnel Management* 19, no. 4 (Winter 1990), pp. 443–486.
13. Ibid.

It's Your Turn

You are responsible for recording income for a midsized public company. Your firm is heavily leveraged with some large debt payments due next year. It has been a good year and income and profits have significantly exceeded projections. However, things do not look so good for next year. Competitors are bringing out new products that outperform the ones your firm is selling. Your firm will introduce products that will match the competition the following year, but they are still under development and thus you expect to lose a significant share of the market next year. Profits could take a big hit at just the wrong time.

It is near the end of your fiscal year. Your boss drops by and you two get into a discussion of the success of the firm this year, but both of you are concerned about next year. If income is in line with your projections, your firm may not be able to obtain the necessary financing to meet its debt obligations. That could put the firm in jeopardy.

Your firm has regularly paid out dividends based upon a percentage of profits. Cutting the dividend may send the wrong message to creditors and the market. However, payment of the dividend will likely deplete cash below the level needed for next year. Your boss mentions the possibility of booking some of this year's income as being received next year. That would stabilize profits over the two years, reduce dividend payouts this year, saving cash needed for next year's payments, and stabilize the firm's stock price.

You believe you can get by the auditors with this scheme to protect the company and jobs. However, you also recognize that this action would not be legal and would deprive current stockholders of dividends and potentially higher stock prices that they have the right to expect with this year's earnings performance. Since time is growing short, you must decide how you are going to record the remaining income for the year. What are you going to do? Why?

14. Peg Holmes, "Communicators Help Build Employee Trust at General Motors," *Communication World* 2, no. 7 (August 1985), pp. 18–21.

15. Jay A. Conger and Rabindra N. Kanungo, "The Empowerment Process: Integrating Theory and Practice," *Academy of Management Review* 13, no. 3 (July 1988), pp. 471–482.

16. Ibid.

17. E. Neilsen, "Empowerment Strategies: Balancing Authority and Responsibility," *Executive Power,* Suresh Srivastra, ed. (San Francisco: Jossey-Bass, 1986), pp. 78–110.

18. Clark H. Johnson, "A Matter of Trust," *Management Accounting* 71, no. 6 (December 1989), pp. 12–13.

19. Ibid.

20. Bill Powell and Martin Kasindorf, "The Tylenol Rescue," *Newsweek* 107, no. 9 (March 3, 1986), p. 52.

21. "Tylenol Begins Making a 'Solid Recovery' " (New Brunswick, New Jersey: Johnson & Johnson, 1986).

22. Johnson, "A Matter of Trust."

23. Felix Kessler, "Tremors from Tylenol Scare Hit Food Companies," *Fortune* 113, no. 7 (March 31, 1986), pp. 59, 62.

24. Thomas R. Nicely, "Pentium FPU Bug," e-mail memo from Nicely to "Whom It May Concern," responding to frequently asked questions (memo dated December 9, 1994).

25. Richard M. Smith, "More History of the Pentium FDIV Bug," report dated December 27, 1994, found under The Pentium Papers on the Mathworks Inc. Internet home page.

26. Alexander Wolfe, "Intel Fixes a Pentium FPU Glitch," *Electronic Engineering Times* (November 7, 1994), p. 1.

27. Don Clark, "Some Scientists Are Angry over Flaws in Pentium Chip, and Intel's Response," *The Wall Street Journal* 131, no. 103 (November 25, 1994), p. B6.

28. Andy Grove, "My Perspective on Pentium-AGS," message posted on the comp.sys.intel newsgroup dated November 27, 1994.

29. Ibid.

30. David Stipp, "Chips Fly over Import of Pentium Flaw," *The Wall Street Journal* 131 (December 16, 1994), p. B8.

31. "IBM Halts Shipments of Pentium-Based PCs Based on Company Research," press release issued by IBM.

32. Jim Carlton, "Humble Pie: Intel to Replace Its Pentium Chips," *The Wall Street Journal* 131 (December 21, 1994), pp. B1, B9.

33. Richard B. Schmitt, "Flurry of Lawsuits Filed against Intel over Pentium Flaw," *The Wall Street Journal* 131 (December 16, 1994), p. B3.

34. "Intel Adopts Upon-Request Replacement Policy on Pentium," press release from Intel dated December 20, 1994.

35. Don Clark, "Intel's 4th-Period Net Fell 37% on Big Charge for Pentium Woes," *The Wall Street Journal* 132, no. 12 (January 15, 1995).

36. Chris Welles, "What Led Beech-Nut down the Road to Disgrace," *Business Week* 3039 (February 22, 1988), pp. 126–127.

37. Ibid.

38. Ibid.

39. Ibid.

40. Ibid.

41. Ibid.

42. Ibid.

43. Ibid.

44. Ibid.

45. "Bad Apples in the Executive Suite," *Consumer Reports* 54, no. 5 (May 1989), pp. 294–296.

46. Ibid.

47. "Justices Decline to Review DES, General Dynamics Cases: Beech-Nut Convictions Also Allowed to Stand," *The Washington Post* 112 (October 31, 1989), pp. D1, D13.

48. Welles, "What Led Beech-Nut down the Road to Disgrace."

49. Ibid.

50. Alix M. Freedman, "Nestle Quietly Seeks to Sell Beechnut, Dogged by Scandal of Bogus Apple Juice," *The Wall Street Journal* (July 6, 1989).

51. Ibid.

52. Robert Johnson, "Ralston to Buy Beech-Nut, Gambling It Can Overcome Apple Juice Scandal," *The Wall Street Journal* (September 18, 1989).

53. Jerri Stroud, "Milnot Is Comfortable in the Slow Lane it Thinks Beech-Nut Deal Will Feed Profits 'Baby-Bust' Shakes up the Market," *St. Louis Post-Dispatch* (August 16, 1998).

54. Bruce Porter, "An Asbestos Town Struggles with a Killer," *Saturday Review of the Society* 1 (March 1973), pp. 26–31.

55. Paul Brodeur, "Annals of Law: The Asbestos Industry on Trial (II-Discovery)," *The New Yorker* 61, no. 17 (June 17, 1985), pp. 45–111.

56. Ibid.

57. Ibid.

58. Ibid.

59. Ibid.

60. Ibid.

61. 90 N.J. 191, 447 A.2d 539.

62. Stephen W. Quickel, "Triumph of Wile," *Business Month* 132, no. 4 (November 1988), pp. 28–31, 34–35.

63. Jeffrey Leib, "Johns-Manville Moniker Returns," *Denver Post* (April 1, 1997).

64. Tom McGhee, "Buffett Agrees to Buy Johns Manville," *Denver Post* (December 21, 2000).

65. Carlton, "Humble Pie: Intel to Replace Its Pentium Chips."

Chapter 3

Moral Standards

We introduce moral standards in this chapter to provide you with tools to use when judging the moral value of a decision. Moral standards are the yardsticks of business ethics. They provide the basis for deciding whether an act is right or wrong. Moral standards can be used to defend the moral worth of an act, or they can be used to expose the moral bankruptcy of a decision.

Before proceeding, a definition of business ethics is in order so that we are all reading from the same script. *Business ethics is the process of evaluating decisions, either pre or post, with respect to the moral standards of the society's culture.* In order to evaluate decisions, we need a toolbox of moral standards. The toolbox needs to be rather large because it must accommodate a number of different standards or yardsticks.

You should note that we will not talk about ethical decisions. Rather, we will discuss the ethical dimension of decisions. In the economic context, decisions possess a number of dimensions. Before an actual decision is made, one or more of the following dimensions will be considered: economic, political, technological, social, and ethical. The specific dimensions considered will depend on the nature of the problem being addressed. A decision concerning employee compensation will not likely include the technological dimension, while a decision regarding a new communication system probably would.

Hopefully, managers will evaluate the moral dimension of a decision prior to the decision being made. Numerous individuals have found it difficult to develop a morally defensible rationale for their decision after the fact. However, other parties will certainly evaluate the moral worth of a decision following its implementation. As indicated previously, the moral yardsticks used to evaluate a decision consist of the moral standards of a society's culture. Note that we are not arguing for the standards of a government because they may or may not reflect the standards of the culture. Consider the gulf between the moral standards of the government and the culture in Nazi Germany.

Business ethics involves the *use* of moral standards when making business decisions; it is the use of standards, not the determination of standards. Business ethics is a type of applied ethics rather than a normative ethics that focuses on determining moral standards. Moral standards consist of specific moral norms and general moral principles. Moral norms prohibit certain types of behavior such as lying, stealing, and killing. Moral principles provide more general guidelines for behavior and are applicable to a wide range of decision situations. We now turn to a discussion of consequentialist and nonconsequentialist principles, which may be used to guide the ethical dimension of decision making.

Consequentialist Principles

Consequentialist principles, also known as teleological principles, focus on the outcome or end results of a decision. A decision is judged to be ethical or unethical based on the consequences of the decision. The interesting question is consequences for whom? The end results may be judged in terms of the decision maker, the firm, the local community, the state, the society, the world, and so on. The evaluation differs significantly depending on who is viewed as the receiver of the results.

Egoism

Egoism is a standard that focuses on self-interest. The usual formulation is to equate egoism with an individual's personal interest. However, the concept of egoism applies equally well when the interest is identified with an organization or even a local community. For example, a decision to move production facilities offshore is made for the self-interest of the firm. Alternatively, a decision to maintain production at the current facilities while working with local employees and suppliers to match costs of offshore suppliers is in the self-interest of the local community.

Decisions based on egoism are made to provide the most favorable consequences for the party of interest regardless of the consequences to other parties. This does not mean that other parties must be harmed by a decision. A decision that benefits an individual or a firm may be beneficial to a country or the world. However, benefits beyond the party of interest are of no concern to the decision maker.

Self-interest may be viewed in the short run or in the long run. The long-run perspective is often called enlightened self-interest because it considers both the direct and the indirect consequences of an act over an extended period of time. Long-run self-interest takes into account the impact of a decision on the relevant stakeholders and the expected reaction of those stakeholders. For example, a decision that increases short-term profits by taking unfair advantage of employees will likely damage employee morale and loyalty and end up costing more in the long run than was gained. A short-run perspective would lead to accepting the decision while an enlightened self-interest position (long run) would reject it due to the projected excess of costs versus benefits.

Egoism appears to reflect the philosophy of Adam Smith (1723–1790) in terms of providing an efficient market allocating mechanism:

> Every individual is continually exerting himself to find out the most advantageous employment for whatever capital he can command. It is his own advantage, indeed, and not that of the society which he has in view. But the study of his own advantage naturally, or rather necessarily leads him to prefer that employment which is most advantageous to the society. . . .
>
> As every individual, therefore, endeavors as much as he can both to employ his capital in the support of domestic industry, and so to direct that industry that its produce may be of the greatest value; every individual necessarily labours to render the annual revenue of the society as great as he can. He generally, indeed, neither intends to promote the public interest, nor knows how much he is promoting it. By preferring the support of domestic to that of foreign industry, he intends only his own security; and by directing that industry in such a manner as its produce may be of the greatest value, he intends only his own gain, and he is in this, as in many other cases, led by an invisible hand to promote an end which was no part of his intention. Nor is it always the worse for the society that it was no part of it. By pursuing his own interest he frequently promotes that of the society more effectually than when he really intends to promote it.[1]

Smith would argue that society's interest is better served when an individual pursues *long-run* self-interest.

We need to be aware also that Smith maintained that certain rules must be followed for the invisible hand to work properly. This is often forgotten by zealots touting perfectly free markets.

> Commerce and manufacturers can seldom flourish long in any state which does not enjoy a regular administration of justice, in which the people do not feel themselves secure in the possession of their property, in which the faith of contracts is not supported by law, and in which the authority of the state is not supposed to be regularly employed in enforcing the payment of debts from all those who are able to pay.[2]

One other point must be considered. Our definition of business ethics referred to "the moral standards of society's culture." Egoism generally has a much narrower focus, and thus a decision could be reached that was supported from an egoism perspective but does not adhere to the moral standards of society's culture. It would thus likely be judged unethical by all except those making the decision.

Utilitarianism

Utilitarianism is most often associated with Jeremy Bentham (1748–1832) and John Stuart Mill (1806–1873). According to the utilitarian principle, a decision is ethical if it provides greater net utility than any other alternative decision. Thus, the decision maker must evaluate each decision alternative, determine the negative and positive utilities arising from the alternative, and then select the one that yields the greatest net utility. You probably recognize this as a type of cost-benefit analysis in which the costs and benefits of all stakeholders are considered. A decision based on the utilitarian principle is ethical if it produces the greatest good for the greatest number. Anything less is wanting.

There are actually two types of utilitarianism, act and rule. Individual decisions are evaluated under act utilitarianism when the moral value of a decision is determined by the consequences of the specific act. Rule utilitarianism prescribes a set of rules that if followed over time will yield the greatest net utility. This may not be the case for a specific act. For example, one rule may be: Do not lie to customers. Under act utilitarianism, if the lie results in significant benefits that outweigh the cost of the lie to the customer, the lie is ethical. However, rule utilitarianism would ask: What is the effect of a lie to a series of customers over time? Trust, customer satisfaction, and business would be lost. Thus, lying does not provide the greatest net utility. One rule then would be: Do not lie to customers. While act utilitarianism examines the total consequences of a single act, rule utilitarianism looks at the consequences over a series of acts. You could refer to act utilitarianism as being short-run focused and rule utilitarianism as having a long-run perspective.

The rules developed under rule utilitarianism become a type of moral code that guides the decision maker in making a series of decisions that will yield the greatest good for the greatest number. Some difficulty may be experienced when two or more rules in the code lead to conflicting actions for a specific decision being considered. A priority system should be developed to handle conflicts among rules contained in the code.

Egoism is concerned with the self-interest of the individual, the firm, the community, and so on, but utilitarianism is concerned with the self-interest of all stakeholders in total. You may consider individual egoism to be at one end of the consequential continuum and utilitarianism to be at the other. Some decisions may be optimal for the entire consequential continuum. Both the individual and society would benefit the most from a specific decision. However, this mutual interest is not guaranteed, especially if egoism is practiced with a short-run perspective.

The relationship between egoism and utilitarianism is shown in Table 3.1. Egoism that considers the self-interest of all stakeholders equates with utilitarianism. Egoism that takes a short-run perspective is similar to act utilitarianism, which evaluates the consequences of one act. (However, act util-

TABLE 3.1   Egoism and Utilitarianism

Time Horizon	Beneficiary					
	Individual	Firm	Community	State	Nation	World
Short term	Egoism	Egoism	Egoism	Egoism	Egoism	Act utilitarianism
Long term	Egoism	Egoism	Egoism	Egoism	Egoism	Rule utilitarianism

itarianism is normally considered to evaluate all the consequences of a single act in terms of the total net utility derived by all stakeholders, whereas egoism evaluates all the consequences based on the actor's self-interest.)

Some Difficulties

Several difficulties are encountered by a manager using a consequentialist approach. First, it is often very difficult if not impossible to foresee all the consequences of a business decision. Accurate forecasts of outcomes are required in situations where very little data or experience is available. The more complex the decision, the harder it becomes. To apply either an egoism or a utilitarian standard correctly, you must be able to evaluate all the consequences of an act. If you cannot, how can you determine if the act maximizes one's own self-interest or maximizes net utility? Of course, some approximations can be made, but the greater the deviation from fact, the less useful the standard.

Second, many decisions have consequences that are not easily measured and often lack common measurement units. For example, installing emission-control equipment on a smokestack to meet current environmental requirements may cost $500,000. Equipment that will reduce emissions to half that amount may cost $1.5 million. Which equipment should be purchased? The costs are quite easy to determine. However, the gain in utility from each piece of equipment is a bit murkier. Would society be better off if the firm used the extra money to increase employment? What damage is done by the emissions?

Third, maximizing net utility may require actions that cause significant harm to a few people. For example, the construction of the Central Pacific Railroad was accomplished using Chinese laborers who were paid next to nothing and treated like machines. Many died or were maimed. In terms of act utilitarianism, a significant positive net utility was created. Linkage of the country by rail greatly enhanced the transportation capabilities of the country, encouraged industrial development, and enhanced national defense. However, this gain was obtained at the expense of the Chinese laborers.

Fourth, the utility obtained from a decision is not constant across members of a stakeholder group. While one dollar, euro, or yen is always one dollar, euro, or yen, a unit of currency provides more utility to a poor person than to a rich person. In addition, some stakeholders gain greater utility from achieving happiness while others realize greater utility from maximizing their material wealth.

Nonconsequentialist Principles

Nonconsequentialist or deontological principles consist of sets of rules. The outcome of a specific decision is irrelevant to the determination of whether the decision is ethical. The rules provide the guide to ethical decision making. Unlike rule utilitarianism, these rules are based on reason, not consequences. (One can argue that the rules are ultimately based on consequences since the reasoning process used to derive the rules must certainly consider the results of applying the rules.) Nonconsequentialist principles can be generally classified as either rights or justice based.

Rights Principles

Rights principles grant you certain moral or human rights because you are a human being. These rights are associated with duties of others not to violate your rights and, in turn, you have duties not to violate their rights. If you have a right to free speech, I have a duty not to violate your right to free speech as long as your speech does not violate my rights. There is disagreement over the composition of human rights, but there is little disagreement over the concept of human rights.

The development of moral rights is generally attributed to Immanuel Kant (1724–1804). Kant created several formulations of his categorical imperative that in essence state that all individuals should be treated as free people and equal to each other. His first formulation states: "Act only according to that maxim by which you can at the same time will that it should become universal law."[3] Maxim means principle. He is arguing that an action is morally right only if you would be willing to have everyone act the same way in a similar situation. Thus, the principle provides both universal (have everyone act) and reversible (you would be the recipient of the acts of others) criteria for determining moral right and wrong.

Kant's second formulation of the imperative states: "Act so that you treat humanity, whether in your own person or in that of another, always as an end and never as a means only."[4] He argues that people should never be treated only as a means to an end but as ends themselves or as means *and* ends. Thus, when using people to accomplish your purposes, you have a duty to respect them as human beings and to promote their ability to realize their desired ends or goals.

Kant considered the categorical imperative to be a moral law. It is an unconditional command that must be obeyed.[5] His categorical imperative provides firm rules for decision making that do not depend on circumstances or results and do not allow for individual exceptions. To Kant they are absolute duties. Kant stressed the importance of duty and contended that a moral act is one performed out of duty only.[6] The fact that the act may provide personal benefit does not have any bearing on moral value.

W. D. Ross differs from Kant in his view of duties as *prima facie* or conditional rather than absolute. He argues that prima facie duties are based on circumstances that have moral significance and that do not depend on consequences or the categorical imperative. These include duties resulting from promises, duties of reparation for previous wrongs, duties of gratitude for previous acts by others, duties of beneficence to others whom we can make better, duties of self-improvement, and duties not to injure others.[7] One can quickly think of examples in which some of the duties will conflict with others. For example, you promise to help a friend move prior to discovering that you are scheduled to be out of town on business that day. *Prima facie* duties are duties that must be honored unless they conflict with a stronger duty. In this case, they can be overridden by the more important duty. Is your trip or the promise to your friend more important?

Rights may be either positive or negative. Positive rights imply that an agent has an overt duty to provide whatever is required to exercise the right. If education is considered a right, some agent (likely the state) has a duty to provide access to education. A lesser duty is associated with negative rights. In this case, the duty is not to interfere with your exercise of the right. If you have a right to free speech, I have a duty not to interfere with your free speech as long as your exercise of free speech does not violate my rights.

While there is no absolute agreement on the exact composition of individual rights, several useful lists are contained in the U.S. Bill of Rights and the United Nations Universal Declaration of Human Rights (see Appendixes A and B). Gerald Cavanagh cites six rights that he believes are basic to business activity. They include:

1. Life and safety.
2. Truthfulness.
3. Privacy.
4. Freedom of conscience.
5. Free speech.
6. Private property.[8]

These rights create *prima facie* duties, with life and safety being the stronger right, other things being equal.

In 1992 Gaston and Copper sent a shipment of fertilizer to Bangladesh.[9] Farmers eager to increase their crop yields spread the material on their fields. Unfortunately, they were spreading hazardous waste containing lead and cadmium dust that had been packaged in bags labeled as fertilizer. Gaston and Copper appear to have violated several human rights. The firm knew that the shipment would create a hazard to human and animal life after it reached Bangladesh. By labeling the shipment as fertilizer, it violated the right to truthfulness when the truth was extremely important.

Justice Principles

Justice is usually associated with issues of rights, fairness, and equality. A just act respects your rights and treats you fairly. Principles of justice may be divided into three types: distributive justice, retributive justice, and compensatory justice.

Distributive Justice

Society has many benefits and burdens that must be distributed among its members. Benefits include income, jobs, wealth, education, and leisure time. Burdens include work, taxes, and social and civic obligations. The specific allocation of benefits and burdens raises questions of distributive justice. Some of the ways in which the allocation can be made include:

1. Equal shares to each person.
2. Based on need.
3. Based on effort.
4. Based on merit.
5. Based on social contribution.

While strong arguments can be made for each of these allocation methods, most proponents agree that equals should be treated equally and unequals should be treated unequally in proportion to the degree of their inequality. This inequality must be based on *relevant* differences among the parties. This concept is often referred to as the formal principle of justice.

On May 6, 1985, Ira Sokolow met Dennis Levine at the posh Palm Too restaurant in New York for lunch.[10] Sokolow told Levine that Nabisco Brands Inc. had hired his firm, Shearson Lehman Brothers, as financial adviser for a promising potential merger with R.J. Reynolds. Prior to returning to work, Levine telephoned Bernard Meier at Bank Leu in Nassau, the Bahamas, and told him to begin buying Nabisco stock.

Levine's insider trading activities violated the formal principle of justice. He obtained information that was not available to other investors, his equals, and used it for personal gain. Dennis Levine was subsequently prosecuted and served time in jail for insider trading, which is illegal in the United States. Insider trading only recently became illegal in Germany, a country that previously had relied upon self-regulation.[11] However, in a number of countries, insider trading is neither illegal nor unacceptable behavior.

John Rawls developed a qualified egalitarian theory of justice in his work *A Theory of Justice.*[12] To develop his theory, Rawls used an innovative conceptual device he called the "veil of ignorance." He argued that valid principles of justice could be agreed on if we could meet for this purpose outside the influence of any society. This would remove the effects of societal pressure from the decision process. Stepping behind the veil of ignorance, we would be in what he called the "original position," not knowing what characteristics we would possess when we reappeared from behind the veil. We would not know our race, sex, age, education level, IQ, or social connections. Being in the original position would prevent us from arguing for principles of justice for personal benefit as we would not know what would benefit us.

Rawls believes we would agree to two principles while in the original position. They are:

1. Each person be permitted the maximum amount of equal basic liberty compatible with similar liberty for others.
2. Social and economic inequalities are allowed only if they benefit everyone.

Rawls does not argue that all persons should benefit equally. He does believe that, if inequalities do occur, the least advantaged person must end up better off than before.

An alternative view of distributive justice is held by libertarians. The cornerstone of their position is that distributive justice is guaranteed only under principles that maximize individual freedom. Their position is well represented in Robert Nozick's *Anarchy, State, and Utopia.*[13] He refers to his philosophy as "entitlement theory," which is based on three principles:

1. A person who acquires a holding in accordance with the principle of justice in acquisition is entitled to that holding.
2. A person who acquires a holding in accordance with the principle of justice in transfer, from someone else entitled to the holding, is entitled to the holding.
3. No one is entitled to a holding except by (repeated) applications of 1 and 2.[14] He refers to property as holdings. In essence, the justness of distribution is based on how it came about regardless of the actual nature of the distribution. He refers to a just distribution as one in which "... everyone is entitled to the holdings they possess...."[15] This would also appear to be consistent with the writings of Adam Smith.

Retributive Justice

Retributive justice is concerned with retribution or punishment for wrongdoing. At issue are the conditions under which it is just to punish someone and the nature of the punishment. According to Aristotle, a person bears moral responsibility for his or her actions unless he or she is forced to take the action or is ignorant of the act's negative consequences.[16] A person should not be held accountable if he or she is unable to halt the wrongdoing due to personal inadequacy or to powerful external force. Ignorance is a justifiable excuse if the person could not be expected to know the act was wrong. For example, farmers should not be punished for killing birds of prey by using the insecticide DDT. They could not have known of the potential damage to the food chain when they began using DDT at the end of World War II.

For punishment to be just, there must be certainty that the individual actually is guilty of wrongdoing. This may be guaranteed through a system of due process. Just punishment must also fit the crime. The severity of punishment should be in proportion to the magnitude of the crime. To be just, punishment must also be consistent across wrongdoers.

Compensatory Justice

Compensatory justice is concerned with compensating the party injured by the wrongful act. Most people tend to agree that the injured party should be returned to the condition that existed prior to the injury. This includes necessary medical treatment, services, and goods that are needed to rectify the injury. The compensation should equal the loss suffered by the injured party and no more.

Problems occur when it is not possible to provide complete compensation. A life lost cannot be restored. Proprietary information cannot be recovered after it has been distributed to competitors. In these cases the best that can be hoped for is that the wrongdoer will pay for the damage done to the extent that it can be fairly estimated.

Situational or Universal Ethics?

Some ethicists argue that an act may be ethical or unethical relative to the situation in which it is encountered. Others argue that the determination of the moral worth of an act is independent of a specific situation, and in fact, the determination applies to all situations thus making it universal. For example, some would argue that insider trading is unethical in some situations and ethical in others depending upon whether a culture condones or condemns the practice. Others would argue that it is unethical regardless of where it is practiced because it puts some traders at an unfair advantage over other traders. Is there a middle ground where some acts are universally considered to be unethical and others may or may not be ethical depending upon where they are encountered?

Integrative Social Contracts Theory

Thomas Donaldson and Thomas Dunfee have advocated integrative social contracts theory as a "realistic, comprehensive, and global normative theory of business ethics. . . ."[17] It allows for moral diversity among various cultures while maintaining certain universal norms. This tolerance of diversity reduces the ethnocentric Western bias that appears in much of the current ethical writing.

A social contract is not a formal written contract. It is an informal agreement concerning behavioral norms that are developed from shared goals, beliefs, and attitudes of groups of people or communities.[18] According to Donaldson, business organizations gain legitimacy via a social contract with society. Specifically he argues that:

> Corporations considered as productive organizations exist to enhance the welfare of society through the satisfaction of consumer and worker interests, in a way which relies on exploiting corporations' special advantages and minimizing disadvantages. This is the *moral foundation* of the corporation when considered as a productive organization. The social contract also serves as a tool to measure the performance of productive organizations. That is, when such organizations fulfill the terms of the contract, they have done well. When they do not, then society is morally justified in condemning them.[19]

The essential elements of social contracts theory are shown in Figure 3.1. Hypernorms are universal and thus impose certain requirements on all business activity. The macro social contract functions at the global level, providing specific conditions under which micro social contracts may be

FIGURE 3.1 **Integrative Social Contracts Theory**

Hypernorms

1. Personal freedom.
2. Physical security and well-being.
3. Political participation.
4. Informed consent.
5. Ownership of property.
6. Right to subsistence.
7. Equal dignity to each human person.

Macro Social Contract   Globally Based

1. Moral free space.
2. Free consent with right to exit.
3. Compatible with hypernorms.
4. Priority rules.

Micro Social Contract   Community Based

Individual Norms (e.g.)
1. Don't lie in negotiations.
2. Honor all contracts.
3. Give hiring preference to native born.
4. Give contract preference to local suppliers.
5. Provide a safe workplace.

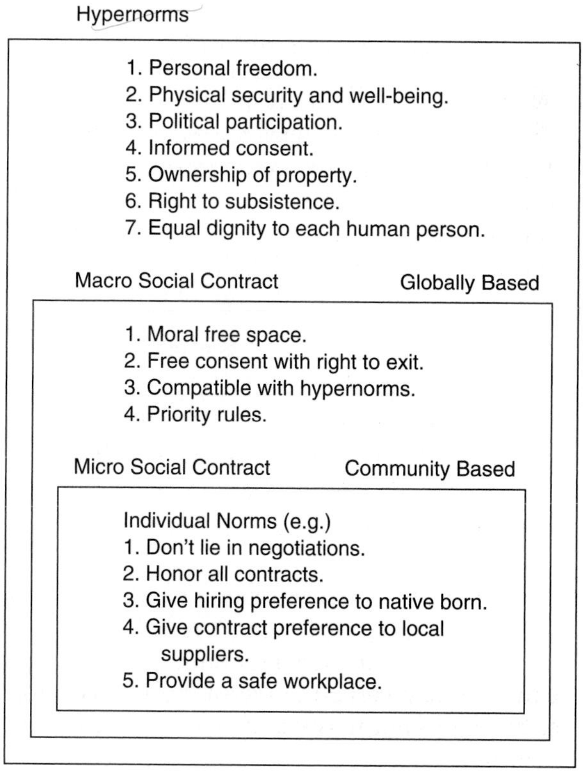

developed. Micro social contracts are unique community contracts developed in the free space, areas not specifically covered by macro social contracts, provided for under the macro social contract to guide business activity. Thus, ethical principles may be tailored to the requirements of specific communities.

Hypernorms

Donaldson and Dunfee envision a series of hypernorms, universal norms, that apply equally to all persons worldwide. Hypernorms provide the basis for evaluating all other norms. They represent the basic principles that are fundamental to human existence and are reflected in a convergence of religious, political, and philosophical thought. Hypernorms include:

- Core human rights, including those to personal freedom, physical security and well-being, political participation, informed consent, and ownership of property, the right to subsistence; and
- The obligation to respect the dignity of each human person.[20]

Hypernorms provide the basic moral structure of the world and as such serve as the foundation for the development of social contracts.

Macro Social Contract

Social contracts exist at two levels. The macro social contract provides global norms (hypernorms), and micro social contracts provide community norms. Communities refer to groups and organizations, both economic and social, although focus primarily upon economic communities. Thus, an industry forms a community, as does a firm. A church forms a community and so does a Lions Club.

According to Donaldson and Dunfee, a macro social contract contains the following terms:

1. Local economic communities are to be allowed moral free space to generate obligatory ethical norms for their members through micro social contracts.
2. Norm-generating micro social contracts must be grounded in consent, buttressed by an absolute right to exit.
3. In order to be obligatory for members of the community, a micro social contract norm must be compatible with hypernorms.
4. Priority rules compatible with principles 1–3 must be employed to resolve conflicts among competing, mutually exclusive micro social contract norms.[21]

The concept of moral free space refers to specific moral areas that have not been prescribed by the macro contract or ruled out by hypernorms. This provides an opportunity for economic communities to develop norms that are adapted to their particular situations via micro social contracts. Thus, Buddhist communities may develop norms that reflect their cultural preferences, and Koreans can develop norms regarding their work behavior that reflect their culture. Micro social contracts provide moral norms that best serve the different communities.

Micro Social Contracts

The unique norms derived from micro social contracts must allow community members who did not agree with the contract to exit the community; the norms must not violate a hypernorm. A conflict of norms may occur when a member of one community decides to do business in another community. For example, nepotism might be a micro social contract norm in an Asian community. Equal opportunity may be a norm in a Western community. Linking the two communities produces an immediate conflict of norms. When two or more norms conflict, a set of previously developed priority rules must be used to indicate which norm should be honored. Donaldson and Dunfee suggest the following priority rules:[22]

1. Transactions solely within a single community, which do not have significant adverse effects on other humans or communities, should be governed by the host community's norms.

   When the president of a U.S. firm travels to Beijing to negotiate a contract for a joint venture with a Chinese firm, the president should observe the Chinese norms and protocols in the negotiations.

2. Community norms for resolving priority should be applied, so long as they do not have significant adverse effects on other humans or communities.

   Once the firm has landed a contract and begins hiring Chinese employees, it should observe equal opportunity norms (the norms of its local community that do not have an adverse effect on the Chinese) in its hiring practices.

3. The more extensive or more global the community which is the source of the norm, the greater the priority which should be given to the norm.

   The plant built in China should meet existing fire, safety, and health standards required of plants located in the developed world. The developed world provides the more global community of reference.

4. Norms essential to the maintenance of the economic environment in which the transaction occurs should have priority over norms potentially damaging to that environment.

   Wages paid in the Chinese plant should be consistent with fair wage levels in the country, not comparable to U.S. levels. U.S. wage levels would distort the existing economic relationships in the Chinese community with unknown results.

5. Where multiple conflicting norms are involved, patterns of consistency among the alternative norms provides a basis for prioritization.

   The firm should refuse to employ child labor even though it is an accepted practice in China and other underdeveloped countries and would increase profit levels. All developed and most developing countries prohibit child labor, providing a consistency of norms.

6. Well-defined norms should ordinarily have priority over more general, less precise norms.

   The smokestack emission standards adhered to by U.S. manufacturing plants should be followed when building the plant in China. China's current standards are significantly less demanding than those in the United States.

Economic communities creating micro social contracts include: informal and formal groups within firms; firms; industries; professional associations; national and international organizations; and so on. Norms created by these contracts may take any form as long as they are consistent with the macro social contract. You might expect many norms to result from the creation of *prima facie* duties à la Ross. As cited previously, these duties include duties resulting from promises, duties of reparation for previous wrongs, duties of gratitude for previous acts by others, duties of beneficence to others whom we can make better, duties of self-improvement, and duties not to injure others.[23]

Community norms created through micro social contracts may also be derived using egoism (often difficult to defend) or utilitarianism standards. They may be rights or justice based. The important caveat is that the norms must not violate the macro social contract. Thus, you would expect to see significant diversity among local moral norms, a fact that makes the development of priority rules mandatory.

Summary

Social contracts theory combines a universalist and a relativist perspective that recognizes moral diversity among cultures. This is accomplished by its two-tier framework. There is a set of universal hypernorms applying to all cultures and multiple sets of relative community norms relating to the multiplicity of communities. When in conflict, hypernorms dominate community-based norms. Hypernorms comprise a set of rights that may not be violated! Community norms may be consequentialist or nonconsequentialist based, but they always are subordinate to hypernorms.

Thus, the theory is neither universalist nor relativist but a hybrid of the two approaches. It appears to represent rather well the type of practices we see in the world today. There are certain practices (hypernorms) such as stealing, killing, and slavery that are not condoned by any community worldwide. However, many community norms are not acceptable in other communities. For example, certain forms of insider trading are acceptable in Hong Kong but not in the United States.

Integrative social contracts theory permits the integration of both deontological and teleological principles into micro social contracts if one desires. In fact, any type of principle may be admitted into micro social contracts as long as it does not violate the requirements of the macro social contract. Social contracts theory permits a great deal of moral flexibility while, at the same time, it maintains specific moral requirements.

Consequentialist standards consider only the well-being of self (egoism) or of society (utilitarianism) when evaluating the moral dimension of a decision. Only the aggregate welfare is considered with no consideration given to how the welfare is distributed or to the effects of the decision on individuals. Some significant measurement problems exist.

Nonconsequentialist standards focus on the individual and the distribution of welfare. The rights principles give prime consideration to individuals with no concern for the aggregate welfare or its distribution. Principles of justice consider the distribution of welfare but neglect the aggregate welfare and effects on individuals.

With the exception of hypernorms, it appears that all the above standards have weaknesses that prevent them from providing universal guidance for the ethical dimension of decision making. Thus, when considering a decision that does not violate a hypernorm, you are advised to use the community norms that apply to the community of interest.

If community norms are not known and cannot be discovered, one might be inclined to use a consequentialist principle (hopefully utilitarian or at least long-run egoism) together with rights and justice principles to evaluate a dilemma. A decision alternative that satisfies these three standards should promote the aggregate welfare and distribute it fairly while not violating individual rights. However, a problem arises when the ethical dimension of a decision would be judged satisfactory under one standard but would be evaluated as unsatisfactory under another. Some priority rules are in order. We can offer some general rules that hold in most cases.[24] Normally, rights principles take precedence over justice and consequentialist principles. Justice principles generally prevail over consequentialist standards. However, we must caution that these rules are not absolute. At times the magnitudes of effects (benefits, harms, injustice) may be large enough to alter the priorities.

Discussion Questions

1. Which of the rights contained in the U.S. Bill of Rights appear to be hypernorms (see Appendix A)?
2. Which of the rights listed in the United Nations Universal Declaration of Human Rights appear to be hypernorms (see Appendix B)?
3. How does the macro social contract differ from micro social contracts?
4. What is the difference between consequentialist and nonconsequentialist principles?
5. Which consequentialist principle do you find most attractive? Why?
6. Which nonconsequentialist principle do you find most attractive? Why?
7. How does Kant's view of duty differ from Ross's view of duty?
8. How does Rawls's view of justice differ from Nozick's view of justice?
9. What is meant by the statement that integrative social contracts theory is both a universalist and a relativist theory of ethics?

It's Your Turn

You are working in a nonunion company. The economy has been doing poorly and your firm has experienced a significant loss of business. Upper management has decided that your company must downsize in order to survive. The department you manage must lay off one person.

Unfortunately you have two people to choose from. Both are very good workers and you would hate to lose either one. However, one must go. One has been with your firm for 15 years. She is married, 55 years old, and has two grown children. She has worked her way up to her current position and is a delightful person to be around. The second person is married, 26 years old with three young children. He has recently purchased a house near your firm. He has great potential, is a quick learner, and also has a wonderful personality.

You must make your decision by tomorrow morning and call the unlucky person into your office to give him or her the bad news. Who are you going to lay off? Why? What are you going to tell him or her?

End Notes

1. Adam Smith, *An Inquiry into the Nature and Causes of the Wealth of Nations* (New York, NY: The Modern Library, 1965), pp. 421, 423.

2. Ibid.

3. Immanuel Kant, *Foundations of Metaphysics of Morals,* trans. by Lewis White Beck (New York, NY: The Liberal Arts Press, 1959), p. 39.

4. Ibid.

5. Ibid.

6. Ibid.

7. W. D. Ross, *The Right and the Good* (London, England: Oxford University Press, 1930), pp. 20–21.

8. Gerald F. Cavanagh, *American Business Values,* 3rd ed. (Englewood Cliffs, NJ: Prentice Hall, 1990), p. 192.

9. Cathleen Fogel, "Break the Toxic Waste Habit," *The Christian Science Monitor* 85, no. 172 (August 2, 1993), p. 19.

10. Douglas Frantz, *Levine & Co.: Wall Street's Insider Trading Scandal* (New York, NY: Henry Holt and Company, 1987)

11. Silfia Ascarelli, "Germany's Law on Insider Trading Takes Effect Today," *The Wall Street Journal* 131, no. 21 (August 1, 1994), p. A14.

12. John Rawls, *A Theory of Justice* (Cambridge, MA: Harvard University Press, 1971).

13. Robert Nozick, *Anarchy, State, and Utopia* (New York: Basic Books, Inc., Publishers, 1974).

14. Ibid.

15. Ibid.

16. *Aristotle's Nicomachean Ethics,* trans. by Hippocrates G. Apostle (Grinnell, IA: The Peripatetic Press, 1984).

17. Thomas Donaldson and Thomas W. Dunfee, "Integrative Social Contracts Theory: A Communitarian Conception of Economic Ethics," *Economics and Philosophy* 11, no. 1 (April 1995), pp. 85–112.

18. Thomas W. Dunfee, "Business Ethics and Extant Social Contracts," *Business Ethics Quarterly* 1, no. 1 (1991), p. 32.

19. Thomas Donaldson, *Corporations and Morality* (Englewood Cliffs, NJ: Prentice-Hall, Inc., 1982), p. 54.

20. Thomas Donaldson and Thomas W. Dunfee, "Toward a Unified Conception of Business Ethics: Integrative Social Contracts Theory," *The Academy of Management Review* 19, no. 2 (April 1994), pp. 252–284.

21. Donaldson and Dunfee, "Integrative Social Contracts Theory."

22. Ibid.

23. Ross, *The Right and the Good,* pp. 20–21.

24. American Business Values, p. 193.

Chapter 4

Ethics and Decision Making[1]

In order to understand the role of ethics in the business environment, we need to become familiar with the part ethics plays in the decision process. Many factors are thought to affect the ethical dimension of business decisions. Some factors are personal, varying by individual decision maker, and others are organizationally based. Factors may oftentimes interact to yield altered effects. This chapter examines a number of factors that are believed to affect business decisions. We draw heavily on the empirical literature discussed in Chapter 5. Although we do not claim to include all relevant factors, we have included all the factors that have been empirically linked to the ethical dimension of decision making.

While much of the discussion in this chapter is applicable to decision making in general, its purpose is to clarify the role ethics plays in the decision process. We view ethics as one of a number of dimensions of the decision process. The ethics component is silent when there is no moral issue associated with the decision, but it becomes relevant when a moral issue surfaces.

The discussion is applicable to decisions made in any of the business disciplines. The actual ethical issues faced by the decision maker are to some extent defined by the type of management position held. For example, a manager in a finance position is likely to face certain ethical issues unique to the job; they will be different from the issues faced by a marketing manager. Higher-level managers are likely to face strategic ethical issues, while lower-level managers are more likely to confront tactical ethical issues. There is evidence indicating that the type of issue faced by the decision maker may influence the ethical quality of the decision. However, the *underlying decision process* appears to be common to all issues.

The discussion evolves from the decision process model shown in Figure 4.1. This model provides a structure for organizing our thoughts. It

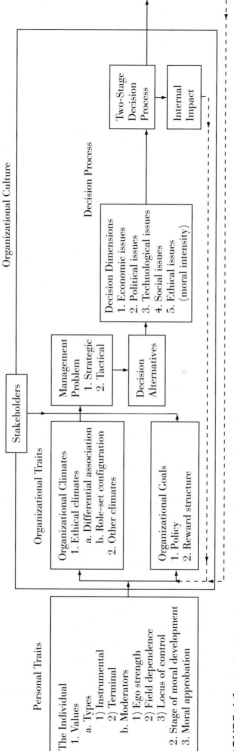

FIGURE 4.1   A Decision Process Model of Ethical Decision Making

also highlights relationships that have been empirically shown to exist or are believed to exist. Its main features include personal traits, organizational traits, and the decision process. Organizational traits and the decision process exist within an organization's culture. We begin with the personal traits of the individual decision maker.

Personal Traits

Business decisions are made by individuals or by committees; thus, the ethics of business in reality is the ethics of the individuals making up the business. A discussion of business ethics then becomes a discussion of the ethics of the individuals who make business decisions. A series of factors is thought to influence a person's ethics: personal values, stage of moral development, and moral approbation, as shown in Figure 4.1. As we shall see later, the actual ethical behavior is also influenced by organizational traits and the decision process occurring within the culture of the organization.

Values

Ethics is revealed through a decision maker's behavior when solving business problems that emerge from the environment. Such behavior evolves from attitudes toward the conditions within the environment that created the problems. The individual's attitudes are based on the personal value system of the decision maker.[2] Thus, the underlying antecedents of behavior are values and, as such, values are the linchpin of ethical decision making![3]

"A value is a belief upon which a man acts by preference."[4] Milton Rokeach states that a value is a prescriptive belief.[5] Thus, ethical values are prescriptive beliefs about what is "right" and "wrong." Values may be based on rules such as the Ten Commandments and are referred to as deontological or rule-based beliefs. Alternatively, values may be based on the perceived outcomes or ends and are referred to as teleological beliefs.

Types of Values

The personal traits section of the model shown in Figure 4.2 suggests that the initial influence on decision making comes from the personal values the decision maker holds. These values are formed and modified over a lifetime of experiences. According to Rokeach, values can be divided into two classes, terminal and instrumental. Terminal values "refer to beliefs or conceptions about ultimate goals or desirable endstates of existence" (e.g., a comfortable life—a prosperous life). Instrumental values "refer to beliefs or conceptions about desirable modes of behavior that are instrumental to the attainment of desirable end-states" (e.g., ambitious—hard-working, aspiring).[6] The terminal and instrumental values used by Rokeach are shown in Table 4.1.

FIGURE 4.2   **Personal Traits**

```
The Individual
1. Values
    a. Types
        1) Instrumental
        2) Terminal
    b. Moderators
        1) Ego strength
        2) Field dependence
        3) Locus of control
2. Stage of moral development
3. Moral approbation
```

Although a decision maker's personal values provide the underpinnings for ethical decisions in private life, in professional life personal values are mediated by other forces inside organizational structures that may alter the role played by personal values in decision making. Philosophers refer to the apparent differences in the two different decision roles as private and public ethics. This concept is illustrated in the following well-known passage from the introduction to *Moral Man and Immoral Society* by Reinhold Niebuhr:

> A sharp distinction must be drawn between the moral and social behavior of individuals and of social groups, national, racial, and economic; and this distinction justifies and necessitates political policies which a purely individualistic ethic must always find embarrassing.[7]

Personal Values Moderators

Three personal traits appear to act as moderators of an individual's personal values in decision-making activities. They are ego strength, field dependence, and locus of control.

Ego Strength   Ego strength is actually another term for self-confidence. Ego strength is associated with personal beliefs. An individual with high ego strength, or a high level of self-confidence, is expected to rely on personal beliefs to a greater extent than persons with low ego strength. A person with high ego strength is expected to rely more on his or her own personal values and beliefs of what is right and wrong and be less influenced by others. Thus, the influence of the organization on the ethical dimension of a decision is less for an individual with high ego strength than for one with lower ego strength.

Field Dependence   Individuals with high field dependency tend to make greater use of information provided by others to clarify issues when situations are ambiguous. Field-independent persons tend to rely on the information they possess or information they develop.

TABLE 4.1   Rokeach Values Survey

Terminal Values (Ultimate goals or desirable end-states)
A comfortable life (a prosperous life)
An exciting life (a stimulating, active life)
A sense of accomplishment (lasting contribution)
A world at peace (free of war and conflict)
A world of beauty (beauty of nature and arts)
Equality (brotherhood)
Family security (taking care of loved ones)
Freedom (independence, free choice)
Happiness (contentedness)
Inner harmony (freedom from inner conflict)
Mature love (sexual and spiritual intimacy)
National security (protection from attack)
Pleasure (an enjoyable, leisurely life)
Salvation (saved, eternal life)
Self-respect (self-esteem)
Social recognition (respect, admiration)
True friendship (close companionship)
Wisdom (a mature understanding of life)

Instrumental Values (Desirable types of behavior to attain end-states)
Ambitious (hard-working, aspiring)
Broad-minded (open-minded)
Capable (competent, effective)
Cheerful (lighthearted, joyful)
Clean (neat, tidy)
Courageous (standing up for your beliefs)
Forgiving (willing to pardon others)
Helpful (working for the welfare of others)
Honest (sincere, truthful)
Imaginative (daring, creative)
Independent (self-reliant, self-sufficient)
Intellectual (intelligent, reflective)
Logical (consistent, rational)
Loving (affectionate, tender)
Obedient (dutiful, respectful)
Polite (courteous, well-mannered)
Responsible (dependable, reliable)
Self-controlled (restrained, self-disciplined)

Source: Milton Rokeach, *The Nature of Human Values,* New York: The Free Press, 1973.

Ethical issues often pose ambiguous dilemmas. In the organizational context, field-dependent individuals will likely be influenced to a greater extent by persons within the organization as they wrestle with difficult ethical issues. This is due to their accepting and using information provided by others within the organization in their decision process. Thus, their decisions are likely to deviate from similar decisions they would make outside the organization when they do not have access to others' information.

Field-independent persons tend to limit the information they use in making decisions to information they own. The information has either been collected earlier or is collected by the individual to help resolve a difficult ethical issue. Decisions made by field-independent individuals are more likely to be based on their personal values and are likely to deviate less from similar decisions they would make outside the organization.

Locus of Control   Locus of control reflects an individual's understanding of the control he or she has over life's events. An "external" believes that life's events are controlled by destiny, fate, or luck. An "internal" believes that life's events are controlled by his or her own actions. An internal is more likely to feel a sense of responsibility for results and thus is more inclined to rely on personal values and beliefs of right and wrong to guide behavior. An external is less likely to feel personal responsibility for the consequences of behavior and thus is more likely to be influenced by forces within the organization.

In summary, the extent to which a decision maker's behavior reflects personal values depends to some extent on the decision maker's ego strength, field dependence, and locus of control. The behavior of individual A, possessing high ego strength, field independence, and an internal locus of control, is likely to mirror closely the person's personal values. The behavior of individual B, possessing low ego strength, field dependence, and external locus of control, is likely to bear little relation to the person's personal values. Thus, we would expect organizational forces to have a much smaller mediating effect on A's personal values than on B's personal values in the decision process.

Stage of Moral Development

Lawrence Kohlberg documented six stages of moral development during his 20-year study of American boys. Individuals appeared to develop sequentially through the stages; however, few people reached the latter two stages. According to Kohlberg, correct behavior for the young child is determined by external rules and standards. As the child matures, correct behavioral guidance gradually evolves to internal control. Kohlberg categorized the moral development stages into three levels—preconventional, conventional, and postconventional—with each level containing two stages.[8]

TABLE 4.2 Kohlberg's Six Stages of Moral Development

Level One:	Preconventional
	Stage One: Right is determined by physical consequences. Right action is taken to avoid punishment.
	Stage Two: Right is what satisfies one's needs. Right action is taken to serve own needs.
Level Two:	Conventional
	Stage Three: Right is what gains approval from others. Right action is taken so others will view you as a good person.
	Stage Four: Right is what is legal. Right action is taken to abide by laws and authority.
Level Three:	Postconventional
	Stage Five: Right is respecting individual's rights and social agreements. Right action is taken to abide by social contracts.
	Stage Six: Right is determined by universal principles. Right action recognizes principles of justice, fairness, and universal human rights.

Source: Lawrence Kohlberg, *Essays on Moral Development, Volume 1, The Philosophy of Moral Development* (New York: Harper & Row, 1981).

The criteria for determining morally correct action differ for each stage, as shown in Table 4.2. The criteria are Stage One—actions that avoid punishment; Stage Two—actions that serve one's needs; Stage Three—actions that gain approval from others; Stage Four—actions that abide by laws and authority; Stage Five—actions taken to abide by social contracts; and Stage Six—actions supported by universal principles.

Kohlberg's moral development stages provide the rationale for morally correct actions. As shown in Table 4.2, the rationale moves from self-centered to group-centered to principled. Philosophically, principled reasoning is preferred. However, all six stages provide rationale for moral action. It is tempting to argue that individuals at higher stages of development are more inclined to make ethical decisions than people at lower stages. However, the data are mixed. At this point, one must be content simply with being able to identify the stage at which a decision maker reasons.

Moral Approbation

Moral approbation is the ". . . desire to avoid moral disapproval."[9] Thomas Jones and Lori Verstegen argue that human beings have a need to be moral; this need may be biological, social, developmental, or religious.[10] It motivates the individual to gain moral approval from others and/or self, or at least to avoid moral disapproval. Moral approbation theory is based on four components of an act: magnitude of consequences, certitude of evil, degree of complicity, and extent of pressure to comply (see Table 4.3).

The magnitude of consequences of an action is the sum of all the harms and/or benefits associated with the act. The greater the net harm associated with the act, the greater the moral responsibility of the actor. In the

TABLE 4.3   Moral Approbation (Approval) Theory Components

Magnitude of consequences—sum of harms and benefits.
Certitude of evil—level of confidence in morality of act.
Degree of complicity—extent of personal involvement.
Extent of pressure to comply—how free to make decisions.

Beech-Nut case in Chapter 2, the benefits included the profits earned and employment opportunities provided by Beech-Nut and Interjuice. The harm included the loss of employment and profit opportunities experienced by Beech-Nut's and Interjuice's competitors. Although these harms and benefits appear to cancel out from a societal perspective, the distribution of the benefits and harms was determined by fraud. In addition, harm of a much greater magnitude was caused by the impact that feeding adulterated apple juice had upon thousands of infants. The vitamins and nutrients that the "apple juice" was supposed to provide were missing.

The degree of moral ambiguity in a situation is referred to as the certitude of evil. The moral responsibility on an individual is greater when an act is clearly immoral than when it is morally ambiguous. There is little question that the Manville Corporation was engaged in immoral activity when it hid the known effects of asbestos. There is no moral ambiguity. However, there *is* moral ambiguity in Intel's early policy of only replacing the Pentium chip for users who would actually encounter the defect. Andy Grove, Intel's President, stated that no chip is perfect. All chips do and will continue to contain bugs. Should Intel have to incur the expense of replacing the chip with a known bug for users who would never encounter the defect? This would reduce corporate earnings, which in turn affects employees and stockholders. On the other hand, should customers be stuck with defective chips even though they would never see the defect?

The degree of complicity describes the extent of personal involvement in causing or failing to prevent an immoral act. The moral responsibility of an individual is directly related to his or her degree of involvement in the act. The Manville Corporation was heavily involved in covering up evidence of the harm caused by asbestos. Johnson & Johnson had no involvement in the Tylenol poisoning incident.

Finally, the extent of pressure to comply refers to the degree of freedom an individual possesses when engaged in an immoral act. The greater the freedom, the greater the moral responsibility. External pressure to perform the act mitigates moral responsibility. External pressure can take the form of economic, physical, or psychological pressure. In the case of Beech-Nut, as with most business decisions, the pressure was economic. The company's baby-food business rarely made a profit and something needed to be done. After Nestlé purchased Beech-Nut, President Neils Hoyvald promised Nestlé that Beech-Nut would be profitable by 1982.[11] That created personal economic pressure for Hoyvald because he would likely be out of a job if he did not deliver on his promise.

According to moral approbation theory, high moral responsibility tends to be associated with moral action due to the desire of the decision maker to be viewed as a morally good person. When moral responsibility is low, the risk of being judged immoral is slight, and thus the motivation to act morally is reduced. Unethical behavior is much more likely when perceived moral responsibility is low rather than when it is high. Jones and Verstegen argue that people respond most ethically when the stakes are high, the action being considered is immoral, they are intimately involved in the decision, and there is no pressure to act.[12]

The personal traits previously discussed portray a complicated mosaic of factors that affect the decision maker. Values represent the basic beliefs underpinning a person's actions. Ego strength, field dependence, and locus of control all represent various relationships with the environment that influence the extent to which an individual will rely upon personal values in decision making. Stage of development depicts the type of rationale used to select actions. Moral approbation characterizes the internal need for approval. Each of these traits may support either ethical or unethical behavior. They may also work at cross-purposes.

Stakeholders

Stakeholders, those groups and individuals both internal and external to the firm who can affect or who are affected by the organization, also have a role in the ethics of the decision-making process. Our discussion of organizational climate cited the influence of peers. Peers are not limited to individuals inside the organization. They may be working for complementary organizations (advertising agency managers), for competing organizations (competitor's salespeople), and so on. In addition, other stakeholders such as stockholders, employees, regulatory bodies (e.g., Federal Trade Commission), public interest groups (e.g., Consumer Federation of America), competitors, and suppliers may exert influence on the decision maker that will affect the ethical aspect of a decision. Another important stakeholder whose influence is little known is the spouse.

Stakeholders influence decisions in both ethical and unethical directions. For example, the Securities and Exchange Commission enforces regulations against insider trading and corporate campaign contributions and thus promotes ethical decision making. A supplier may offer a significant personal benefit to the decision maker if the decision maker commits the firm to a contract with the supplier, thus promoting unethical decision making. For example, Lockheed Corporation was fined $24.8 million for bribing an Egyptian lawmaker.[13] In 1990, Lockheed had paid Leile Takla $1 million to help sell three C-130 aircraft to the Egyptian government. Lockheed hid the payment via phony and incomplete records. The company told Pentagon investigators that the payment was a "termination" fee, not a commission. The payment of a commission was illegal in both Egypt and the United States.

Organizational Culture

Organizational culture may be referred to as the common set of assumptions, beliefs, and values that has developed within the organization to cope with the external and internal environment and that is passed on to new members to guide their actions within these environments.[14] Culture has several important functions: First, it provides a sense of identity among organization members; second, it promotes a commitment of the members to something larger than self (to the organization); third, it provides for stability of the organizational social system; and fourth, it provides rationale and direction for behavior.[15]

Hewlett-Packard (HP) has been known for its strong culture, which is based on a philosophy of business commonly referred to as "the HP way."[16] The HP way includes a set of underlying organizational values that serve as the bedrock of the firm's culture. These values are:

1. Trust and respect for individuals.
2. Focus upon a high level of achievement and contribution.
3. Conduct business with uncompromising integrity.
4. Achieve common objectives through teamwork.
5. Encourage flexibility and innovation.[17]

Certain management practices became associated with the HP way, including one of the most well-known—Management by Wandering Around (MBWA). This technique, favored by HP's founders and many of its managers, was formally recognized ". . . in a presentation by John Doyle (formerly Executive Vice President for Business Development) in which he told a group of HP managers that to keep better informed and to manage smarter they did not need to get an MBA; they needed to do more MBWA."[18] The firm's concern for employees is demonstrated in stories such as the one told by Bill Hewlett regarding an early employee who was forced to take a two-year leave of absence due to contracting tuberculosis. "Here we had the opportunity to observe the devastating impact that it had on his family . . . Consequently, we established a plan for catastrophic medical insurance to protect our employees. . . ."[19] Stories such as these, together with the actions of management and peers, quickly acquainted new employees with the HP culture.

Culture in our model serves as the glue binding the organization together in common identity and actions. It influences the thoughts and feelings of the decision maker and provides a guide for behavior. It is manifested in norms, ceremonies, legends, myths, and rituals within the organization. An understanding of the culture of a corporation should help explain the decision maker's response to the various stimuli that occur during the decision process.

A culture characterized as open and democratic may delegate authority and responsibility to lower levels of the organization. Delegation increases the opportunity of lower-level decision makers to engage in unethical decision making. However, the opportunity could be diminished if the shared values of the culture work against morally questionable behavior. Conversely, a more autocratic culture with more morally permissive values could result in a lower level of ethical behavior.

Organizational Traits

While organizational culture serves as the overall glue of the organization, specific aspects of an organization's culture deserve individual treatment to enhance our understanding of ethical decision making. Among these are organizational climate and organizational goals, components that are shown in Figure 4.3.

Organizational Climate

Organizational climate or atmosphere may be thought of ". . . as a shared and enduring . . . perception of the psychologically important aspects of the work environment."[20] Benjamin Schneider argued that there are, in fact, many organizational climates.[21] Our discussion is limited to ethical climates, although numerous other climates have been studied. These include autonomy/control, degree of structure, nature of rewards, consideration, warmth, and support.[22]

Ethical Climates Bart Victor and John Cullen believe that the nine ethical climates shown in Table 4.4 may exist within organizations.[23] The specific climate depends on the ethical criteria and the level of reference used in resolving problems. (See Chapter 5 for a more complete discussion.) The nine climates are identified as self-interest, company interest, efficiency, friendship, team interest, social responsibility, personal morality, rules and operating procedures, and laws and professional codes. More than one ethical climate may exist within a firm. For example, different geographi-

FIGURE 4.3   Organizational Traits

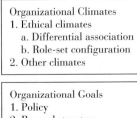

Organizational Climates
1. Ethical climates
   a. Differential association
   b. Role-set configuration
2. Other climates

Organizational Goals
1. Policy
2. Reward structure

TABLE 4.4　Ethical Climates

Ethical Criteria	Level of Reference		
	Person	**Company**	**Society**
Egoism	Self-interest	Company interest	Efficiency
Benevolence	Friendship	Team interest	Social responsibility
Principle	Personal morality	Rules and operating procedures	Laws and professional codes

Adapted from Bart Victor and John B. Cullen, "The Organizational Bases of Ethical Work Climates," *Administrative Science Quarterly* 33 (March 1988), pp. 101–125.

cal or organizational units may possess different climates. The ethical climate within an organizational unit may have a strong impact on the way a decision maker approaches the ethical dimension of business problems.

There appears to be increasing agreement in the empirical literature that a decision maker's relationship to superiors and peers will affect the ethical dimension of a decision. This effect can be expected to differ depending on the ethical climate in which the relationship exists. For example, the effect in a self-interest climate is likely to be much less than in a team-play climate.

Differential Association　One dimension of this decision maker/superior/peer relationship included in the model involves the degree to which members of an organization associate with each other. Edwin Sutherland and Donald Cressey developed the theory of differential association, which states that a person tends to adopt the behavior and beliefs of those he or she associates with according to the ratio of contacts with the individuals.[24] Thus, a manager's behavior and beliefs are likely to be much closer to those of her or his immediate peers than to peers in another department or division.

Role-set Configuration　A second dimension of the relationship involves the actual role played by the manager. The role of an individual in an organization is dependent on the relationship of the individual to other individuals (people to whom the manager relates) in the organization. The role in reality is a set of roles that creates the relationships the individual enjoys with others by virtue of his or her social status within the organization.[25]

The components of the role set included in the model are organizational distance and relative authority. Organizational distance refers to the number of distinct intra- and interorganizational boundaries that separate the decision maker and other individuals to whom the decision maker relates. As the organizational distance between the decision maker and others increases, the influence of other individuals decreases. The influence of an individual in another division will be less than an individual in another department, other things being equal.

According to the relative authority component in the business setting, top management would have more influence than peers on the decision maker's behavior. One likely reason is that members of top management wield more power via control of promotions and rewards. Thus, the perceived behavior of superiors should be an important factor influencing the ethics of decisions.

Organizational Goals

In addition to organizational climate, organizational goals impact the ethical dimension of decision making. Since there are a great many organizational goals that are not likely to influence the ethical aspect of decisions, our discussion is limited to those that have been shown to have an impact on policy and reward structures.

Organizational goals may be viewed as being similar to organizational terminal values. Rokeach argues that ". . . institutional values are socially shared cognitive representations of institutional goals and demands."[26] These goals can be expected to exert a strong influence on the development of corporate codes and policy and thus on management's behavior.

Policy   There appears to be substantial evidence indicating that certain types of organizational policy can significantly affect the ethical behavior of managers within the corporation. Policy may take the form of codes of conduct and/or stated operating policy by top management. Whatever the form, policies serve as the laws of the firm, providing guidance and a means for management control.

While the form of the policy is not important, the communication of the policy is. To be effective, policies must be well known by all members in the organization. They must also be enforced. A well-thought-out and enforced set of policies concerning ethical behavior will likely have a powerful impact on the ethics of the decision maker.

The Boeing Company published a 74-page manual entitled "Business Conduct Policy and Guidelines."[27] The first page contained the letter from Chairman and CEO Frank Shrontz (now retired) shown in Figure 4.4. Notice the importance he placed on integrity, the personal characteristic Barry Posner and Warren Schmidt found managers most admired in others.[28] The manual was distributed to all new employees, suppliers, consultants, and contract labor. It was also available to customers and public organizations on request.

Reward Structure   In addition to policy, the reward structure also appears to affect the ethical aspects of decision making. One would expect that the effect of the reward or the punishment would depend on the likelihood of receiving it and the magnitude of the reward or punishment. Here again, the communication of requirements for and awarding of rewards and punishments will likely have a significant influence on the ethics of the decision maker.

Decision Process

The stage is now set with the individual decision maker possessing an array of personal values, the function of which is influenced by the culture of an organization with particular reference to the climate and goals of the

FIGURE 4.4 **Letter from Boeing Chairman and CEO Frank Shrontz**

Frank Shrontz Chairman Chief Executive Officer	The Boeing Company P.O. Box 3707 Seattle. WA 98124-2207

June 1, 1991

BOEING

Dear Boeing Employee:

For three quarters of a century, The Boeing Company has maintained its commitment to the highest standards of integrity. Integrity in the broadest sense must govern our actions in all relationships, including those with customers, suppliers, and each other. Our commitment includes compliance with all laws and regulations.

This revised edition of the Boeing *Business Conduct Policy and Guidelines* will help you recognize and properly respond to situations that may arise in the performance of your job. It is important that you read this booklet and keep it for future reference.

I ask each of you to work continuously to improve our products and services while adhering to the highest standards of ethics and business conduct.

Frank Shrontz

Frank Shrontz

---

organization as well as its stakeholders. The recognition of a problem requiring action provides an opportunity for examining the role of ethics in decision making. The problem may involve reacting to changes in the environment or taking a proactive stance with respect to future opportunities. The components of this section are shown in Figure 4.5.

FIGURE 4.5 **Decision Process**

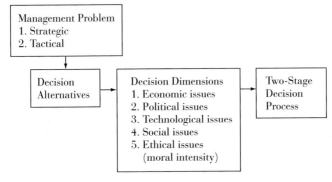

Management Problem

As the model focuses on ethical issues in decision making, the management problems of interest must have an ethical component to be considered. The problem may be major, such as the siting of a new plant, or minor, such as the number of units of a product to ship to a warehouse next month. Such decisions would be made at varying levels of the hierarchy within the organization. In some cases, overt acts must be taken to engage in unethical behavior. In others the acts may simply be ones of omission.

Management problems can generally be classified as either strategic or tactical. Strategic problems involve long-term commitments of resources: for example, where to locate a new manufacturing plant. Tactical problems consist of short-term resource deployments supporting strategic decisions, such as how many production lines to operate in the plant next month. Tactical decisions tend to be made by lower-level managers, while strategic decisions are made by upper-level managers. While a decision of either type that results in unethical behavior is not to be condoned, strategic decisions that are questionable from an ethical perspective tend to be much more damaging.

Strategic decisions create a venue for numerous future tactical decisions. Thus, one unethical strategic decision is likely to lead to a series of unethical tactical decisions, while an unethical tactical decision is unlikely to influence many other tactical decisions and certainly should not affect strategic decisions. In addition, as strategic decisions are made by higher levels of management, an unethical strategic decision sends the message to subordinates that unethical decisions are okay. As stated earlier, superiors' behavior is a prime influence on the ethical behavior of subordinates.

Decision Alternatives

The recognition of a management problem motivates the decision maker to search for solutions. A set of solution alternatives is generated that comprises the alternatives considered by the decision maker. The specific set depends on the manager and the manager's organization. The contents of the set reflect the personal values of the decision maker as well as the organization's culture and the influence of relevant stakeholders. Certain alternatives found to be acceptable in some organizations may be considered unacceptable in others.

An organization's policy can have a significant influence on the decision alternatives considered by the decision maker. Effective corporate policy that encourages ethical behavior and discourages unethical behavior tends to eliminate unethical decision alternatives from the set being considered. Conversely, ineffective policy or policy that takes the low road tends to encourage the inclusion of questionable alternatives in the set of solutions being considered. In addition to policy, a reward structure that encourages ethical behavior and punishes unethical behavior tends to prevent unethical solutions from being included. The converse should be true as well.

Professional codes of conduct of organizations to which the decision maker belongs can also eliminate unethical alternatives. Policy, positive reward structures, and professional codes tend to remove the opportunity to engage in unethical behavior. If the set of alternative actions being considered by the decision maker contains no unethical actions, an ethical decision is guaranteed!

Decision Dimensions

Once the set of decision alternatives has been established, each one is evaluated on the basis of the following relevant criteria or hurdles: economic, political, technological, social, and ethical. While we know the general criteria used, we do not know their role in the actual evaluation process. One would assume that the relative importance of the criteria may be situational. For example, when one chooses between two alternative marketing channels, economic criteria may be critical. For a decision regarding the development of new computer chips, the technological criteria may take precedence. Although all the criteria may be important in the decision process, our focus will be primarily on ethical criteria following a short discussion of each type of criteria.

Economic Issues For most decisions, economic issues (short-term and long-term profitability) will be important criteria, particularly for commercial organizations. The hope is that the criteria utilized would include a longer time perspective than is currently in use by many firms exposed for ethical transgressions. Longer-term criteria tend to correlate more closely with ethical decisions. For example, organizations utilizing get-rich-quick schemes are not in business long enough to be concerned with the impact of their actions on customers or society. Organizations following a long-run business strategy must be concerned with customers and society in order to be successful. Sharp practices will result in a loss of customers and/or the creation of public policy that restricts an organization's actions.

Political Issues   Relevant political considerations are found both inside and outside the organization. Internal considerations may include the impact that a decision alternative has on the decision maker's present and future political actions within the organization. This impact may result in a change in political power or an alteration in a current or future negotiating position. External considerations may include the relationship of the decision to current public policy as well as the impact the decision may have on the political power and the negotiating capabilities of the organization with respect to future public policy and the firm's stakeholders.

Technological Issues   Technological issues consist of determining what is technologically feasible both currently and in the foreseeable future. Technology applies to a number of areas in the business environment (e.g., new composite materials for manufacturing products or new communication techniques for promotion). The boundary may be somewhat stationary, but more than likely it is continually shifting. A decision that satisfies technological considerations at one point in time may not be satisfactory at a future date. A decision that does not take future technology into consideration may be obsolete before it is implemented.

Social Issues   The potential impact of the decision on both the local and the greater society as well as the reaction of these groups to the decision comprise the relevant social issues. Because economic organizations operate at the pleasure of society, societal factors may be quite important to the decision maker. Decisions that are viewed as having a positive impact or reception may result in favorable public policy, a reduction in unfavorable public policy, a positive economic experience, a more favorable pool of employment talent, and so on.

Ethical Issues   Ethical issues deal with what is morally right and wrong with a decision alternative. The judgment is based on the moral standards of the decision maker.[29] Moral standards consist of moral norms and moral principles. Moral norms are specific standards that require, allow, or prohibit specific types of behavior. For example, moral norms prohibit lying, theft, and murder. Moral norms may be classified as either hypernorms or community norms. Moral principles are more general standards used to evaluate private and public behavior. These standards include principles of justice, principles of rights, and principles of utility. A decision contains an ethical component when there is a question of whether one or more decision alternative violates a moral standard. (For a more complete discussion of moral standards, see Manuel Velasquez.[30])

Jones argues that the moral intensity of an alternative has an important bearing on the actual decision outcome.[31] Moral intensity is comprised of six dimensions:

1. Magnitude of consequences—the total harm and/or benefits created by the act.
2. Social consensus—extent to which society agrees the act is good or evil.

3. Probability of effect—likelihood that the harm or benefit will actually occur.
4. Temporal immediacy—the elapsed time prior to the beginning of the consequences of the act.
5. Proximity—the social, cultural, psychological, or physical closeness of the decision maker to the recipients of the act's benefits and harms.
6. Concentration of effect—the proportion of people affected by the act.[32]

Moral intensity increases when the magnitude of consequences increases, a stronger social consensus exists, the probability of effect is greater, the temporal immediacy is shorter, the proximity is closer, and/or the concentration of effect is greater. While the functional relationship between moral intensity and its components appears logical, the nature of the relationship is open to speculation.

Jones offers several propositions concerning moral intensity. He argues that the likelihood of recognizing a moral component within a decision alternative is directly related to the magnitude of the act's moral intensity. More sophisticated reasoning is applied to problems in which alternatives have high moral intensity. The probability of establishing moral intent increases as the act's moral intensity increases. The chances of choosing an ethical alternative increase as the moral intensity of the alternatives under consideration increases.[33]

Two-Stage Decision Process

Minimum Performance Level   Although the specific role played by the decision dimensions is unknown, there is sufficient evidence to indicate that the actual decision process may occur in two stages. (See James Bettman's discussion of the phased heuristic decision processes for a more complete discussion.[34]) In Stage One, the decision maker applies a minimum performance rule to each dimension that specifies the minimum acceptable performance level for each of the decision dimensions. An economic performance rule might be: A decision alternative must project an ROI of X percent for further consideration. An ethical performance rule might be: Any alternative that creates a conflict of interest will be dropped from consideration.

The minimum performance level may be less than the desirable level and when considered by itself would lead to rejection of the alternative. However, it would be an acceptable level if the marginal performance can be compensated for by superior performance on other decision dimensions: for example, economic or technological. Thus, we have three regions of performance: unacceptable, marginal, and acceptable. These regions are delineated by the minimum performance level and the desirable performance level. See Figure 4.6 for an example of the regions concept.

Total Benefit Test   Decision alternatives that survive the first phase (minimum performance rule test) may then be subjected to the second phase, a

FIGURE 4.6   Example of Decision Dimension Performance Regions

Economic Dimension	Ethical Dimension	
(ROI)	(Examples)	
11%	Provide good jobs	◄— Acceptable
10	Create social value	Region
9	Honest presentation	
	Desirable Performance Level	
8	Minimum deception	
7	Moderate bribery	◄— Marginal
6	Moderate deception	Region
	Minimum Performance Level	
5	Major bribery	
4	Gross deception	◄— Unacceptable
3	Unfair discrimination	Region

total benefit test yielding the overall value of each alternative. The first step in calculating total benefits is to assign a relative importance weight w to each of the five decision dimensions. Then the total benefit of each alternative is evaluated individually. For each decision dimension, expected benefit b is estimated. The relative value v of the decision dimension is calculated by multiplying the importance weight w by the benefit b ($v = w \times b$). The relative values v of the dimensions are then summed to arrive at the total benefit T provided by the decision alternative, as shown in Figure 4.7.

Most readers will recognize this procedure as being similar to calculating a grade-point average. The importance weight w translates as the number of credit hours awarded for a course and the benefit b becomes the grade earned in the course. The product obtained by multiplying credit hours by earned grade point yields the total number of points earned in the course or, in our case, the relative value v of the decision dimension for a specific alternative. The final grade point is determined by adding the products derived for each course and then dividing by the total number of course hours taken. Because only the total benefit needs to be calculated, the products v for each dimension are added to obtain T. No subsequent division takes place to determine the average benefit per unit of importance. (To determine the average benefit per unit of importance, one would divide T_j by Σw_i yielding a measure analogous to grade-point average per credit hour. However, in this case the measure has little meaning).

After the benefit for each decision alternative being considered has been derived, one would expect that the decision maker would select the alternative with the highest T.

While the minimum performance level of a decision dimension represents the lowest level of the dimension a decision maker will tolerate, it

FIGURE 4.7 **Total Benefit Calculation**

$$T_j = \Sigma_{ij} w_i b_{ij}$$

where T = the total benefit of a decision alternative
w = the importance weight assigned to a decision dimension
b = the benefit assigned to a decision dimension for a decision alternative
i = index indicating specific decision dimension
j = index indicating specific decision alternative

does not represent a generally accepted or desired level. For example, the minimum level for the ethics dimension might be alternatives that do not cause death to consumers (or at least an unacceptable number of deaths). Other unethical acts resulting in misrepresentation of products or bribery may not be condoned. The desirable performance level would identify the beginning of actions that result in truthful representation without payoffs. However, the alternatives falling within the marginal region (between the minimum and desirable performance levels) may have positive benefits on other dimensions that are large enough to more than offset the negative benefits of the ethics dimension.

The evaluation of the negative benefits of the ethical dimension is likely to be based on the magnitude of the effect in conjunction with the likelihood of its occurrence. The attractiveness of a decision alternative decreases as the size of the potential negative consequences increases and/or the likelihood of the consequences increases. For example, the fine for engaging in some unethical and illegal act may be rather stiff, while the likelihood of getting caught may be almost nil. Thus, the negative benefit may tend to be considered as relatively small. This evaluation process may explain why some business decisions are made that, when considered on the ethics dimension alone, would be immediately rejected. The alternative may be just above the minimum acceptable level but below the desirable level and thus likely to be rejected if ethics is the only consideration. However, the benefits of the other dimensions may simply overwhelm the negative ethics dimension, resulting in a selected alternative. The calculus of Stage Two deserves extensive study.

The type of issue faced by the decision maker also appears to influence the ethical nature of the decision. One may speculate that this is due to the minimum performance level for the ethical decision dimension being set higher for some ethical issues than for others. As stated earlier, the potential issues and thus the opportunities faced by a decision maker are to some extent delineated by the type of management position held and the hierarchical level of the position.

The selection and implementation of a decision alternative result in an internal and/or an external impact that may influence future decisions. Internal impacts may affect both the organization's climate and the organization's goals. External impacts may alter the set of decision alternatives considered in the future. Alternatives resulting in positive impacts will likely be included in future sets, while those yielding negative impacts are likely to be excluded.

Summary

Our model borrows from several previous models of business ethics. The model incorporates the essence of the O. C. Ferrell and Larry Gresham model.[35] The teleological and deontological evaluations in the Shelby Hunt and Scott Vitell model are provided for in the evaluation of decision alternatives based on the decision maker's personal values and mediating factors.[36] The ethical judgment-intentions section is replaced by the two-stage decision process. Most of the situational moderators in the Linda Trevino model are subsumed within the organizational culture, organizational climate, and organizational goal portions of our model.[37] The individual moderators are included in the personal traits section.

The addition of personal values as a major input into the decision-making process offers a means of understanding how organizational forces interact with individual decision makers to influence the ethical aspects of their decisions. The type of interaction that occurs likely depends on the composition and strength of the decision maker's personal values as well as the strength and the nature of the organizational mediating factors. Although the specific relationships among these variables remain to be discovered, the framework is in place.

An understanding of the personal values—organizational mediating factors relationship—helps explain the development of public ethics as separate from an individual's private ethics. The existence of public ethics as distinct from private ethics as well as the relationship between the two has been an issue in the philosophical literature since it was first raised by scholars in the classical Greek Academy.

The incorporation of the two-stage decision process in the model provides a construct that appears to explain the types of ethical decision-making behavior that occur in business. Managers indicate there are specific actions that they will not countenance—thus, the minimum performance rule. Yet there are numerous examples of decisions being made that cannot be justified when considered on ethical grounds alone. Although the total benefit test in actuality may or may not be quite linear as our example portrays, the conceptual process appears to yield the types of decisions that are being made.

Discussion Questions

1. Which personal traits do you believe to be most important in influencing the ethics of a decision?
2. How can organizational policy work against ethical decision making?
3. How might you use the concept of moral approbation to improve the ethics of decision making in an organization?

It's Your Turn

You are working for a small underdeveloped country that is experiencing an AIDS epidemic. Unfortunately, drugs available from foreign vendors to combat the disease are too expensive for people in your country to purchase and your firm does not have the expertise to develop such a drug.

Last night you were surfing the Web of a major American pharmaceutical company and came upon the formula it uses to manufacture its treatment for AIDS. Its webmaster apparently made a mistake and left that information unprotected. Using that formula, your firm could begin manufacturing an AIDS treatment drug within a month and sell it to your countrymen at a price they could afford.

Would you use the formula and begin producing the drug for sale within your country? Why or why not?

4. An organization's culture is said to be revealed by its norms, ceremonies, legends, myths, and rituals. How might these signals affect the ethical decision making in an organization?

5. Which ethical climates do you believe promote ethical decision making?

6. How can management influence the development of an ethical climate?

7. How can organizational goals influence ethical decision making? (You might consider the Sears auto-repair case.)

8. What role do stakeholders play in the ethics of decision making?

9. How would hypernorms relate to Stage One of the decision process?

10. Which decision dimension appears to have been dominant in the Johnson & Johnson Tylenol case?

11. Stage Two of the decision process is portrayed as being linear. Can you think of situations where it may be nonlinear?

End Notes

1. The material in this chapter draws heavily from David J. Fritzsche, "A Model of Decision Making Incorporating Ethical Values," *Journal of Business Ethics* 10, no. 12 (1991), pp. 841–852. © 1991 Kluwer Academic Publishers. Reprinted by permission of Kluwer Academic Publishers.

2. Patrick E. Connor and Boris W. Becker, "Values and the Organization: Suggestions for Research," *Understanding Human Values: Individual and Societal,* M. Rokeach, ed. (New York: The Free Press, 1979).

3. Milton Rokeach, *The Nature of Human Values* (New York: The Free Press, 1973).

4. Gordon W. Allport, *Pattern and Growth in Personality* (New York: Holt, Rinehart & Winston, 1981).

5. Rokeach, *The Nature of Human Values.*

6. Milton Rokeach, "From Individual to Institutional Values: With Special Reference to the Values of Science," *Understanding Human Values: Individual and Societal,* M. Rokeach, ed. (New York: The Free Press, 1979).

7. Reinhold Niebuhr, *Moral Man and Immoral Society* (New York: Charles Scribner, 1932).

8. Lawrence Kohlberg, *The Philosophy of Moral Development* (New York: Harper & Row, 1981).

9. Thomas M. Jones and Lori J. Verstegen, "A Moral Approbation Model of Ethical Decision Making in Organizations," paper presented at the 1992 Society for the Advancement of Socio Economics held at the University of California, Irvine, March 27–29.

10. Ibid.

11. Ibid.

12. Ibid.

13. Andy Pasztor, "Lockheed Pleads Guilty to Conspiring to Violate Anti-bribery Regulations," *Wall Street Journal* 132, no. 20 (January 30, 1995), p. A9A.

14. Edgar H. Schein, "Coming to a New Awareness of Organizational Culture," *Sloan Management Review* 25, no. 2 (Winter 1984), pp. 3–16.

15. Linda Smircich, "Concepts of Culture and Organizational Analysis," *Administrative Science Quarterly* 28, no. 3 (September 1983), pp. 339–358.

16. John P. Kotter and James L. Heskett, *Corporate Culture and Performance* (New York, NY: The Free Press, 1992).

17. "Communicating the HP Way: A Guide for HP Managers, Trainers, and Other Communicators" (Hewlett-Packard Company, 1989).

18. Ibid.

19. Ibid.

20. Blake E. Ashforth, "Climate Formation: Issues and Extensions," *Academy of Management Review* 10, no. 4 (October 1985), pp. 837–847.

21. Benjamin Schneider, "Organizational Climate: An Essay," *Personnel Psychology* 28 (1975), pp. 447–479.

22. Bart Victor and John B. Cullen, "The Organizational Bases of Ethical Work Climates," *Administrative Science Quarterly* 33, no. 1 (March 1988), pp. 101–125.

23. Ibid.

24. Edwin H. Sutherland and Donald R. Cressey, *Principles of Criminology*, 8th ed. (Chicago: Lippincott, 1970).

25. Robert K. Merton, "The Role-Set: Problems in Sociological Theory," *British Journal of Sociology* 8, no. 2 (1957), pp. 106–120.

26. Rokeach, "From Individual to Institutional Values."

27. "Business Conduct Policy & Guidelines," manual published by The Boeing Company (June 1, 1991).

28. Barry Z. Posner and Warren H. Schmidt, "Values and the American Manager: An Update," *California Management Review* 26, no. 3 (1984), pp. 202–216.

29. Manuel G. Velasquez, *Business Ethics: Cases and Concepts* (Englewood Cliffs, NJ: Prentice-Hall, Inc., 1982).

30. Ibid.

31. Thomas M. Jones, "Ethical Decision Making by Individuals in Organizations: An Issue-Contingent Model," *The Academy of Management Review* 16, no. 2 (April 1991), pp. 366–395.

32. Ibid.

33. Ibid.

34. James R. Bettman, *An Information Processing Theory of Consumer Choice* (Reading, MA: Addison-Wesley Publishing Company, 1979).

35. O. C. Ferrell and Larry G. Gresham, "A Contingency Framework for Understanding Ethical Decision Making in Marketing," *Journal of Marketing* 49, no. 3 (Summer 1985), pp. 87–96.

36. Shelby D. Hunt and Scott Vitell, "A General Theory of Marketing Ethics," *Journal of Macromarketing* 6, no. 1 (Spring 1986), pp. 5–16.

37. Linda K. Trevino, "Ethical Decision Making in Organizations: A Person-Situation Interactionist Model," *Academy of Management Review* 11, no. 3 (July 1986), pp. 601–617.

Chapter 5

The Empirical Evidence[1]

Business ethics empirical research began to appear in the 1960s. The first widely recognized data-based publication was authored by Raymond Baumhart in 1961.[2] Interest in the area grew slowly through the 1960s and 1970s and then began to grow at a rapid rate during the latter half of the 1980s and 1990s, a rate that has continued into the current century. This chapter reviews the body of knowledge that has developed, with a focus upon ethics and the decision-making process. We will organize the discussion around the process model presented in Chapter 4. Preference will be given to studies of business practitioners.

We begin our review by focusing upon the individual. The question we are seeking to answer is: What individual characteristics are associated with ethical decision making? We start by examining the personal traits of decision makers.

Note: Much of the research is based on surveys. All the surveys used some type of questionnaire to collect data from a sample of the population being studied. The findings of any study are dependent on the wording of the questions and the specific group of people who actually respond to the questionnaire.

The findings of two studies can differ due to variations in question wording that leads people to respond differently to the questions. The results of a survey can differ from the actual population being studied to the extent that the group of people who respond are not representative of the population. Thus, more confidence can be placed in findings that have been supported by several studies.

Personal Traits

Personal traits studied in business ethics research have been limited to personal values, stages of moral development, and selected demographic traits.

Personal Values

Most studies of personal values have used the Rokeach Values Survey developed by Milton Rokeach, which consists of a terminal values scale and an instrumental values scale.[3] Terminal values are viewed by Rokeach as describing ultimate goals and instrumental values as depicting modes of behavior to obtain the goals. The values contained in the two scales are shown in Table 5.1. Ethics researchers have used the instrumental values scale more often than either the terminal values scale or the combined scales.

In a survey of 6,000 executives and managers belonging to the American Management Association, Warren Schmidt and Barry Posner found that the two values managers regarded most highly were being responsible and being honest.[4] These values were reflected in the personal characteristic managers most admired in others, integrity.[5] Other highly regarded values frequently cited by managers include being capable, imaginative, and logical. Graduates of an executive MBA program surveyed by William Frederick and James Weber cited the same top three values with "honest" being first and "responsible" second.[6] The relative importance of the first four values in the Schmidt and Posner study are identical to those found in an unpublished study of marketing managers by the author with "capable" replacing "logical" as the fifth value. The latter study found the Rokeach terminal values self-respect, family security, freedom, accomplishment, and happiness most frequently mentioned by marketing managers as one of their most important values. The order of the first three values is corroborated by the Frederick and Weber study (see Table 5.2). The evidence provides remarkable agreement among the top three instrumental and terminal values reported by business managers.

John Newstrom and William Ruch state that ethical beliefs tend to be personal.[7] In their study, some respondents cited a specific action as being highly ethical while others considered the action as highly unethical. Ishmael Akaah and Edward Riordan also found that executives and researchers differ in terms of ethics judgments.[8] When faced with a decision regarding the ethical thing to do, Baumhart also noted disagreement among executives.[9] David Fritzsche and Helmut Becker examined managers' rationale for indicated decisions with respect to specific ethical dilemmas.[10] They found a variety of rationale supporting alternative decisions with the

TABLE 5.1   Rokeach Values Survey

Terminal Values
A comfortable life (a prosperous life)
An exciting life (a stimulating, active life)
A sense of accomplishment (lasting contribution)
A world at peace (free of war and conflict)
A world of beauty (beauty of nature and arts)
Equality (brotherhood)
Family security (taking care of loved ones)
Freedom (independence, free choice)
Happiness (contentedness)
Inner harmony (freedom from inner conflict)
Mature love (sexual and spiritual intimacy)
National security (protection from attack)
Pleasure (an enjoyable, leisurely life)
Salvation (saved, eternal life)
Self-respect (self-esteem)
Social recognition (respect, admiration)
True friendship (close companionship)
Wisdom (a mature understanding of life)

Instrumental Values
Ambitious (hard-working, aspiring)
Broad-minded (open-minded)
Capable (competent, effective)
Cheerful (lighthearted, joyful)
Clean (neat, tidy)
Courageous (standing up for your beliefs)
Forgiving (willing to pardon others)
Helpful (working for the welfare of others)
Honest (sincere, truthful)
Imaginative (daring, creative)
Independent (self-reliant, self-sufficient)
Intellectual (intelligent, reflective)
Logical (consistent, rational)
Loving (affectionate, tender)
Obedient (dutiful, respectful)
Polite (courteous, well-mannered)
Responsible (dependable, reliable)
Self-controlled (restrained, self-disciplined)

Source: Milton Rokeach, *The Nature of Human Values,* New York: The Free Press, 1973.

TABLE 5.2 Most Important Personal Values

Instrumental Values	Terminal Values
Responsible	Self-respect
Honest	Family security
Capable	Freedom

rationale being predominately utilitarian in nature. However, Ishmael Akaah's and Shelby Hunt and Arturo Vasquez-Parraga's data indicate that marketing professionals base their ethics judgments on both consequentialist and nonconsequentialist principles, with consequentialist principles dominating.[11]

The personal nature of ethical beliefs appears to be linked to individual value structures. As implied previously, not all individuals place the same importance on specific values. As values affect behavior, different value structures tend to lead to different ethical beliefs. W. Harvey Hegarty and Henry Sims detected a preconditioned set of values as the strongest individual variable affecting ethical behavior.[12]

While we know the values that managers deem to be important, the missing link in ethics research on values and value structures is the determination of the values or value structures that support ethical behavior and the values or value structures that are associated with unethical behavior. That information is critical if values are to be used for employment and training purposes.

Stage of Moral Development

Lawrence Kohlberg studied the rationale American boys use for making ethical decisions.[13] His research led to the development of the six-stage model of moral development shown in Table 5.3. The model was described in more detail in Chapter 4. Weber examined managers' reasoning using Kohlberg's theory of moral development. He found that most managers reasoned at the conventional level at either Stage Three or Stage Four.[14] Managers in small firms or those who were self-employed tended to reason at a higher stage than managers working for large or medium-size organizations. It is also interesting to note that the level of reasoning was not constant across ethical dilemmas. Moral reasoning tended to be at a lower stage of development for some dilemmas than for others.

Interest in the stage of moral development model rests on the assumption that people reasoning at higher stages of development will tend to make decisions that are more ethical or more decisions that are ethical than those reasoning at lower levels. Thus, to promote ethical behavior, one needs to help managers reach higher levels of moral development.

Kohlberg's research investigated the rationale for making ethical decisions. He did not examine the rationale for unethical decisions. Thus, at

TABLE 5.3   Kohlberg's Stages of Moral Development

Level One:	Preconventional
	Stage one: Right is determined by physical consequences. Right action is taken to avoid punishment.
	Stage two: Right is what satisfies one's needs. Right action is taken to serve own needs.
Level Two:	Conventional
	Stage three: Right is what gains approval from others. Right action is taken so others will view you as a good person.
	Stage four: Right is what is legal. Right action is taken to abide by laws and authority.
Level Three:	Postconventional
	Stage five: Right is respecting individual's rights and social agreements. Right action is taken to abide by social contracts.
	Stage six: Right is determined by universal principles. Right action recognizes principles of justice, fairness, and universal human rights.

Source: Lawrence Kohlberg, *Essays on Moral Development, Volume 1, The Philosophy of Moral Development* (New York: Harper & Row, 1981).

each stage of development, his subjects were making moral decisions. His research did not address the issue of whether individuals operating at higher stages of development were more or less likely to make ethical decisions than were individuals operating at lower stages. Research addressing this latter issue has yielded mixed results. Einar Marnburg's recent findings offer no support for the assumption.[15]

While the stage of moral development model provides an attractive theoretical construct for researchers and educators, the question of whether moving decision makers to higher levels will enhance ethical behavior remains. This is an area worthy of further research.

Demographics

Several demographic traits of decision makers may influence decisions. Scott Kelley, O. C. Ferrell, and Steven Skinner found that female researchers perceive themselves to be more ethical than male researchers.[16] This is supported by Akaah who concluded that female marketing professionals demonstrated higher research ethics.[17] However, Gary Powell, Posner, and Schmidt concluded that males perceived themselves as more concerned about ethics relative to their peers and superiors.[18] Fritzsche found females to be more likely to pay bribes, engage in conflict of interest, and to request a subordinate to engage in unethical behavior. On the other hand, males were more likely to ask for a bribe.[19] Thus, gender differences in ethical behavior, if they exist, appear to be complex. Numerous studies have yielded conflicting results.[20] Behavioral differences may be due more to shifting gender roles than to actual gender.

Age and/or tenure appears to have some bearing on the ethics of decision making. According to James Harris, top management was the least tolerant of fraud with the tolerance for unethical behavior decreasing as years of service with the firm increased.[21] First-level managers and females were less tolerant of self-interest behavior. Paul Mihalek, Anne Rich, and Carl Smith state that middle-level accounting managers are most likely to be placed in situations where there are pressures to compromise ethics.[22] However, Posner and Schmidt state that pressures appear to be stronger to compromise personal principles at lower levels in the organization.[23] In the Kelley et al. study, researchers 50 and over and researchers with 10 years' or more tenure with the firm perceived themselves as more ethical. Middle-level managers appeared to have lower standards than top management in a study by Kam-Hon Lee.[24]

Justin Longenecker, Joseph McKinney, and Carlos Moore found younger respondents to be more ethically permissive than older respondents.[25] Career stage was found to be important by John Barnett and Marvin Karson, with early stages appearing to be less ethical.[26] The evidence suggests that upper-level and older managers appear to be more ethical than younger and lower-level managers. This may to some extent be accounted for by younger and lower-level managers being placed in situations where the pressure to make ethical compromises is greater. While the numerous scandals involving top management that have been reported in recent years tend to refute this evidence, the scandals make headlines and have touched a relatively small number of managers. We do not normally hear about unethical behavior occurring at lower levels unless it has a major impact upon a firm.

Sharyne Merritt did not find level of education to be related to ethical standards or behavior.[27] Merritt did find respondents with business degrees to be associated with lower ethical standards but not lower ethical behavior. However, in the Kelley et al. study, researchers with a graduate degree perceived themselves as less ethical.[28]

Stakeholders

Harvard Business Review readers provided a ranking of the company stakeholders for Steven Brenner and Earl Molander.[29] The priority of stakeholders in descending order was : customers, stockholders, employees, local community, society, suppliers, and government. Executives from manufacturing firms told Scott Vitell and Troy Festervand that customers come ahead of stockholders.[30] Vitell and Anusorn Singhapakdi examined factors influencing the relative importance of stakeholders; these factors are discussed later in this chapter in the codes-of-conduct section under organizational goals. Marc Epstein et al. found some support for ethical behavior within the firm among stockholders, even though it might reduce short-term profits.[31] However, there appeared to be more concern about illegal behavior than unethical behavior. Little more is known about the role stakeholders play in the ethical dimension of the decision process. However, it is interesting to note that customers appear to occupy the number-one position of importance.

One measure used by customers to evaluate the ethics of a firm is its advertisements. Joel Davis found that consumers evaluate the ethics of the firm and of the advertising message when a company promotes a product as environmentally friendly.[32] Messages that were more specific enhanced the ethical image of the firm. Messages that had greater emphasis enhanced the ethical image of the message. The images of both the firm and the message were significant predictors of consumer response to advertising.[33]

Wallace Davidson et al. examined the role stockholders play after the disclosure that a firm has engaged in illegal actions.[34] While no impact was evident when examining illegal activities in total, when actions were analyzed individually, the market penalized firms that were accused of specific transgressions. Firms that engaged in bribery, tax evasion, theft of trade secrets, financial reporting violations, or violations of government contracts experienced a decrease in stock price within 20 days of the announced transgression. The duration of this penalty is unknown.

Apparently the penalty is not a major deterrent since Melissa Baucus and Janet Near found that a firm that has incurred a violation is more likely to become a repeat offender.[35] This finding was supported by Davidson et al., with more than half the firms accused of crimes in the 1980s having been accused of crimes in the 1970s.[36]

The question that has not been answered: What are the risks of ignoring or giving lower priority to one group of stakeholders over another? This includes both short-term and long-term effects.

Organizational Traits

Much of the business ethics research has focused on organizational traits. The research has primarily centered on organizational climate and organizational goals.

Organizational Climates

An understanding of an organization's climate provides clues to the types of behavior that would be successful in achieving both an individual's and the organization's goals. Thus, a decision maker's perception of an organization's climate will likely influence the ethical dimension of behavior. Posner and Schmidt found that managers perceive unethical behavior to be dependent on an organization's climate, especially the actions of one's immediate boss and peers.[37] They also state that when faced with a significant ethical dilemma, decision makers tend to seek help from others. Specifically, they found that managers seek advice from their boss, spouse, and colleagues. It is interesting to note that a number of studies have found respondents believing they are more ethical than their peers.[38] This also appears to be true of firms with respondents believing their firm is more ethical than most firms in the industry.[39] Some writers have speculated that the ethics respondents attribute to their peers may serve as a realistic proxy for the ethics of the respondents. In any case, the ethics of peers apparently has a significant influence on the ethics of the decision maker. No studies have investigated the effect of a spouse's ethics on the decision maker.

Ferrell and Mark Weaver found that respondents believed top management had ethical standards that were lower than their own.[40] Brenner and Molander stated that a major area of conflict with superiors is over ethical issues with superiors pressing for unethical behavior.[41] Fritzsche and Becker found that respondents indicated their standards were higher than top management when the consequences of the act were less risky.[42] However, when the consequences involved a higher degree of risk, the respondents reported their actions would more closely parallel the actions they believed their superiors would take. One explanation could be that as the consequences of an unethical action become more severe, decision makers at all levels tend to make decisions that are more ethical. As is the case with peers (discussed previously), the ethics of top management appears to have a significant influence on the ethics of the decision maker.

Loren Falkerberg and Irene Herremans examined the role of the formal and informal system on organizational ethics.[43] They found that the informal system has more influence on ethical behavior. However, formal policies and procedures were also credited with an important role in guiding the behavior of individuals. Role models appeared to be the major determinant of the level of ethical behavior, with role models often being managers or supervisors.[44]

They also found that when a crisis hits, a firm is likely to move into survival mode and do what is necessary to survive whether it is ethical or not.[45] The decision criteria specified in formal policies or procedures may be lost or forgotten. When profit margins are low, informal norms supporting poor or unsafe operating practices and/or lower product standards are likely to develop.[46] Only minimum regulatory requirements may be met if not altogether ignored. When good times return and the firm is experiencing high profit margins, the formal system is less likely to be concerned with controlling costs. This provides opportunities to engage in graft, fraud, and kickbacks, which may be supported by factions within the informal system.[47] Thus, different sets of ethical issues may arise during good times than during bad times.

Ethical Climates

Bart Victor and John Cullen proposed a series of ethical climates that they described as a dimension of the work climate.[48] They stated that ethical climates in an organization ". . . influence what ethical conflicts are considered, the process by which such conflicts are resolved, and the characteristics of their resolution."[49] The nine different ethical climates that they

TABLE 5.4   **Ethical Climates**

	Level of Reference		
Ethical Criteria	**Person**	**Company**	**Society**
Egoism	Self-interest	Company interest	Efficiency
Benevolence	Friendship	Team interest	Social responsibility
Principle	Personal morality	Rules and operating procedures	Laws and professional codes

Adapted from Bart Victor and John B. Cullen, "The Organizational Bases of Ethical Work Climates," *Administrative Science Quarterly* 33 (March 1988), pp. 101–125.

identified are shown in Table 5.4. The vertical dimension identifies three different ethical criteria that members of an organization may use to resolve ethical problems. The principled (deontological) approach follows rules or laws. The benevolence (utilitarian) criterion is concerned with the well-being of others. The egoism method is concerned with self-interest. The horizontal dimension describes three different levels of reference decision makers may use in the analysis. The individual level considers only the self. A local orientation is concerned with the firm, and the cosmopolitan level takes into consideration the total society.

The nine climates are identified as self-interest, company interest, efficiency, friendship, team interest, social responsibility, personal morality, rules and operating procedures, and laws and professional codes. Victor and Cullen's research documented the existence of five of the nine dimensions they hypothesized. The names they gave to the five dimensions in their empirical study and the comparable hypothesized names in parentheses follow: instrumentalism (egoism and all levels of analysis), caring (benevolence and all levels of analysis), independence (personal morality), rules (rules and operating procedures), and law and code (laws and professional codes). Different names were used so the empirical results would not be confused with the theoretical classification. The question of whether the benevolence and egoism dimensions can be subdivided further is a subject for future research.

Organizational climate factors influencing the decision maker are summarized in Table 5.5.

Interesting questions are: What climates tend to be associated with ethical behavior and what climates tend to be associated with unethical behavior? Linda Trevino et al. found the self-interest climate to be positively related to unethical conduct.[50] There was also some indication of a negative relationship between unethical conduct and the laws and professional code's climate for firms that did not have an ethics code. This latter climate was perceived to be the dominant climate in a high-technology firm studied by Fritzsche.[51]

TABLE 5.5 Ethical Climate Factors Influencing Decision Makers

Ethical Climate References: Peers, Top Management	
Differential Association Theory:	
(An ethical orientation)	A decision maker tends to adopt the ethical behavior and ethical beliefs of those he or she associates with according to the ratio of contacts with the individuals.
Role-set Configuration:	
A. Organizational distance	The number of distinct intra- and interorganizational boundaries that separate the decision maker and referent other. Distance decreases the influence of referent others on the decision maker.
B. Relative authority	Top management as referent others have more influence than peers on the decision maker's behavior.

Differential Association A simplified explanation of differential association theory maintains that a person tends to adopt the general behavior and beliefs of those he or she associates with according to the ratio of contacts with the individuals. For our purposes, the person tends to adopt the *ethical* behavior and beliefs of those he or she associates with.

Newstrom and Ruch found that respondents held beliefs close to those of their superiors.[52] In a study of advertising executives, Dean Krugman and Ferrell discovered that respondents believed their ethical standards to be the same or lower than those of top management.[53] A further analysis of the data by Mary Zey-Ferrell and Ferrell indicated that behavior of peers was the major predictor of respondents' ethical behavior for advertising agency respondents, while the beliefs of top management were the major predictor of corporate advertising managers' ethical behavior.[54] An earlier study by Weaver, Zey-Ferrell and Ferrell had cited the behavior of peers to be an important influence on ethical behavior.[55] This led them to propose Edwin Sutherland and Donald Cressey's theory of differential association as a partial explanation of ethical behavior.[56] Decision makers such as ad agency managers who associate more closely with peers tend to adopt the ethical behavior of their peers. Decision makers such as corporate advertising managers who associate more closely with superiors tend to adopt their superiors' ethical standards.

Role-Set Configuration In addition, Zey-Ferrell and Ferrell cited role-set theory as a partial explanation of ethical behavior.[57] They dealt with the organizational distance and the relative authority dimensions of role-set theory in their analysis. They found support for the assertion that as organizational distance (the number of distinct intra- and interorganizational boundaries that separate the decision maker and another person) between the decision maker and another person increases, the influence of the other person decreases.

The relative authority dimension in the business setting maintains that top management would have more influence than peers on the decision maker's behavior. Both the Baumhart and the Brenner and Molander studies found the perceived behavior of superiors to be the most important factor influencing unethical decisions.[58] MIS professionals indicated that top management has a significant impact on ethical behavior according to Vitell and Donald Davis.[59] Zey-Ferrell and Ferrell concluded that their sample of advertising managers supported the relative authority proposition, but their sample of ad agency executives did not support the proposition.[60] However, the differential association theory explained this deviation.

Hunt, Lawrence Chonko, and James Wilcox and Chonko and Hunt found that the actions of top management to encourage ethical behavior were the best single predictor of respondents' perceived ethical problems.[61] A survey of advertising agency executives by Chonko, Hunt, and Roy Howell indicated that the executives perceived conformity with the American Advertising Federation principles to be higher at agencies where top management promoted high ethical standards.[62] According to Akaah and Riordan, actions by top management that encourage ethical behavior and discourage unethical behavior can influence the behavior of marketing professionals.[63] They also found that when fewer ethical problems were perceived in the professional's organization, disapproval of unethical/questionable research practices increased. In addition, Hunt, Chonko, and Wilcox found that reprimands by top management can significantly reduce unethical research behavior, and Chonko and Hunt cite the influence of reprimands in reducing unethical behavior in marketing management.[64] Hegarty and Sims found that the threat of punishment tended to counter the effect provided by rewards for unethical behavior in the decision-making process.[65]

Thus, both peers and top management appear to influence significantly the ethical behavior of managers, with top management wielding the greatest influence. Ethical behavior can be encouraged and unethical behavior can be discouraged by the actions of top management and of peers. Unfortunately, the converse is also probably true.

Organizational Goals

You would expect organizational goals to guide the development of corporate codes and policies. Thus, the ethical aspect of codes and policies should flow directly from the organization's goals. George England reported in 1967 that organizational efficiency, high productivity, and profit maximization were the goals managers deemed most important.[66] In 1983, respondents in a study by Schmidt and Posner cited effectiveness, the organization's reputation, and high morale as the three most important organizational goals with good organizational leadership, efficiency, and high productivity close behind.[67] Profit maximization had moved to last place. Data collected more recently by the author closely follow this pattern, with the exception that profit maximization was approximately in the middle of the 11 goals evaluated in terms of relative importance.

Also in a study by Fritzsche, the two organizational goals service to the public and the organization's value to the community were associated with indicated ethical behavior, while profit maximization and organizational stability were associated with questionable/unethical behavior.[68] It should be noted that the goals were associated with specific ethical issues and did not apply to ethical decision making in general. The former goals would be associated with England's social-welfare organizational goal that was evaluated as the least important of the organizational goals evaluated in his study. However, these goals appear to be more important than profit maximization in the Schmidt and Posner study.[69] The latter goals were ranked in the first and second importance groups in the England study but had fallen to the lower half in the Schmidt and Posner study. This pattern is consistent with the Fritzsche study. One might conclude that we have seen a shifting of organizational goals over the period of time from the latter half of the 1960s to the first half of the 1980s.

Does the shifting of organizational goals mean firms are becoming more ethical? There is little empirical research available on the relationship between organizational goals and the ethical dimension of decision making. However, given the number of scandals continually surfacing, one would think not. One must also be careful when drawing conclusions from the press.

Policy   There appears to be substantial evidence indicating that corporate policy can significantly affect the ethical behavior of managers within the organization. Policy may take the form of codes of conduct and/or stated operating policy by top management. Respondents from the Baumhart study indicated that top management must set the tone for ethical behavior.[70] Mark Weaver and Ferrell found corporate policy to be linked with ethical beliefs and behavior of corporate employees.[71] Ferrell and Weaver state that the establishment and rigorous enforcement of corporate policy concerning ethics should improve the frame of reference for ethical behavior.[72] However, the respondents did not believe that such action would encourage conduct that is more ethical than the respondents' existing personal beliefs.

Bodo Schlegelmilch and Jane Houston state that large British firms are becoming more interested in developing codes.[73] The firms' reason for establishing codes was to define and clarify policy and to communicate policy information to interest groups. Two conditions were listed by the British firms as necessary to attain corporate ethical excellence: (1) an ethical corporate culture and (2) individual integrity and autonomy within the corporation. Cornelius Pratt and E. Lincoln James found that few advertising firms and departments appeared to have policies on gift giving to potential clients, lying to clients about their account status, seeking confidential information using deception, and reporting outdated data as current.[74] There was strong support among practitioners for their firm to create policies regarding these issues. Vitell and Singhapakdi found that marketers tend to value their company's interest more highly when a code of ethics exists.[75] Clients' interests also tend to become more important when a code of ethics is strictly enforced. When codes of ethics are enforced, ethical problems are perceived as being more serious.[76] However, Rich et al. found that pressure was greater in firms having codes to achieve targeted income and return-on-investment targets.[77]

An experimental study by Hegarty and Sims indicated that a clear organizational policy had a deterring effect on unethical behavior.[78] Respondents from the Brenner and Molander study generally supported ethical codes but did not believe ethical codes alone would improve business ethics.[79] The enforcement of ethical codes appeared to be a major area of concern. Meaningful ethical codes effectively administered appear to limit the opportunity of management to make unethical decisions. Work by Zey-Ferrell, Weaver and Ferrell, and Zey-Ferrell and Ferrell indicates that managers' perceptions of the opportunity to engage in unethical behavior is a significant predictor of the ethical behavior of the decision maker.[80]

Professional codes also appear to play a role in decision-making behavior. Singhapakdi and Vitell discovered that marketing practitioners who were in agreement with the professional values stated in the American Marketing Association's code of ethics disagreed with unethical behavior described in three vignettes.[81]

The American Institute of Certified Public Accountants Code of Professional Conduct was found to be a primary guide used by CPAs in their reactions to ethical dilemmas according to Gregory Claypool et al.[82] In a study of accountants in a large CPA firm by Jeanne David et al., the code was considered to be important to extremely important.[83] Two of the most important components of the code were demonstrating commitment to professionalism and maintaining independence. It is interesting to note that males, nonauditors, and upper management indicated a stronger belief in the importance of the code and its individual components.[84] S. Douglas Beets found that the beliefs of a majority of public accountants were consistent with the Code of Professional Conduct.[85] However, Mihalek et al. discovered that 42 percent of their sample from the National Association of Accountants were not aware of the code of conduct for management accountants, and an additional 49 percent were only somewhat familiar with the code.[86]

Finally, Gary Weaver et al. found that major American companies have developed some type of corporate ethics policy.[87] However, the implementation and enforcement of the policy vary greatly by company. This includes policy dissemination, organizational structure of the ethics component, involvement of the CEO, procedures for dealing with ethical problems, and so on. As the number of environmental influences (e.g., media attention, attendance at Conference Board ethics meetings, and familiarity with the United States Sentencing Guidelines) increased, the scope of ethics programs broadened.[88] Top management's commitment to ethics was also related to a broader scope but to a lesser extent than environmental influences. However, top management commitment was more strongly related to a program's control orientation.[89] When ethics programs were examined by their degree of integration into the organizational activities of a firm, top management's commitment appeared to determine whether the programs became an integral part of a firm's operations or whether they simply existed as stated policy.[90]

Codes of conduct and/or policies supporting ethical behavior appear to enhance ethical behavior, especially if they are strictly enforced, a condition that requires top-management commitment. Professional codes also appear to be effective if they are well known to members of the profession. In keeping with the differential association theory, we would expect professional codes to be more effective in situations where professionals view themselves as more closely associated with their profession than with their employer (e.g., certain specialties in accounting and law). These professions normally have strong professional associations that develop acceptable standards of behavior.

We have discussed various aspects of organizational culture. The unifying effects of culture are evidenced in the work of Paul Nystrom. He stated that knowledgeable employees tend to agree with the importance placed on moral values by a firm's management.[91] This important consensus differs among firms even when they are of similar age, domain, location, and size. The pattern of company differences held for both financial-service firms and manufacturing companies. Organizational values and indicated ethical behavior were found to be positively related in a study by Akaah and Daulatram Lund.[92]

Culture Ethnic Differences

Differences in ethnic cultures may also play some role in ethical behavior. Jeffrey Blodgett et al., using Hofstede's cultural typology in a study of American and Taiwanese sales agents, found that uncertainty avoidance was positively related to ethical sensitivity toward stakeholders, while power distance and individualism/masculinity were negatively related to ethical sensitivity toward stakeholders.[93]

Hegarty and Sims concluded that foreign nationals tended to be less ethical.[94] Becker and Fritzsche and Fritzsche et al. found differences in behavior across cultures, but the differences tended to depend on the ethical issue faced.[95] Fritzsche cited foreign nationals as perceiving the United States as having lower ethical standards.[96] Diana Robertson and Schlegelmilch found that U.S. firms tended to consider ethical issues to be more important than did British firms.[97] In Great Britain, ethics policies were generally communicated by senior executives, while in the

United States, ethics policies were most frequently communicated by human resources and legal departments. American firms were especially concerned with employee behavior that could harm the firm, while British firms were more concerned with issues that impacted external stakeholders as well as employees; British firms tended to be more protective of employee rights, with the exception of issues of privacy.

Alan Dubinsky et al. examined differences in perceptions among U.S., Japanese, and Korean salespeople.[98] They found differences in perceptions among managers from all three countries as to whether specific problem situations presented ethical questions. U.S. managers' perceptions differed from those of Japanese and Korean managers regarding whether their company had a policy covering the situations. There were no differences between Japanese and Korean managers' perceptions regarding company policy. However, there were differences among all three groups of managers concerning whether their company should have a policy for each situation.

Fritzsche et al. explored differences in indicated ethical behavior among managers from the United States, Japan, Korea, and Taiwan.[99] U.S. managers appeared to be more concerned with ethical issues. Japanese and Korean managers tended to treat bribery as an entry fee to a business proposition. Japanese and U.S. managers were more concerned with the legality and risky nature of environmental pollution. South Korean managers were much less concerned with producing a dangerous product than were the managers from the other three countries. There was less certainty in the responses from the Asian managers and more of a spirit of compromise among the Japanese and Taiwanese managers. Overall, Japanese managers appeared to be more similar to their American counterparts than to the other Asian managers. This may be due to the fact that they are both from developed countries. Chiaki Nakano also found many similarities between American and Japanese managers. The major differences were that Japanese managers' ethical orientation appeared to be more situational, and Japanese managers' decisions tended to be driven by company policy, while American managers tended to be driven by personal codes of behavior.[100] While Laura Whitcomb et al. found the Chinese to respond similarly to Americans in three out of five ethical dilemmas, the rationale for responses differed for all five dilemmas.[101] An interesting summary by M. Dolecheck and C. Dolecheck concluded that managers in Hong Kong tend to equate ethics with acting within the law, while managers in the United States perceive ethical behavior as going beyond simply complying with the law.[102]

Ethnic Similarities

Similarities also exist across cultures. Lee found no difference in the ethical standards of marketing practices between British and Chinese managers doing business in Hong Kong.[103] Robert Armstrong et al. found little difference in perceived ethical problems and management practices between Australian and American managers engaged in international marketing.[104]

The data show both similarities and differences in ethical behavior and beliefs. More research is needed to support or refute the findings to date. Research across ethnic cultures is much more complex than research within a culture. The most obvious difference in most cases is language. It is very difficult to create questionnaires in two or more languages that are identical in meaning. It is even difficult in two countries that speak the same language because word usage differs by country. Also, a number of countries speak more than one language. Differences in cultures also make research difficult because the way people approach problems, express themselves, and make decisions varies in ways that are difficult to assess using standard research methodologies.

Decision Processes

The decision process is driven by management problems. When a problem occurs, a series of possible alternative solutions are considered. For example, in the Intel Pentium case discussed in Chapter 2, the problem was how to deal with customers who had purchased a defective Pentium processor. One alternative was to ignore them. A second was to replace the processor for users who were actually affected by the defective one. A third was to replace the processor upon request, which was the alternative finally selected.

The types of problems that occur and the methods used to resolve them are discussed next. There is some overlap between the material on types of problems presented here and in Chapter 1. The material presented below is more comprehensive.

Management Problems

Substantial evidence, cited next, indicates that the type of issue faced by the decision maker may influence the ethical dimension of the decision. For example, bribery appears much more common than theft. The potential issues faced by the decision maker are to some extent defined by the type of management position held. A manager in a finance position is likely to face certain ethical issues specific to the job (e.g., insider trading) that will be different from the issues faced by a marketing manager (e.g., deceptive advertising). In addition, higher-level managers are likely to face issues (e.g., plant closings) that lower-level managers do not confront and vice versa. Of course, certain general ethical dilemmas are common in all types of management positions.

Several studies have examined the nature of the ethical issues faced by business executives. *Harvard Business Review* readers were polled in 1961 (Baumhart) and again in 1976 (Brenner and Molander).[105] These readers represented managers from all business disciplines. Marketing researchers were surveyed by Hunt, Chonko, and Wilcox; marketing managers were interviewed by Chonko and Hunt; and advertising agency executives

TABLE 5.6   Ethical Issues Faced by Business Executives

Harvard Business Review Readers	Marketing Managers	Advertising Agency Executives
Gifts; gratuities, bribes; "call girls"	Bribery	Treating clients fairly
Price discrimination, unfair pricing	Fairness	Creating honest non-misleading, socially desirable ads
Dishonest advertising	Honesty	Representing clients whose products/ services are unhealthy, unneeded, useless, or unethical
Misc. unfair competitive practice	Price	Treating suppliers, vendors, and media fairly
Cheating customers, unfair credit practices, overselling	Product	Treating employees and management of agency fairly
Price collusion by competitors	Personnel	Treating other agencies fairly
Dishonesty in making and keeping contracts	Confidentiality	Other issues
Unfairness to employees, prejudice in hiring	Advertising	
Other issues	Manipulation of data	
	Purchasing	
	Other issues	

were queried by Hunt and Chonko.[106] Australian international marketing executives and U.S. District Export Council practitioner members were interviewed by Armstrong et al.[107] The important issues elicited from the respondents in each of the studies are reported in Table 5.6.

The issues are listed in the order of their frequency of response. It should be noted that in all the studies the frequency does not represent the frequency of occurrence of such problems in ongoing business operations. Both studies of *Harvard Business Review* readers asked readers to cite the unethical practice in their industry that they would most like to see eliminated. In the other studies, the respondents were asked to list the ethical issue that posed their own most difficult ethical or moral dilemma. Thus, the issues represented ethical situations that respondents listed as major concerns.

It is interesting to note that the *Harvard Business Review* studies cited mostly marketing issues even though the respondents came from a wide

TABLE 5.6 Ethical Issues Faced by Business Executives *(continued)*

Marketing Researchers	Australian International Marketing Manager	U.S. District Export Council Practitioners
Research integrity	Bribery	Bribery
Treating outside clients fairly	Government interference	Cultural differences
Research confidentiality	Customs clearance	Pricing
Marketing mix and social issues	Transfer of funds/ cultural differences	Gifts/favors/ entertainment
Personnel issues	Pricing	Questionable commissions
Treating respondents fairly	Technology/copyright	Product/technology
Treating others in company fairly	Immoral entertainment	Involvement in politics
Interviewer dishonesty	Product use	Tax evasion
Gifts, bribes, and entertainment		Illegal/immoral activities
Treating suppliers fairly		
Legal issues		
Misuse of funds		
Other issues		

range of functional areas. This may be due to the fact that managers engaged in marketing functions have a greater opportunity to be involved in unethical behavior, since they are dealing with boundary-spanning activities. The emphasis on the ethics of marketing activity is supported by two studies that found that the opportunity to engage in unethical behavior is an important predictor of ethical behavior.[108] The emphasis may also result from unethical behavior in marketing activities being more damaging to the firm because it is more visible to outsiders such as customers, suppliers, and government.

Cultural differences in the Armstrong et al. study dealt with differences in acceptable business practices such as gifts, favors, political contributions, and so on. Some portions of the gifts/favors/entertainment and questionable commissions categories may be found under the bribes category in the first three studies.

Chonko and Hunt found that the primary ethical conflict faced by marketing managers involves balancing the demands of the corporation against the needs of the customer.[109] Similar results were reported by Hunt, Chonko, and Wilcox in a survey of marketing researchers.[110] Manufacturing executives reported that marketing situations cause the most ethical conflict and represent much of the unethical conduct the executives would like to see eliminated.[111] Two-thirds of the advertising agency executives believed that their ethical problems negatively influenced their job performance and their relations with their co-workers.[112] A survey by Chonko and John Burnett of salespeople, sales managers, and sales support personnel dealing with sources of role conflict found that conflict was greatest in ethical situations.[113] Given that the nature of the sales job makes it highly competitive, the finding by Hegarty and Sims that competitiveness tends to decrease ethical decision behavior would tend to support the existence of significant role conflict.[114]

An optimistic note was sounded in studies by Hunt, Chonko, and Wilcox and by Chonko and Hunt that indicated that marketing executives do not believe that unethical behavior leads to success in marketing management or marketing research.[115] Respondents indicated that many opportunities exist to engage in unethical behavior, but few people actually do. However, both studies found that a large proportion of the respondents believed that successful managers engage in unethical behavior. MIS professionals also believe there are many opportunities to engage in unethical behavior, but few managers do.[116] They further believe that ethics and success are complementary factors. It is interesting to note that Douglas Lincoln, Milton Pressley, and Taylor Little found that marketing executives exhibit beliefs that are more ethical than those of finance or production executives.[117]

Different Solutions

Several studies have examined differences in response by ethical issues using vignettes to portray specific ethical dilemmas. Fritzsche and Becker found the response to a bribery issue to be significantly different from responses to issues dealing with conflict of interest and paternalism.[118] In addition, the response dealing with whistle-blowing and personal integrity issues was significantly different from the response to conflict of interest and bribery issues. Although no statistical testing across issues was done, Becker and Fritzsche collected additional data from samples in two foreign countries and found the same general pattern of response with the exception that the whistle-blowing response was closer to the conflict of interest and the paternalism issues.[119] A study by Fritzsche using some of the same vignettes, along with a new vignette dealing with lying, yielded a similar pattern as did a later study by Lund.[120] The response to the lying vignette was more in line with the conflict-of-interest response. Advertising practitioners' perceptions of ethics varied significantly by type of issue confronted in a study by Pratt and James.[121] Finally, George Zinkham, Michael Bisesi, and Mary Jane Saxon also found responses to differ by issue.[122]

When examining specific ethical issues, Krugman and Ferrell and Ferrell and Mark Weaver also found differential response across issues.[123] In addition, they report that respondents appeared to consider ethics as a matter of degree rather than as a right or a wrong. In their studies, practices that required more overt action such as manipulating a situation to make a superior look bad were deemed to be more unethical than practices that were less overt in nature such as taking personal time or not reporting violations of company policy by others. Some support for the concept of ethics being a matter of degree was found in a study by Fritzsche and Becker that indicated that decisions were more ethical for dilemmas as the degree of risk associated with the decision increased.[124] Further partial support was found in an experimental study by Fritzsche that altered the consequences of ethical dilemmas over three levels.[125]

Some of these differences may be explained by the degree of moral intensity associated with the dilemmas.[126] Singhapakdi et al. and Joseph Paolillo and Vitell found moral intensity to be a significant factor in indicated ethical decision making. Not all of the dimensions posited by Tom Jones were equally influential, but all dimensions tended to be significant.[127] The most important dimensions appear to be (1) magnitude of consequences, (2) probability of effect, (3) temporal immediacy, and (4) concentration of effect.

Summary: What We Have Learned

We can be quite confident of some of the empirical findings. The results that have been supported by several studies using similar and/or different methodologies are quite persuasive. Other findings are interesting indicators but await corroboration before we place too much confidence in them. The results that we are inclined to trust include the following:

1. The Rokeach instrumental values—responsible, honest, and capable—and terminal values—self-respect, family security, and freedom—are deemed most important by the majority of managers.
2. Older managers and/or managers with longer tenure tend to behave more ethically.
3. Top management establishes the ethical climate of the firm by example and by enforcement.
4. Beliefs concerning the ethical nature of specific acts vary among managers.
5. The response to ethical issues tends to differ depending on the type of ethical issue faced by the decision maker.
6. A relevant code of ethics seriously implemented by an organization positively affects the ethical behavior of decision makers.

7. Managers believe they are more ethical than their peers.
8. Managers believe they are more ethical or at least as ethical as their superiors.
9. Organizational goals have changed, with present emphasis placed on effectiveness, reputation, and morale by many managers.
10. One of the greatest ethical concerns involves balancing the needs of the organization and the customer.
11. Managers can identify valid lists of unethical behavior that they find reprehensible.

Support for Ethics in Business

It is encouraging to discover that most managers would like to see at least some unethical acts eliminated. This should not be surprising, given that managers place such emphasis on integrity in others and cite being responsible and honest as their two most important instrumental values. This is reinforced by the relative importance placed on the terminal value of self-respect.

Given that there are some differences of opinion on what is ethical and what is not, it is not surprising to find that successful managers engage in unethical behavior. It is important to learn that managers do not perceive unethical behavior as leading to success. For those few who do, the threat of punishment appears to counter the perceived rewards. The differences in behavior across specific issues raise more serious questions. For example, why is there a greater tendency to engage in bribery, an issue that is of major concern to managers, than to engage in other behaviors that create a conflict of interest? Is bribery an issue in which a utilitarian rationale is used, with the only beneficiary being the firm?

A key factor in ethical decision making appears to be values: values of the decision maker, the decision maker's peers, and the decision maker's superiors. One may include the decision maker's spouse, although little is known of this relationship. The decision maker's values may not be as important as peer or top-management values. While research indicates that decision makers believe they are more ethical than their peers and possibly top management, the ethical behavior of peers and the ethical beliefs of top management appear to be good predictors of the behavior of decision makers.

This relationship may have several explanations. First, differential association theory states that the decision maker will accept the ethical values, at least in the work environment, of the individuals most closely associated with, whether they be peers or top management. One may speculate that a sales force would be more likely to adopt the values of peers rather than superiors. Second, the organizational distance theory maintains that associates who are organizationally more distant from the decision maker will have less influence on ethical values. Third, the relative authority theory states that the greater the authority a superior has over a decision maker, the more likely the decision maker is to adopt the ethical values of the superior. While these three concepts can be applied to explain most of the contradictions in the empirical data with respect to the ethical beliefs of the three parties, we do not know their relative importance. When there is conflict, for example, between the differential association theory and the relative authority theory, which construct takes precedence?

The role of gender is unclear. Some of the findings are contradictory. It may be that gender has no bearing on the ethical dimension of decision making. One may be able to make a strong case that gender is not a relevant variable. On the other hand, a positive relationship between age and/or management tenure and the ethical dimension appears to be surfacing. Many hypotheses are possible to explain this relationship.

Finally, the data concerning ethnic culture and ethics are somewhat mixed. However, the data are available for a small number of cultures. While some differences have appeared, the more interesting findings are the number of studies that suggest little or no difference across cultures. The surface has just been skimmed on this line of research, with much left to discover.

Enhancing Ethical Behavior

Organizational policy explained in a comprehensive code of ethics appears to be an effective vehicle for maintaining ethical behavior in the firm. To be effective, the code must become part of the standard operating procedures of the organization and not simply a code of ethics for resolving ethical problems. This policy, of course, reflects the values of top management, and thus decision makers tend to adopt the ethical values of top management. Such policy should permeate the firm, and thus it does not matter whether the decision maker takes cues from peers or top management; their ethical values will be similar.

Specific attention should be given to marketing activities when developing policy that affects ethical behavior, since the greatest opportunity for unethical behavior appears to lie in the marketing arena. By developing policy to promote ethical behavior, one is denying the opportunity to engage in unethical behavior. Policy development should also recognize that potential response to ethical issues differs by issue. Thus, more attention should be given to issues such as bribery that tend to invite unethical behavior. Unethical behavior tends to be its own deterrent when the risk involved becomes excessive. Thus, mid-level and low-level risk behavior should probably receive the greatest attention in policy development.

Guidance needs to be provided regarding the appropriate ways of balancing the demands of the many stakeholders on the decision maker. This is particularly true with reference to the needs of the firm and its customers. This may become less difficult as organizational goals shift in relative emphasis away from profit maximization toward organizational effectiveness, maintaining a good reputation, and high morale. Differences in cultures also need to be addressed by organizations that operate internationally. Specifically, foreign nationals need to be provided with policy guidance when operating in a new culture.

Summary: What We need to Learn

While there are many interesting ethical issues to investigate, this chapter has pointed out four areas needing further study.

1. What values or value structures are associated with ethical behavior and what values or value structures are associated with unethical behavior?
2. Do managers operating at higher stages of moral development actually make decisions that are more ethical, or a higher percentage of decisions that are more ethical?
3. When evaluating the impact that a decision alternative will have upon stakeholders, what priority should each stakeholder be given?
4. What impact does each ethical climate have upon the ethical dimension of decision making?

Developing our knowledge in these areas should significantly enhance our capability to influence ethical behavior in the workplace.

Discussion Questions

1. Which set of personal values, terminal or instrumental, has more influence on the ethics of decision making?
2. Why do people who have worked for an organization a long time tend to be more ethical than people who have worked for the firm a short time?
3. Why do you think respondents tend to indicate that they are more ethical than their peers?
4. Which of the ethical climates documented by Victor and Cullen would appear to reinforce ethical behavior? Which would reinforce unethical behavior? Why?
5. Would the differential association theory support the finding that respondents are more ethical than their peers?
6. Under what conditions would codes of conduct be most likely to promote ethical behavior within a firm?
7. Why are there differences in ethical behavior across cultures?
8. Why are there similarities in ethical behavior across cultures?
9. Where in the firm are the most serious ethical problems likely to occur?
10. Where in the firm are the most frequent ethical problems likely to occur?

End Notes

1. Much of the material in Chapter 5 is taken from David J. Fritzsche, "Marketing/Business Ethics: A Review of the Empirical Research," *Business and Professional Ethics Journal* 6, no. 4 (1987), pp. 65–79.

Your firm is a medium-sized job shop making structural components for truck manufacturers. Your sales office has landed a large order from a new domestic customer that must be filled in one month and will require your total manufacturing capacity. Your firm has been attempting to do business with this customer for four years and believes future business could be very profitable.

At the present time your production lines are running at half capacity. The primary run, which is for a manufacturer in Europe, must be shipped in one month. The manufacturer has fallen on hard times and is counting on your shipment to enable it to meet several customer deadlines that are crucial to its survival.

To fulfill the new order, your firm must shift production from the foreign customer's job to the domestic customer's job, putting off the former until the latter is finished. However, this might result in the foreign customer failing. Would you switch production to the domestic customer's job? Why or why not?

2. Raymond C. Baumhart, SJ, "How Ethical Are Businessmen?" *Harvard Business Review* 39, no. 4 (July–August 1961), pp. 6–19, 156–176.

3. Milton Rokeach, *The Nature of Human Values* (New York: The Free Press, 1973).

4. Warren H. Schmidt and Barry Z. Posner, "Managerial Values and Expectations: The Silent Power in Personal and Organization Life," AMA Survey Report (New York: American Management Association, 1982).

5. Barry Z. Posner and Warren H. Schmidt, "Values and the American Manager: An Update," *California Management Review* 26, no. 3 (1984), pp. 202–216.

6. William C. Frederick and James Weber, "The Values of Corporate Managers and Their Critics: An Empirical Description and Normative Implications," *Research in Corporate Social Performance and Policy* 9, William C. Frederick, ed., (Greenwich, CT: JAI Press Inc., 1987).

7. John W. Newstrom and William A. Ruch, "The Ethics of Management and the Management of Ethics," *MSU Business Topics* 23, no. 1 (Winter 1975), pp. 29–37.

8. Ishmael P. Akaah and Edward K. Riordan, "Judgments of Marketing Professionals about Ethical Issues in Marketing Research: A Replication and Extension," *Journal of Marketing Research* 26, no. 1 (February 1989), pp. 112–120.

9. Baumhart, "How Ethical Are Businessmen?"

10. David J. Fritzsche and Helmut Becker, "Linking Management Behavior to Ethical Philosophy: An Empirical Investigation," *Academy of Management Journal* 27, no. 1 (1984), pp. 166–175.

11. Ishmael P. Akaah, "Influence of Deontological and Teleological Factors on Research Ethics Evaluations," *Journal of Business Research* 39 (1997), pp. 71–80; and Shelby D. Hunt and Arturo Z. Vasquez-Parraga, "Organizational Consequences, Marketing Ethics, and Salesforce Supervision," *Journal of Marketing Research* 30 (1993), pp. 78–90.

12. W. Harvey Hegarty and Henry P. Sims, Jr., "Some Determinants of Unethical Decision Behavior: An Experiment," *Journal of Applied Psychology* 63, no. 4 (1978), pp. 451–457.

13. Lawrence Kohlberg, *The Philosophy of Moral Development* (New York: Harper & Row, 1981).

14. James Weber, "Managers' Moral Reasoning: Assessing Their Responses to Three Moral Dilemmas," *Human Relations* 43, no. 7 (1990), pp. 687–702.

15. Einar Marnburg, "The Questionable Use of Moral Development Theory in Studies of Business Ethics: Discussion and Empirical Findings," *Journal of Business Ethics* 32 (2001), pp. 275–283.

16. Scott E. Kelley, O. C. Ferrell, and Steven J. Skinner, "Ethical Behavior among Marketing Researchers: An Assessment of Selected Demographic Characteristics," *Journal of Business Ethics* 9, no. 8 (August 1990), pp. 681–688.

17. Ishmael P. Akaah, "Differences in Research Ethics Judgments Between Male and Female Marketing Professionals," *Journal of Business Ethics* 8, no. 5 (May 1989), pp. 375–381; and Peter Arlow, "Personal Characteristics in College Students' Evaluations of Business Ethics and Corporate Social Responsibility," *Journal of Business Ethics* 10, no. 1 (January 1991), pp. 63–69.

18. Gary N. Powell, Barry Z. Posner, and Warren H. Schmidt, "Sex Effects on Managerial Value Systems," *Human Relations* 37, no. 11 (1984), pp. 909–921.

19. David J. Fritzsche, "An Examination of Marketing Ethics: Role of the Decision Maker, Consequence of the Decision, Management Position, and Sex of the Respondent," *Journal of Macromarketing* 8, no. 3 (Fall 1988), pp. 29–39.

20. Maureen L. Ambrose, "Sex Differences In Business Ethics: The Importance of Perceptions," *Journal of Management Issues* 11, no. 4 (Winter 1999), pp. 454–474.

21. James R. Harris, "Ethical Values of Individuals at Different Levels in the Organizational Hierarchy of a Single Firm," *Journal of Business Ethics* 9, no. 9 (September 1990), pp. 741–750.

22. Paul H. Mihalek, Anne J. Rich, and Carl S. Smith, "Ethics and Management Accountants," *Management Accounting* 69, no. 6 (December 1987), pp. 34–36.

23. Barry Z. Posner and Warren H. Schmidt, "Ethics in American Companies: A Managerial Perspective," *Journal of Business Ethics* 5 (1987), pp. 383–391.

24. Kam-Hon Lee, "Ethical Beliefs in Marketing Management: A Cross-Cultural Study," *European Journal of Marketing* 15, no. 1 (1981), pp. 58–67.

25. Justin G. Longenecker, Joseph A. McKinney, and Carlos W. Moore, "The Generation Gap in Business Ethics," *Business Horizons* 32, no. 5 (September–October 1989), pp. 9–14.

26. John H. Barnett and Marvin J. Karson, "Managers, Values, and Executive Decisions: An Exploration of the Role of Gender, Career Stage, Organizational Level, Function, and Importance of Ethics, Relationships and Results in Managerial Decision-Making," *Journal of Business Ethics* 8, no. 10 (October 1989), pp. 747–771.

27. Sharyne Merritt, "Marketing Ethics and Education: Some Empirical Findings," *Journal of Business Ethics* 10, no. 8 (August 1991), pp. 625–632.

28. Kelley, Ferrell, and Skinner, "Ethical Behavior among Marketing Researchers."

29. Steven N. Brenner and Earl A. Molander, "Is the Ethics of Business Changing?" *Harvard Business Review* 55, no. 1 (January–February 1977), pp. 57–71.

30. Scott J. Vitell and Troy A. Festervand, "Business Ethics: Conflicts, Practices, and Beliefs of Industrial Executives," *Journal of Business Ethics* 6, no. 2 (1987), pp. 111–122.

31. Marc J. Epstein, Ruth Ann McEwen, and Roxanne M. Spindle, "Shareholder Preferences Concerning Corporate Ethical Performance," *The Journal of Business Ethics* 13, no. 6 (June 1994), pp. 447–453.

32. Joel J. Davis, "Good Ethics Is Good for Business: Ethical Attribution and Response to Environmental Advertising," *Journal of Business* 13, no. 11 (November 1994), pp. 873–885.

33. Ibid.

34. Wallace N. Davidson III, Dan L. Worrell, and Chun I. Lee, "Stock Market Reactions to Announced Corporate Illegalities," *Journal of Business Ethics* 13, no. 12 (December 1994), pp. 979–987.

35. Melissa S. Baucus and Janet P. Near, "Can Illegal Corporate Behavior Be Predicted? An Event History Analysis," *Academy of Management Journal* 34 (March 1991), pp. 9–36.

36. Davidson, Worrell, and Lee, "Stock Market Reactions."

37. Barry Z. Posner and Warren H. Schmidt, "Values and the American Manager: An Update," *California Management Review* 26, no. 3 (1984), pp. 202–216.

38. Baumhart, "How Ethical Are Businessmen?"; Newstrom and Ruch, "The Ethics of Management"; Brenner and Molander, "Is the Ethics of Business Changing?"; Mark K. Weaver and O. C. Ferrell, "The Impact of Corporate Policy on Reported Ethical Beliefs and Behavior of Marketing Practitioners," *Contemporary Marketing Thought*, 1977 Educators' Proceedings, #41, Barnett A. Greenberg and Danny N. Bellenger eds. (Chicago: American Marketing Association, 1977), pp. 477–481; O. C. Ferrell and Mark K. Weaver, "Ethical Beliefs of Marketing Managers," *Journal of Marketing* 42, no. 3 (July 1978), pp. 69–73; Dean M. Krugman and O. C. Ferrell, "The Organizational Ethics of Advertising: Corporate and Agency Views," *Journal of Advertising* 10, no. 1 (1981), pp. 21–30, 48; David J. Fritzsche and Helmut Becker, "Ethical Behavior of Marketing Managers," *Journal of Business Ethics* 2, no. 4 (1983), pp. 291–299; Leyland F. Pitt and Deon Nel, "The Wearer's Merit—A Comparison of the Attitudes of Suppliers and Buyers to Corruption in Business," *Industrial Marketing & Purchasing* 3, no. 1 (1988), pp. 30–39; Cornelius B. Pratt, "PRSA Members' Perceptions of Public Relations Ethics," *Public Relations Review* 17, no. 2 (1991), pp. 145–159; Vince Howe, K. Douglas Hoffman, and Donald W. Hardigree, "The Relationship between Ethical and Customer-Orientated Service Provider Behaviors," *Journal of Business Ethics* 13, no. 7 (July 1994), pp. 497–506.

39. Lawrence B. Chonko, Shelby D. Hunt, and Roy D. Howell, "Ethics and the American Advertising Federation Principles," *International Journal of Advertising* 6, no. 3 (1987), pp. 265–274; and William Cohen and Helena Czepiec, "The Role of Ethics in Gathering Corporate Intelligence," *Journal of Business Ethics* 7, no. 3 (1988), pp. 199–203.

40. Ferrell and Weaver, "Ethical Beliefs of Marketing Managers."

41. Brenner and Molander, "Is the Ethics of Business Changing?"

42. Ferrell and Weaver, "Ethical Beliefs of Marketing Managers."

43. Loren Falkerberg and Irene Herremans, "Ethical Behaviours in Organizations: Directed by the Formal or Informal Systems?" *Journal of Business Ethics* 14, no. 2 (February 1995), pp. 133–143.

44. Ibid.

45. Ibid.

46. Ibid.

47. Ibid.

48. Bart Victor and John B. Cullen, "A Theory and Measure of Ethical Climate in Organizations," *Research in Corporate Social Performance and Policy 9,* William Frederick, ed., (Greenwich, CT: JAI Press Inc., 1987), pp. 51–71.

49. Ibid.

50. Linda Klebe Trevino, Kenneth D. Butterfield, and Donald L. McCabe, "The Ethical Context in Organizations: Influences on Employee Attitudes and Behaviors," *Business Ethics Quarterly* 8 (1998), pp. 447–476.

51. David J. Fritzsche, "Ethical Climates and the Ethical Dimension of Decision Making," *Journal of Business Ethics* 24 (2000), pp. 125–140.

52. Newstrom and Ruch, "The Ethics of Management."

53. Krugman and Ferrell, "The Organizational Ethics of Advertising."

54. Mary Zey-Ferrell and O. C. Ferrell, "Role-Set Configuration and Opportunity as Predictors of Unethical Behavior in Organizations," *Human Relations* 35, no. 7 (1982), pp. 587–604.

55. Mary Zey-Ferrell, Mark K. Weaver, and O. C. Ferrell, "Predicting Unethical Behavior among Marketing Practitioners," *Human Relations* 32, no. 7 (1979), pp. 557–569.

56. Edwin H. Sutherland and Donald R. Cressey, *Principles of Criminology,* 8th ed. (Chicago: Lippincott, 1970).

57. Zey-Ferrell and Ferrell, "Role-Set Configuration and Opportunity."

58. Baumhart, "How Ethical Are Businessmen?"; Brenner and Molander, "Is the Ethics of Business Changing?"

59. Scott J. Vitell and Donald L. Davis, "Ethical Beliefs of MIS Professionals: The Frequency and Opportunity for Unethical Behavior," *Journal of Business Ethics* 9, no. 1 (1990), pp. 63–70.

60. Zey-Ferrell and Ferrell, "Role-Set Configuration and Opportunity."

61. Shelby D. Hunt, Lawrence B. Chonko, and James B. Wilcox, "Ethical Problems of Marketing Researchers," *Journal of Marketing Research* 21, no. 3 (August 1984), pp. 309–324; Lawrence B. Chonko and Shelby D. Hunt, "Ethics and Marketing Management: An Empirical Examination," *Journal of Business Research* 13, no. 4 (1985), pp. 339–359.

62. Chonko, Hunt, and Howell, "Ethics and the American Advertising Federation Principles."

63. Akaah and Riordan, "Judgments of Marketing Professionals."

64. Ibid.

65. Hegarty and Sims, "Some Determinants of Unethical Decision Behavior."

66. George W. England, "Personal Value Systems of American Managers," *Academy of Management Journal* 10, no. 1 (1967), pp. 53–68.

67. Warren H. Schmidt and Barry Z. Posner, "Managerial Values in Perspective," AMA Survey Report (New York: American Management Association, 1983).

68. Author's unpublished manuscript.

69. Schmidt and Posner, "Managerial Values in Perspective."

70. Baumhart, "How Ethical are Businessmen?"

71. Weaver and Ferrell, "The Impact of Corporate Policy."

72. Ferrell and Weaver, "Ethical Beliefs of Marketing Managers."

73. Bodo B. Schlegelmilch and Jane Houston, "Corporate Codes of Ethics in Large UK Companies: An Empirical Investigation of Use, Content, and Attitudes," *European Journal of Marketing* 23, no. 6 (1989), pp. 7–24.

74. Cornelius B. Pratt and E. Lincoln James, "Advertising Ethics: A Contextual Response Based on Classical Ethical Theory," *Journal of Business Ethics* 13, no. 6 (June 1994), pp. 455–468.

75. Scott J. Vitell and Anusorn Singhapakdi, "Factors Influencing the Perceived Importance of Stakeholder Groups in Situations Involving Ethical Issues," *Business & Professional Ethics Journal* 10, no. 3 (Spring 1991), pp. 53–72.

76. "Marketing Ethics: Factors Influencing Perceptions of Ethical Problems and Alternatives."

77. Anne J. Rich, Carl S. Smith, and Paul H. Mihalek, "Are Corporate Codes of Conduct Effective?" *Management Accounting* 72, no. 3 (September 1990), pp. 34–35.

78. W. Harvey Hegarty and Henry P. Sims, Jr., "Organizational Philosophy, Policies, and Objectives Related to Unethical Decision Behavior," *Journal of Applied Psychology* 64, no. 3 (1978), pp. 331–338.

79. Brenner and Molander, "Is the Ethics of Business Changing?"

80. Zey-Ferrell and Ferrell, "Role-Set Configuration and Opportunity." Zey-Ferrell, Weaver, and Ferrell, "Predicting Unethical Behavior among Marketing Practitioners."

81. Anusorn Singhapakdi and Scott J. Vitell, "Personal and Professional Values Underlying the Ethical Judgment of Marketers," *Journal of Business Ethics* 12, no. 7 (1993), pp. 525–533.

82. Gregory A. Claypool, David F. Fetyko, and Michael A. Pearson, "Reactions to Ethical Dilemmas: A Study Pertaining to Certified Public Accountants," *Journal of Business Ethics* 9, no. 9 (1990), pp. 699–706.

83. Jeanne M. David, Jeffrey Kantor, and Ira Greenberg, "Possible Ethical Issues and Their Impact on the Firm: Perceptions Held by Public Accountants," *Journal of Business Ethics* 13, no. 12 (December 1994), pp. 919–937.

84. Ibid.

85. S. Douglas Beets, "Personal Morals and Professional Ethics: A Review and an Empirical Examination of Public Accounting," *Business and Professional Ethics Journal* 10, no. 2 (Summer 1991), pp. 63–84.

86. Paul H. Mihalek, Anne J. Rich, and Carl S. Smith, "Ethics and Management Accountants," *Management Accounting* 69, no. 6 (December 1987), pp. 34–36.

87. Gary R. Weaver, Linda Klebe Trevino, and Philip L. Cochran, "Corporate Ethics Practices in the Mid-1990's: An Empirical Study of the Fortune 1000," *Journal of Business Ethics* 18 (1999), pp. 283–294.

88. Gary R. Weaver, Linda Klebe Trevino, and Philip L. Cochran, "Corporate Ethics Programs as Control Systems: Influences of Executive Commitment and Environmental Factors," *Academy of Management Journal* 42, no. 1 (1999), pp. 41–57.

89. Ibid.

90. Gary R. Weaver, "Integrated and Decoupled Corporate Social Performance: Management Commitments, External Pressures, and Corporate Ethics Practices," *Acaedmy of Management Journal* 42, no. 5 (1999), pp. 539–552.

91. Paul C. Nystrom, "Differences in Moral Values between Corporations," *Journal of Business Ethics* 9, no. 12 (1990), pp. 971–979.

92. Ishmael P. Akaah and Daulatram Lund, "The Influence of Personal and Organizational Values on Marketing Professionals' Ethical Behavior," *Journal of Business Ethics* 13, no. 6 (June 1994), pp. 417–430.

93. Jeffrey G. Blodgett, Long-Chuan Lu, Gregory M. Rose, and Scott J. Vitell, "Ethical Sensitivity to Stakeholder Interests: A Cross-Cultural Comparison," *Journal of the Academy of Marketing Science* 29, no. 2 (2001), pp. 190–202.

94. Hegarty and Sims, "Some Determinants of Unethical Decision Behavior"; Hegarty and Sims, "Organized Philosophy, Policies, and Objectives Related to Unethical Decision Behavior: A Laboratory Experiment."

95. Helmut Becker and David J. Fritzsche, "A Comparison of the Ethical Behavior of American, French, and German Managers," *The Columbia Journal of World Business* 22, no. 4 (1987), pp. 87–97; and David J. Fritzsche, Y. Paul Huo, Sakae Sugai, Stephen Dun-Hou-Tsai, Cheong Seok Kim, and Helmut Becker, "Exploring the Ethical Behavior of Managers: A Comparative Study of Four Countries," *Asian Pacific Journal of Management* 12, no. 2 (October 1995), pp. 37–62.

96. David J. Fritzsche, "Ethical Issues in Multinational Marketing," *Marketing Ethics: Guidelines for Managers,* Gene R. Laczniak and Patrick E. Murphy, eds. (Lexington, MA: D. C. Heath and Company, 1985), pp. 85–96.

97. Diana Robertson and Bodo B. Schlegelmilch, "Corporate Institutionalization of Ethics in the United States and Great Britain," *Journal of Business Ethics* 12, no. 4 (1993), pp. 301–312.

98. Alan J. Dubinsky, Marvin A. Jolson, Masaaki Kotabe, and Chae Un Lim, "A Cross-national Investigation of Industrial Salespeople's Ethical Perceptions," *Journal of International Business Studies* 22, no. 4 (Fourth Quarter 1991), pp. 651–670.

99. Fritzsche et al, "Exploring the Ethical Behavior of Managers."

100. Chiaki Nakano, "A Survey Study on Japanese Managers' Views of Business Ethics," *Journal of Business Ethics* 16 (1997), pp. 1737–1751.

101. Laura L. Whitcomb, Carolyn B. Erdener, and Cheng Li, "Business Ethical Values in China and the U.S.," *Journal of Business Ethics* 17 (1998), pp. 839–852.

102. M. Dolecheck and C. Dolecheck, "Business Ethics: A Comparison of Attitudes of Managers in Hong Kong and the United States," *Hong Kong Manager* 1 (1987), pp. 28–43.

103. Lee, "Ethical Beliefs in Marketing Management."

104. Robert W. Armstrong, Bruce W. Stening, John K. Ryans, Larry Marks, and Michael Mayo, "International Marketing Ethics: Problems Encountered by Australian Firms," *European Journal of Marketing* 24, no. 10 (1990), pp. 5–18.

105. Baumhart, "How Ethical Are Businessmen?"; Brenner and Molander, "Is the Ethics of Business Changing?"

106. Hunt, Chonko, and Wilcox, "Ethical Problems of Marketing Researchers"; Chonko and Hunt, "Ethics and Marketing Management." Shelby D. Hunt, "Ethical Problems of Advertising Agency Executives," *Journal of Advertising* 16, no. 4 (1987), pp. 16–24.

107. Armstrong et al, "International Marketing Ethics."

108. Zey-Ferrell, Weaver, and Ferrell, "Predicting Unethical Behavior among Marketing Practitioners"; Zey-Ferrell and Ferrell, "Role-Set Configuration and Opportunity."

109. Chonko and Hunt, "Ethics and Marketing Management."

110. Hunt, Chonko, and Wilcox, "Ethical Problems of Marketing Researchers."

111. Vitell and Festervand, "Business Ethics: Conflicts, Practices, and Beliefs of Industrial Executives."

112. Vitell and Festervand, "Ethical Problems of Advertising Agency Executives."

113. Lawrence B. Chonko and John J. Burnett, "Measuring the Importance of Ethical Situations as a Source of Role Conflict: A Survey of Salespeople, Sales Managers, and Sales Support Personnel," *Journal of Personal Selling and Sales Management* 3, no. 1 (May 1983), pp. 41–47.

114. Hegarty and Sims, "Some Determinants of Unethical Decision Behavior."

115. Hunt, Chonko, and Wilcox, "Ethical Problems of Marketing Researchers"; Chonko and Hunt, "Ethics and Marketing Management."

116. Vitell and Davis, "Ethical Beliefs of MIS Professionals."

117. Douglas J. Lincoln, Milton M. Pressley, and Taylor Little, "Ethical Beliefs and Personal Values of Top Level Executives," *Journal of Business Research* 10, no. 4 (1982), pp. 475–487.

118. Fritzsche and Becker, "Ethical Behavior of Marketing Managers."

119. Becker and Fritzsche, "A Comparison of the Ethical Behavior of American, French, and German Managers."

120. Fritzsche, "An Examination of Marketing Ethics;" and Daulatram B. Lund, "An Empirical Examination of Marketing Professionals' Ethical Behavior in Differing Situations," *Journal of Business Ethics* 24 (2000), pp. 331–342.

121. Pratt and James, "Advertising Ethics."

122. George M. Zinkham, Michael Bisesi, and Mary Jane Saxon, "MBAs' Changing Attitudes toward Marketing Dilemmas: 1981–1987," *Journal of Business Ethics* 8, no. 12 (1989), pp. 963–974.

123. Krugman and Ferrell, "The Organizational Ethics of Advertising." Ferrell and Weaver, "Ethical Beliefs of Marketing Managers."

124. Fritzsche and Becker, "Ethical Behavior of Marketing Managers."

125. Fritzsche, "An Examination of Marketing Ethics."

126. Thomas M. Jones, "Ethical Decision-Making by Individuals in Organizations: An Issue-Contingent Model," *Academy of Management Review* 16, no. 2 (1991), pp. 366–395.

127. Joseph G. P. Paolillo and Scott J. Vitell, "An Empirical Investigation of the Influence of Selected Personal, Organizational, and Moral Intensity Factors on Ethical Decision Making," *Journal of Business Ethics* 35 (2002), pp. 65–74; Anusorn Singhapakdi, Scott J. Vitell, and George R. Frank, "Antecedents, Consequences, and Mediating Effects of Perceived Moral Intensity and Personal Moral Philosophies," *Journal of the Academy of Marketing Science* 27, no. 1 (1999), pp. 19–36; Anusorn Singhapakdi, Scott J. Vitell, and Kenneth L. Kraft, "Moral Intensity and Ethical Decision-Making of Marketing Professionals," *Journal of Business Research* 36 (1996), pp. 245–255.

Chapter

Making Moral Decisions

We believe two conditions are necessary for a manager consistently to include ethics in the decision-making process: (1) The organizational culture must support ethical decision making; and (2) the manager must possess tools for evaluating the ethical dimension of a decision. A manager normally has little influence on the culture of an organization unless he or she is part of the top-management team. However, the manager has a great deal of control over the tools available for evaluating decisions. If the appropriate tools are not available, managers may obtain them by reading the business ethics literature, attending executive development programs on ethics, and/or by enrolling in a course on business ethics at a nearby university. A culture that supports ethical decision making encourages managers to obtain the necessary tools to operate successfully within the culture.

Organizational Culture

In Chapter 4 organizational culture was referred to as the common set of assumptions, beliefs, and values that has developed within the organization to cope with the external and internal environment. Culture as an organizational concept was borrowed from social anthropology, which focuses on the beliefs, values, speech, and artifacts of groups of people and the manner in which these traits are transmitted from generation to generation. Organizations also have certain common characteristics that provide internal guidance and are shared and perpetuated by their members. Thus, the concept of organizational culture was a natural extension of the concept of culture from social anthropology.

John Kotter and James Heskett argue that there are two levels of corporate culture.[1] The deeper level of culture consists of values that are shared by members of the organization. These values tend to be relatively stable over time and are passed on to new members as the composition of the organization changes. The values are generally so ingrained in the organization that members are often not aware that they exist unless the values are brought to their attention. Thus, the values may be difficult for outsiders to discover because they are not actually visible, even though they underlie most actions taken within the firm. Even direct questioning may not yield values to which employees unconsciously adhere.

The second level of culture consists of norms that guide the behavior of organizational members in their day-to-day activities. Behavioral norms are visible in the members' dress, language, and demeanor. Behavioral norms develop from the shared values of the organization, although an individual value may not be identifiable from specific behavior. Norms often develop as a result of a combination of values. While behavioral norms generally are not easy to change, shared values are considered to be much more difficult to change.[2]

Culture evolves throughout the life of an organization. It originates as the beliefs and values of the founders become shared with other members of the organization. The values of the founders provide the basis for an initial set of beliefs concerning how the organization should relate to its external environment.[3] These beliefs include the initial core mission, goals, and strategy. They also involve the methods used to implement, evaluate, and fine-tune the strategy. These beliefs and values guide what is considered appropriate behavior for the organization's success and survival. For example, the founders may place high value on professionalism in dealing with customers. As this value develops into a shared value of the firm, the belief may emerge that a professional image is critical to success. To convey the image, service representatives are asked to dress in conservative three-piece suits. If early service experience is successful, such dress becomes a behavioral norm for the firm. It is perceived as an important factor in the firm's success and survival.

In addition to the founder's influence, major developments in a firm's culture may also occur when a dynamic new leader takes over the reins. In some organizations, the culture developed by the founders was weak and ineffective; in others, the culture that served the firm well in its early years did not fit the changing environment in later years. The Boeing Company was founded in 1916, yet the Boeing culture is most closely identified with William Allen, a dynamic leader who took over the presidency in 1945.[4] Johnson & Johnson was founded in 1887. General Robert Wood Johnson, the son of one of the founders, is credited with creating the highly successful Johnson & Johnson culture.[5] He became head of the corporation in 1932.

Cultural values also provide guidance for the firm in integrating its internal environment.[6] They provide common terminology and concepts necessary for internal communication. Culture creates a consensus of the membership boundaries of the organization and thus defines who is included and who is excluded. The rules for acquiring, maintaining, and losing power as well as for obtaining rewards and punishment are part of an organization's culture. Appropriate peer relationships are prescribed by culture. Finally, culture provides an ideology for the firm. The ideology may consist of the shared assumptions of the firm, future aspirations and ideals, current realities, and possibly rationalizations for unexplained behavior.

The internal environment is organized to function successfully and to cope with a corporation's external environment. The shared beliefs concerning the relevant characteristics of the external environment guide the structure and operating relationships created within the internal environment. For example, if the cultural leaders value consensus in decision making, managers will spend time listening to points of view, developing a proposal, and getting colleagues to support the proposed decision. "Lone Ranger" decision making becomes an unacceptable mode of behavior. Consensus building becomes a behavioral norm for the organization.

Thus, culture functions to promote the survival of the firm by influencing both its external and internal behavior. It promotes consistency of behavior in a manner that the members of the organization believe to be successful. When the environment changes and such behavior ceases to be successful, values are called into question and possibly adjusted to more successfully meet the changed environment. Adjustment is generally a very slow process. At times it may be too slow to insure survival of the firm. On the other hand, too rapid a change may lead to overshooting the mark and results in cultural instability.

The support that an organization's culture provides to a manager considering the ethical dimension of a decision is dependent on the shared values that make up the culture. Chapter 7 will examine several firms that have very supportive cultures; opposite examples can also be found. Some have asked if an organization's culture should support ethics. Does this shortchange the stockholders by reducing the economic performance of the business, a prime interest of any investor? We now turn to look at the available evidence.

High-Performing Cultures Promote Ethical Behavior

A value has been defined as "a lasting belief that a certain mode of conduct or goal is better than the opposite conduct or goal."[7] In Chapter 3 business ethics was referred to as the process of evaluating a business decision with respect to the moral standards of a culture. Values that support moral standards, both moral norms and moral principles, tend to influence behavior in a moral direction. The belief is that behavior that supports the standards is better than behavior that does not. If the shared values of an organization are consistent with the moral standards of the culture, the organization's culture will support ethical behavior. That does not mean that all behavior within the organization will be ethical, as we will discover in Chapter 7. It does mean that behavior within the organization will *tend* to be ethical.

Thus, a key factor in the ethics of an organization is the set of values believed to be important by the members of the firm. If the shared values of the firm support moral standards, the culture is supportive of ethical decision making. If the values do not support the standards, the culture does not support ethical decision making.

Kotter and Heskett found that three conditions appear to exist at firms that realize high performance over the long run (see Table 6.1). First, the firm must have a strong corporate culture. This is a necessary but not sufficient condition because some organizations with strong cultures simply march over the cliff together.[8] Second, the culture needs to fit the environment in which the firm operates.[9] A firm operating in a rapidly changing, turbulent, high-tech environment requires a culture significantly different from a firm operating in a stable, mature industry. Third, the culture must be able to help the firm foresee environmental changes and adjust successfully to those changes.[10] The culture should encourage and empower managers to provide the leadership to change strategies and tactics whenever necessary in order to satisfy the needs of their key constituencies, especially customers, employees, and shareholders.[11] The culture should also recognize and encourage good leadership, for it is leadership that provides the change mechanism for keeping the culture current with its

TABLE 6.1 **Some Characteristics Of High-Performance Firms**

Cultural Characteristics
1. There is a strong corporate culture.
2. The culture fits the environment in which the firm operates.
3. The culture helps the firm foresee environmental changes and adjust successfully to those changes.
Value System Emphasis
(Key constituencies: customers, employees, and shareholders.)
1. Sincere caring for key constituencies.
2. Concern of long duration.
3. Emphasis on integrity.
Corporate Behavior
Corporations with high-performing cultures are organizations that possess shared values that promote ethical behavior.

Cultural characteristics and value system emphasis reported in John P. Kotter and James L. Heskett, *Corporate Culture and Performance* (New York, NY: The Free Press, 1992), pp. 15–57.

environment. Edgar Schein states that ". . . the unique and essential function of leadership is the manipulation of culture."[12]

Our interest centers on the satisfaction of the needs of the firm's key constituencies. Kotter and Heskett found that the value system of high-performing firms evidenced a sincere caring for their key constituencies.[13] This concern was of long duration, not some recent addition to the culture. A key aspect seemed to be a sincere effort to be fair to the stakeholders. They cited a recurring ". . . emphasis on 'integrity' or 'doing the right thing.' "[14] These terms should be familiar. Justice is associated with fairness and integrity is associated with honesty. It appears that a strong case can be made for high-performance companies being ethical organizations. This is the strongest justification yet for the statement that good ethics is good business. Corporations with high-performing cultures are organizations that possess shared values that promote ethical behavior! We can conclude that ethics is a necessary but not a sufficient condition for high performance.

This provides a strong argument for promoting ethical behavior, but it provides an even stronger argument for creating a high-performance culture, since this will promote ethical behavior as well as promote the long-term survival of the firm. A manager working in a high-performance culture is aware of the support for ethical behavior. The manager working in a nonsupportive culture faces a dilemma: Is it time to change firms or can the culture be altered?

As stated previously, cultural change is a long and difficult process. The main force for change must come from top-management leadership. If there is evidence of change being attempted from the top, middle-level managers can lend crucial support. In fact, top management must obtain the support of a large number of middle managers in order to successfully create cultural change.[15] With support from the top, managers can take a leadership position within their groups, departments, or divisions to support and effect the kind of change that will lead to a high-performance culture. By building consensus among management peers, a manager helps to broaden the support for change and thus increases the chances that a successful alteration can be accomplished. However, this is not without some personal risk. If the change effort fails and the top-management champion leaves, a manager may find himself or herself left in an untenable position within the firm.

The question of whether a manager should support a cultural-change action depends on the current conditions within the firm and future prospects. If the manager is locked into the firm either for geographic or financial reasons, the chances of the success of the change effort must be weighed carefully and balanced against current ethical performance. If the manager has other employment options, the potential cost of the change action must be weighed against the chances of success and the current ethical performance of the firm as well as the ethical performance of alternative employers.

Ethics Tools

Just as a carpenter needs a saw and a hammer to build a house, a manager needs ethics tools to evaluate the ethical dimension of a decision. The tools we advocate consist of the theory presented in Chapter 3 and a decision support model that integrates the theory into applications.

Chapter 4 introduced the idea that the ethical dimension of a decision alternative has a minimum performance level below which the decision maker will reject the alternative outright as being unacceptable. Immediately above the minimum performance level, the decision alternative is marginally acceptable and may be either accepted or rejected based on the economic, political, technological, and social criteria, even though the decision maker may not be pleased with the ethical dimension. At some point above the minimum performance level, the decision maker will be entirely satisfied with the ethical dimension of the decision alternative. We identified this as the desirable performance level. Thus, we have a three-level ethical dimension: unacceptable, marginally acceptable, and acceptable. One would expect that decision alternatives that clearly violate hypernorms or community norms would fall into the unacceptable category. Those on the borderline present more difficult problems.

Decision Support Model

The decision support model utilized is a highly modified version of the Manuel Velasquez et al. model shown in Figure 6.1.[16] The model incorporates both hypernorms and community norms into the decision application. It also factors in the five decision dimensions introduced in the decision process model in Chapter 4.

Before making a decision, the manager collects information about the problem and the alternatives being considered. The information sought includes the stakeholders affected by the decision as well as the potential positive and negative impacts upon each stakeholder resulting from each decision alternative. The amount and detail of the information collected depends on the availability of the information and the time remaining before the decision must be made. The shorter the interval, the less information can be collected and vice versa. More information would be collected for major decisions, such as altering a firm's strategy, than for minor ones such as altering the reporting procedures for injuries occurring on the job. The type and amount of information collected also depends on costs. Readily available information usually costs less and thus tends to be collected. Less-accessible information may be disregarded unless it is considered critical to the success of the decision. Some desired information may be impossible to obtain, such as the cost of releasing a harmful chemical into the environment. In these cases, best estimates must be used.

FIGURE 6.1   **Decision Support Model**

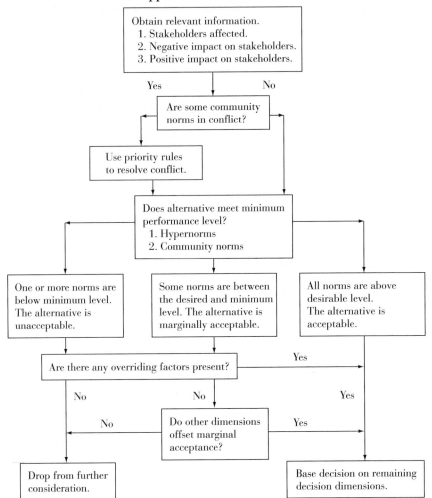

Managers should incorporate all relevant hypernorms into their decision-alternative evaluation. In addition, all applicable community norms need to be considered. The specific set of community norms used depends on the local economic communities impacted by the decision. The norms of all affected communities should be included. The inclusion of multiple community norms (whether from one or more communities) raises the possibility of norms' conflicts.

When community norm conflicts are discovered, the manager needs to determine the priority rules that apply. By utilizing the appropriate priority rules, a consistent set of community norms can be developed for use in evaluating the decision alternatives. For example, age discrimination is an accepted practice in Europe, but in the United States it is prohibited. A French general manager of a U.S. firm located in Italy wants to limit new hires in an expansion program to people under 40 years old. The policy violates a norm of the parent U.S. firm but not of firms operating in Italy. Recalling the discussion of priority rules in Chapter 3, well-defined norms should generally have priority over less-precise norms. The norm barring discrimination is well defined, while the norm allowing it occurs by default. In addition, the Italian community will not be harmed by following the norm prohibiting discrimination on the basis of age. The nondiscrimination norm should take priority; the evaluation process can begin using an internally consistent set of norms.

An alternative judged unacceptable using any norm is dropped from further consideration. An alternative judged acceptable on all norms is a desirable alternative from an ethical perspective. Alternatives that are considered marginally acceptable on one or more norms require further investigation. A marginally acceptable alternative may become an acceptable alternative if specific overriding factors are present. A marginally acceptable alternative may become a chosen alternative even though the ethics dimension remains only marginally acceptable if the strength of other dimensions compensates for the weak ethics dimension.

Overriding Factors

Specific overriding factors exist that will convert a marginally acceptable alternative into an acceptable alternative. In some cases, one norm becomes more important than another and thus overrides the marginal acceptance. (It should be noted that a community norm can never override a hypernorm.) For example, a steel manufacturing firm, in an effort to reduce workplace injuries, may decide that its employees must submit to random drug tests. While the decision maker may not like random testing because it violates privacy rights, random testing may be judged marginally acceptable under the right to privacy because, if handled correctly, the employees will not actually be harmed by the testing. Because steel manufacturing involves hazardous work, employees impaired by drug use while operating mechanical equipment pose a danger to fellow employees. Their actions could lead to injury (or death) that would harm individuals, their families, and the surrounding community. Thus, under the hypernorm concerning physical security and well-being, drug testing to prevent impaired employees from operating equipment would appear to be acceptable. The decision maker may decide that the personal-safety benefits gained outweigh the personal loss of privacy and judge the random testing as ethically acceptable. The personal-safety norm would override the right-to-privacy norm in this case.

A second overriding factor is referred to as incapacitation, which means that an individual is unable to select a specific alternative. This may be due to lack of information or to coercion. Most business decisions are made with less than complete information due to time and cost constraints and/or unavailability of the needed information. If certain information regarding a specific alternative is simply not available, that information cannot be used to evaluate the ethical dimension of the alternative.

Continuing with the example of the steel firm, suppose that the firm retained to do the drug testing hired two new people to perform the tests. The two new employees made many errors, resulting in a number of innocent people being fired because of false test results. Several careers were ruined and families were destroyed. The decision to test was made based on the assumption that the testing procedure would be handled correctly. It was not! While the firm hired to run the tests had an excellent record, the performance of its new employees was poor. If the decision maker had possessed information concerning the testing outcome, the personal-safety norm would never have overridden the right-to-privacy norm's marginal acceptability. In this case, the lack of information incapacitated the decision maker from judging the alternative correctly. What appeared to be an ethically acceptable alternative turned out to be unacceptable.

Coercion can also incapacitate the decision maker so that an alternative is judged acceptable when it would otherwise be considered unacceptable. The threat of physical or political harm can be so strong that the decision maker is forced to take actions that would be readily dismissed if he or she were operating free of duress.

Decision Dimensions

In addition to the ethical dimension of business decisions, you will remember from Chapter 4 that there are four other dimensions: economic, political, technological, and social. An alternative with sufficient benefits from any one or a combination of these dimensions may offset a marginally acceptable ethical judgment and become an alternative of choice. A business is an economic institution and must make a satisfactory profit to exist. If a decision alternative appears sufficiently profitable or in some other manner enhances the economic performance of the organization, the economic benefits may be sufficient to offset a marginally acceptable ethical dimension. The firm will then be forced to operate at an ethical level not desirable to the manager but dictated by economics.

Closing a plant that requires firing many in the workforce would appear to be a marginally acceptable alternative on the ethics dimension. While the closing would not likely be judged unacceptable, one would expect it to be judged marginally acceptable due to the disruption and pain it would cause long-time employees who have given much of their lives to the firm. Thus, when Weyerhaeuser Company announced that it was closing its Everett, Washington, pulp mill effective March 29, 1992, one would expect the ethical dimension to have been judged marginally acceptable.[17] The mill produced primarily bleached kraft market pulp. The closure was a result of overcapacity in the market, resulting in a severe decline in pulp price, rising raw material costs, and the large investment required to meet current environmental regulations. The mill was small and outdated in a market with substantial capacity. Thus, the economic dimension overwhelmed the marginal ethical judgment and the alternative of closing the plant was accepted. To the company's credit, it helped workers locate new jobs, and it paid termination benefits to 285 workers who were laid off.

A significant benefit within the political dimension can turn a marginally acceptable decision within the ethical dimension into an acceptable decision alternative. General Motors had long believed that its presence in South Africa was a positive force for change of the apartheid system. In 1985, a GM spokesman discussing critics' calls for General Motors to disinvest its South African operations stated, "It makes no sense economically or morally."[18] GM had taken a number of steps to weaken apartheid, including bringing strong pressure on the Port Elizabeth Town Council (where one of its operations was located) to eliminate whites-only beaches and offering financial and legal assistance to nonwhite employees who were prosecuted for violating whites-only laws.[19] GM had also maintained the highest rating under the Sullivan principles for seven straight years.[20] To withdraw from South Africa would eliminate these activities and likely decrease the well-being of the blacks employed by the company. To GM, leaving South Africa was a marginally acceptable decision. However, strong political forces were at work to remove all U.S. firms from South Africa. Congress passed legislation tightening the sanctions. New York and San Francisco passed laws limiting purchases from companies doing business with the South African government. Numerous activist groups were bringing pressure for divestiture. As a result, GM announced on October 20, 1986, that its South African operations would be sold to a group of investors headed by local management. The strength of the political dimension had turned the marginally acceptable alternative into an acceptable alternative.

The technological dimension can also offset a marginally acceptable ethical dimension. Immunex Corporation and the Fred Hutchinson Cancer Research Center in Seattle, Washington, decided to test gene therapy on human subjects in their quest to find a treatment for the acquired immune deficiency syndrome (AIDS).[21] The procedure involved inserting special genetically altered cells into a series of patients in an attempt to treat the virus. The procedure created one billion virus-fighting cells in a patient's body, but there was also some risk of immune reaction. If the immune response was too strong, it could cause inflammation of the brain and lungs. Such effects would certainly not be desirable and under ordinary circumstances would be considered unacceptable on the ethical dimension. However, given the terminal nature of AIDS, there may be justification for experimental treatments that would not normally be permitted under less dire circumstances. Thus, the ethics dimension may be judged to be marginally acceptable. If the gene therapy would lead to a cure for AIDS, a significant technological breakthrough would be achieved. The benefit of the potential breakthrough would likely compensate for the marginal acceptance on the ethical dimension and turn the alternative into an acceptable option.

Finally, a strong judgment on the social dimension can provide significant support for an alternative that is marginally acceptable on the ethical dimension. McDonald's Corporation has a history of being environmentally conscious. In the mid-1970s, prior to introducing polystyrene plastic containers, McDonald's hired the Stanford Research Institute (SRI) to conduct a study comparing the environmental impact of paperboard packaging versus polystyrene plastic packaging.[22] SRI concluded that polystyrene was more environmentally positive when evaluated from the point of production to disposal. Over the years, McDonald's had directed its polystyrene suppliers to remove chloroflourocarbons from their production processes and to reduce the thickness of the foam containers.[23]

In February 1990, McDonald's began a test recycling operation in 450 of its stores in New England.[24] It subsequently announced that it would purchase recycled materials for use in the construction and remodeling of its stores. The firm had been working with its suppliers who had agreed to build seven polystyrene recycling plants in the United States.[25] The plan was to extend its recycling program nationally. During this time, McDonald's was coming under increasing pressure from the Environmental Defense Fund, the National Toxics Campaign, numerous women's clubs, and school-children to stop using polystyrene packaging.[26] In late 1990, McDonald's responded to the social pressure by announcing that it was replacing its polystyrene containers with poly-coated paper.[27]

Edward Rensi, president of McDonald's U.S.A., appeared to have some misgivings concerning the decision. In his statement, Rensi said, "Although some scientific studies indicate foam packaging is environmentally sound, our customers don't feel good about it."[28] The firm appeared to be reacting to social pressure rather than its environmental convictions. If polystyrene packaging had been found to be environmentally superior to paperboard, recycling the polystyrene should have been much superior to poly-coated paper that cannot be recycled due to the plastic coating. Although the decision to use the coated paper was not unacceptable, it was marginally acceptable, particularly if the recycling effort was successful. Social pressure converted the marginally acceptable decision into an acceptable decision that was implemented. The end result appears to be more damaging to the environment, but the social dimension of the decision overrode the ethically marginal judgment.

When all decision alternatives are judged acceptable from an ethical perspective, the alternative selection is based on the remaining four decision dimensions: economic, political, technical, and social. If an alternative is judged marginal on one or more of the ethical norms, a check is made to see if there are any overriding factors to convert it to an acceptable level. If there are not, the other decision dimensions are examined to see if one or more are sufficiently strong to offset the marginal judgment of the ethical dimension. If none is found, the alternative is dropped from consideration. An alternative judged as unacceptable on any ethical norm is examined to see if there are any overriding factors that would convert it to an acceptable level. If there are none, it is dropped from further consideration.

Summary

For a manager to consistently consider ethics in decision making, the organization's culture must support ethical behavior, and the manager must possess tools to evaluate the ethical dimension of a decision alternative. We believe the more important of the two is the organization's culture. A culture that supports ethical behavior motivates managers to obtain the required decision tools. They can be developed relatively quickly when compared to changing a culture. Ethics tools can be developed via training programs and self-study.

Changing a culture that does not support ethical behavior is another matter. A cultural change of any significance can take many years, and there is no guarantee the desired change can be effected. Kotter and Heskett argue that to successfully change to a performance-enhancing culture, managers must be found who possess three characteristics: They must be effective leaders, have an outsider's perspective, and have an insider's resources.[29] They further state that combination is not found in many people today.

Discussion Questions

1. What is the difference between ethical norms that are in conflict and an evaluation in which the strong acceptance based on one norm overrides the marginal acceptance based on another norm?
2. What are the benefits of using a decision support model for evaluating the ethics of decision alternatives?
3. What opportunities do lower-level managers have for raising the ethical performance of a firm?
4. Can you think of other dynamic leaders of companies who have made significant contributions to their cultures? How did this happen?
5. What benefits does a strong culture provide a firm?
6. Why is a strong culture not sufficient to ensure long-term success?
7. What is the relationship between high-performance firms and their key constituencies? How does this relate to ethics?
8. Are there times when the interests of key constituencies are in conflict? (Long run or short run?)
9. Are there times when extreme benefits on one or more of the other four decision dimensions could justify selecting an alternative that is clearly unethical?

End Notes

1. John P. Kotter and James L. Heskett, *Corporate Culture and Performance* (New York, NY: The Free Press, 1992), p. 4.
2. Ibid.

It's Your Turn

Your firm makes upscale casual clothing. The decision was made last year to move half of your production off-shore, and you have been assigned the task of deciding where to relocate the manufacturing operations. After extensive investigation, you have decided to contract with a manufacturer in Southeast Asia.

You have narrowed the search to two firms. Firm A employs people aged 10 to 60. All employees work a 10-hour day with the weekends off. The pay scale is on the high side for the country. Working conditions are better than average for the country, and employees younger than 16 are placed so that they will not be exposed to dangerous working conditions. Upon further investigation, you find that the younger children are working because their family needs their income to survive. The only alternative to work is to sell their children.

Firm B employs people aged from 16 to 75. Employees work a 10-hour day six days a week. Pay tends to be on the low side for the country and working conditions are described as poor. All employees are treated the same regardless of their age. People work for the company because they have no alternative.

Both firms manufacture clothing that meets your company's standards. You need to make your recommendation at a meeting today. What factors should you consider in making your decision? What weight should each factor be given? Which firm will you recommend? Why?

3. Edgar H. Schein, *Organizational Culture and Leadership* (San Francisco: Jossey-Bass Publishers, 1985), p. 210.
4. "Corporate Ethics: A Prime Business Asset," James Keogh, ed. (New York: The Business Roundtable, 1988), p. 12.
5. Ibid, p. 82.
6. Schein, *Organizational Culture and Leadership,* pp. 65–82.
7. Gerald F. Cavanagh, *American Business Values,* 3rd ed. (Englewood Cliffs, NJ: Prentice Hall, 1990), p. 2.
8. Kotter and Heskett, *Corporate Culture and Performance,* pp. 15–27.
9. Ibid, pp. 28–43.
10. Ibid, pp. 44–57.
11. Ibid, p. 50.
12. Schein, *Organizational Culture and Leadership,* p. 317.
13. Kotter and Heskett, *Corporate Culture and Performance,* p. 52.
14. Ibid.
15. Ibid, p. 146.
16. Manuel Velasquez, Gerald F. Cavanagh, and Dennis J. Moberg, "Organizational Statesmanship and Dirty Politics: Ethical Guidelines for the Organizational Politician," *Organizational Dynamics* (Fall 1983), pp. 65–80.
17. "Weyco's Everett Mill Succumbs," *Pulp and Paper* 66, no. 3 (March 1992), p. 27.
18. William Holstein, Jim Jones, and Boyd Frances, "U.S. Companies Are Pulling Out—Apartheid Is Likely to Stay," *Business Week,* June 24, 1985, pp. 56, 57.

19. Karen Paul and Sharyn Duffy, "Corporate Responses to the Call for South African Withdrawal," *Research in Corporate Social Performance and Policy* 10 (Greenwich, Connecticut: JAI Press, 1988), pp. 211–240.

20. Ibid. The Sullivan principles, a set of standards designed to prevent racist practices by U.S. multinational firms operating in South Africa, were developed by Leon Sullivan, a black American minister.

21. Marilyn Chase, "Gene Therapy Test in AIDS May Begin within Months," *Wall Street Journal* 219, no. 32 (February 11, 1992), p. B2.

22. Scott Hume, "McDonald's," *Advertising Age* 62, no. 5 (January 29, 1991), p. 32.

23. Ibid.

24. Ibid.

25. Phyllis Berman, "McDonald's Caves In," *Forbes* 147, no. 3 (February 4, 1991), pp. 73–74.

26. Ibid.

27. Ibid.

28. Hume, "McDonald's."

29. Kotter and Heskett, *Corporate Culture and Performance*, p. 91.

Chapter 7

Ethics in Practice

This chapter highlights several firms that have been cited as among the best in the business community.[1] These firms are noted for their general business performance and behavior as well as for their commitment to ethical behavior. Included are The Boeing Company, a project management firm; Hewlett-Packard, a high-technology company; and Johnson & Johnson, a consumer products producer.

This chapter also examines actions taken by five other firms. Each action has been selected to represent one of the following types of ethical issues: bribery, coercion, deception, theft, and unfair discrimination. Using the modified Velasquez et al. model discussed in Chapter 6, this chapter examines the ethical dimension of the decision. Where the action is judged to be unethical, the focus is on what went wrong, what may have led to the unethical behavior, and how top management could have acted to encourage ethical behavior, rather than what actually occurred.

Ethical Companies

The Boeing Company

Boeing has been widely recognized as a well-run, successful, ethical organization. The firm, which began operations in 1916, is the world's largest producer of commercial aircraft. Other primary business activities include military aircraft, helicopters, and aerospace equipment. The firm grew significantly in the 1990s by acquiring Rockwell International Corporation's aerospace and defense units in 1996 and merging with the McDonnell Douglas Corporation in 1997.

Boeing's strong set of values can be traced back to William Allen, the CEO who took the reins at the end of World War II. Allen faced the formidable challenge of transforming Boeing from a wartime producer to a peacetime aircraft manufacturer. He is remembered for his sincerity, honesty, and integrity. The night he agreed to serve as company president, Allen developed a list of resolutions that reflected his personal values:

Must keep temper—always—never get mad.

Be considerate of my associates' views.

Don't talk too much . . . let others talk.

Don't be afraid to admit that you don't know.

Don't get immersed in detail—concentrate on the big objectives.

Make contacts with other people in industry—and keep them.

Try to improve feeling around Seattle toward the company.

Make a sincere effort to understand labor's viewpoint.

Be definite; don't vacillate.

Act—get things done—move forward.

Develop a postwar future for Boeing.

Try hard, but don't let obstacles get you down. Take things in stride.

Above all else be human—keep your sense of humor—learn to relax.

Be just, straightforward; invite criticism and learn to take it.

Be confident. Having once made a move, make the most of it. Bring to the task great enthusiasm, unlimited energy.

Make Boeing even greater than it is.[2]

Boeing became known as an ethical, reputable company under Allen's guidance. In 1964, Allen created an ethics committee comprised of upper management and members of the board that reported directly to the board of directors.[3] At the same time, Boeing drafted and implemented an ethics policy that reinforced the company's commitment to high values.

Allen's successor, T. A. Wilson, carried on the tradition of high standards established by Allen. The firm experienced continuing success until the commercial and military airplane markets collapsed in 1969–1970. During the next few years, Boeing downsized its labor force by two-thirds. Wilson's efforts became totally focused on maintaining the viability of Boeing.

Unknown to Wilson, several Boeing employees were engaged in foreign payments that came to light in the aircraft industry foreign payments scandals of 1974.[4] Such payments were in direct violation of Boeing standards. It became clear that the high standards of operation established during the Allen years had deteriorated. Wilson took immediate action. Boeing thoroughly reviewed its sales policies, developed sales training programs that reinforced the company's standards, and developed an auditing mechanism to insure compliance.

In 1981 Boeing began an effort to upgrade its ethics program. This led to a presentation in 1984 by the vice president of contracts and general counsel entitled "Pressures on Your Ethical Barometer."[5] The presentation discussed the competitive and internal organizational pressures that could lead to ethics violations. It also stressed the importance of managing the company's ethical culture. Only days after the presentation, Boeing Computer Services Company (BCS) was notified by the Department of the Interior that it had access to government inside information prior to submitting a bid to construct a financial system for the National Park System.[6] Because this was a violation of federal procurement rules, BCS's Federal Systems Group (FSG) was suspended from further business with any branch of the federal government. FSG worked on many government contracts held by Boeing; thus, the entire Boeing company was affected.

BCS quickly located the offending employees and took disciplinary action. It also made plans to initiate a major ethics program and thus got the suspension lifted. The program consisted of revising marketing procedures, implementing an employee-training program, appointing an ethics adviser whom employees could contact to report ethics violations, and creating internal audit procedures for screening all future government proposals. The BCS transgression underlined the need for management to manage the ethical climate of the organization.

Three lessons were learned from the foreign payments and the insider information incidents. First, the ethics involved when dealing with government agencies differs from the ethics of dealing with commercial firms. Second, employees who deal with outside parties require special attention so that they do not become ethical liabilities. Third, maintaining high ethical standards can be central to a firm's survival.[7]

Work continued on the ethics program and in 1985 Boeing revised and consolidated its ethics policy statements into a booklet entitled "Business Conduct Guidelines."[8] Business conduct was divided into five areas: marketing practices; offering of business courtesies; conflict of interest; acceptance of business courtesies; and the use of company time, materials, equipment, and proprietary information. The current edition added four additional areas: marketing to the U.S. government sector, relationships with suppliers, former U.S. government employees—conflict of interest, and buying and selling securities—insider trading.[9] In addition, training programs in a number of operating divisions were implemented. In 1986 Boeing added the Office of Business Practices to its corporate headquarters.[10] Boeing continues to upgrade its ethics program. Over the years, the program has been principle and value based rather than policy or rule focused.

Boeing states that the purpose of the program is to:

1. Communicate the Boeing values and standards of ethical business conduct to employees.
2. Inform employees of company policies and procedures regarding ethical business conduct.

3. Establish companywide processes to assist employees in obtaining guidance and resolving questions regarding compliance with the company's standards of conduct and the Boeing values.
4. Establish companywide criteria for ethics education and awareness programs and to coordinate compliance oversight activities.[11]

The Ethics and Business Conduct Committee, whose members are appointed by The Boeing Company Board of Directors, has oversight responsibility for the program. Members of the committee include the company chairman and chief executive officer, the president and chief operating officer, the presidents of the operating groups, and the senior vice presidents. The vice president of ethics and business conduct administers the program.

On June 16, 1992, Raymon L. Pedersen, a rivet supervisor in the manufacturing department of The Boeing Commercial Airplane Group, was indicted on charges of mail fraud, interstate travel to promote commercial bribery, and extortion.[12] Pedersen was accused of accepting $46,500 from VSI Corporation and $22,000 from Huck Manufacturing to promote the use of their aerospace fasteners. The latter payment was extorted from Huck using the threat of stopping the installation of Huck parts on Boeing aircraft. He was also accused of receiving $35,000 for supplying VSI with confidential business information about one if its competitors.[13] The indictment came 11 days after the president and two former top executives of VSI pleaded guilty to providing prostitutes, cash payments, and other gifts to win business from Boeing and other aerospace companies.[14] You can be sure that Pedersen is no longer employed by Boeing.

Recent events have cast a shadow on Boeing's ethics program. The Project on Government Oversight cited Boeing as being involved in 36 cases of misconduct between 1990 and 2003, resulting in fines, penalties, and settlements of $358 million.[15] It should be noted that in the murky world of federal contract rules not every dispute is the result of unethical actions. There may be honest disagreements over what is covered and what is not. In addition, a number of the cases were inherited with the recent acquisitions and merger. However, the name on the cases today is still Boeing.

The latest case to come to light involved a contract competition between Boeing and Lockheed to build a new Air Force rocket known as the EELV. Boeing's Huntington Beach, California, rocket division, part of McDonnell Douglas prior to the merger in August 1997, won the competition in 1998, giving it 19 out of 28 planned launches valued at $1.88 billion.[16] The remaining nine launches were given to Lockheed. Following the competition, it was discovered that Boeing had in its possession 25,000 pages of confidential Lockheed documents describing Lockheed's EELV project.[17] The Air Force subsequently punished Boeing by shifting seven of the launches previously awarded to Boeing to Lockheed and giving Lockheed three additional launches that had yet to be awarded.[18] That cost Boeing approximately $1 billion. It also suspended three Boeing space subsidiaries from receiving new government contracts for at least 60 to 90 days.

Boeing was extremely apologetic, running a full-page ad in major newspapers, admitting its shortcomings and promising to make amends. Boeing has also admitted to receiving 8,800 pages of confidential Lockheed documents pertaining to its competition with Lockheed to build satellites for New Skies Satellites N.V. of the Netherlands.[19] On July 30, 2003, Boeing held a mandatory four-hour ethics training program for approximately 75,000 employees at its St. Louis Boeing Integrated Defense System.[20] It also appointed former Senator Warren B. Rudman to conduct an independent review of company ethics policies and competitive information handling.

Boeing's rapid growth beginning in the mid 1990s via mergers and acquisitions may have contributed to its ethical lapses. It acquired Rockwell's aerospace and defense business in 1996 with 21,000 employees.[21] It merged with McDonnell Douglas in 1997, adding 64,000 more people.[22] In 2000, Boeing purchased Hughes Space and Communications with 9,000 people, Jeppesen Saunders Inc. with 1,400 people, and Hawker deHavilland of Australia with 950 people.[23] The result was 96,000 people coming from five different organizational cultures. Folding these disparate cultures into the Boeing culture could not be accomplished overnight. It should be noted that the majority of the cases of misconduct cited previously came to light after the acquisitions began and involved some personnel from the acquired firms. Hopefully, through its training programs and renewed emphasis upon ethics, Boeing can recover its reputation for integrity.*

Hewlett-Packard Company

Hewlett-Packard Company (HP) was founded in 1939 by William Hewlett and David Packard. The direction of the company was set in the 1950s when objectives were developed that provided the foundation for the core values of the organization:[24]

- Recognize that profit is the best measure of a company's contribution to society and the ultimate source of corporate strength;
- Continually improve the value of the products and services offered to customers;

*As this book went to press, two significant events occurred at Boeing.CFO Michael Sears was dismissed along with a senior executive in the company's missile defense unit, Darleen Druym. Boeing learned that Sears had talked with Druym about potential employment at Boeing while she was working as an acquisitions officer in the Pentagon for the Air Force. Her work involved Boeing business, most notably negotiations involving the leasing of 100 Boeing 767 aerial tankers. A few days later, as reported in The Wall Street Journal, December 2, 2003, CEO Phil Condit resigned stating that "the controversies and disturbances of the past year were obscuring the great accomplishments of this company."

- Seek new opportunities for growth, but focus efforts on fields in which the company can make a contribution;
- Provide employment opportunities that include the chance to share in the company's success;
- Maintain an organizational environment that fosters individual motivation, initiative, and creativity;
- Demonstrate good citizenship by making contributions to the community;
- Emphasize growth as a requirement for survival.

The core values formed the basis of what has become known as "The HP Way," described by Bill Hewlett as follows:

> I feel that in general terms it is the policies and actions that flow from the belief that men and women want to do a good job, a creative job, and that if they are provided the proper environment they will do so. But that's only part of it. Closely coupled with this is the HP tradition of treating each individual with consideration and respect, and recognizing personal achievements.[25]

Employees see the values and ethics of the company evidenced in the behavior of the company's managers and executives. The values are part of the strong culture, which is reinforced on a daily basis.

The core content of HP's values has been reflected in three documents. The primary document, "Corporate Objectives" developed in 1957, provides a summary of HP's approach that was developed for managers who no longer have day-to-day contact with top management due to size and geographic remoteness. The Corporate Objectives document was organized into the following sections: profit, customers, fields of interest, growth, our people, management, and citizenship.[26] This document and the lessons communicated by the corporate culture provided the primary communication of organizational values. Two lesser documents included "Communicating the HP Way" and the "Standards of Business Conduct." Ethics was not prominently labeled in any of the documents, but moral values were clearly communicated. Values relating to employee treatment were highly visible.

HP is currently reinventing itself and is thus creating a new set of guiding documents. The corporate objectives have been revised to include the following sections: customer loyalty, profit, market leadership, growth, employee commitment, leadership capability, and global citizenship.[27] The new document is designed to reflect the continuing values of the organization while adapting them to the changed environment in which the company operates. There is also a document entitled "Business Ethics" that focuses upon integrity and the dedication to the principles of honesty, excellence, responsibility, compassion, citizenship, fairness, and respect.[28] This more overt declaration of ethics appears to be a response to the times.

HP has recently completed its first "Social and Environmental Responsibility Report."[29] The report focuses upon the workplace, the environment, and sustainability. The firm is developing significant programs to reduce material and energy usage. It is also developing a number of recycling programs focusing upon "end-of-life" issues.

In keeping with the changing business environment, HP has developed a "Supplier Code of Conduct" that all of its suppliers must follow.[30] The code requires suppliers to adhere to all laws protecting the environment, worker health and safety, and labor and employment practices in the countries in which they operate. In addition, they must establish management systems that insure compliance with the laws and regulations.

The firm's confidence in and respect for its employees continues to be constantly stressed. Employees are given a great deal of freedom. They select which eight-hour shift they want to work, beginning at 6, 7, or 8 A.M. HP does not use time clocks. Employees are given specific job objectives and may negotiate with their supervisor to determine how the objectives will be met.

Open communication is stressed. Everyone in the firm is on a first-name basis. Company offices are created using low partitions so that one may talk to the person in the next office simply by leaning over the partition. Management strongly encourages open communication both up and down the levels in the firm. HP also has an "Open Door Policy," which is described in company documents in these words:

> All employees have the right, if in their opinion they feel such steps are necessary, to discuss their concerns with the level of management they feel is appropriate to handle the situation. Any effort to prevent an employee from going to higher-level managers, through intimidation or any other means, is absolutely contrary to company policy and will be dealt with accordingly. Using the open door policy will not in any way impact any evaluations of employees or subject them to any other adverse consequences.[31]

HP advocates employee sharing of benefits and responsibilities. Equal sharing of rewards through a profit-sharing plan and a stock-purchase plan is stressed. Offices are generally the same size, with supervisors sharing offices with their secretaries. Carpeting is a rarity and parking spaces are generally unassigned. The company fosters a sense of teamwork and partnership in its everyday business operations. Decisions are generally made through consensus and persuasion in small work groups.

HP demonstrates a strong concern for the individual employee. It has gone to great lengths to avoid layoffs. Growth has been deliberately slowed at times so the firm could manage expansion without subsequent layoffs. The firm has been able to get voluntary agreements from employees to take a pay and hour cut to avoid laying off part of its workforce. While jobs come and go, management has generally been able to accommodate the workforce via shifts. The company takes the position that it provides employment security, not job security.[32] Thus, if a worker's job disappears, HP will offer to provide training for another position within the firm. In addition, the firm strongly encourages employee development. The company promotes from within and provides extensive training and educational opportunities.

Honesty and integrity are basic HP core values. HP does not tolerate dishonesty among its employees. The "Standards of Business Conduct" cites four areas of employee obligations: obligations to HP, to customers, to competitors, and to suppliers.[33] Obligations to HP include avoiding conflicts of interest, maintaining the confidentiality of company information, and reporting and avoiding payments to foreign sales agents or government officials. Customer obligations encompass trade practices, price discrimination, unfair methods of competition, government procurement, and confidentiality of information. Competitor obligations include competitor relations, obtaining competitive information, and commenting about competitors. Supplier obligations encompass honoring confidential information and discriminating among suppliers on relevant bases. General managers are responsible for their employees' familiarization with the standards.

HP's internal audit department has developed an audit program to monitor employee awareness of the standards, to uncover any violations of the standards, and to make sure steps are taken to rectify the deficiencies. The audit team also has an extensive annual interview with each of the top managers from each work group.

In September 1987, company officials were alarmed by rumors of drug use at its Santa Clara, California, sales office. At 5 A.M. on Friday, September 18, a team of private security guards with two golden retrievers and one Labrador retriever entered the sales office.[34] The guards and dogs searched the building, including management offices, looking for drugs. No locked files, desks, or offices were opened. As the 300 employees arrived for work, they were asked to open their handbags and parcels. No drugs were found and employees were upset by the invasion of privacy and lack of trust. However, in March 1987 drugs were found in a shipping and receiving office in Boise, Idaho. Twenty employees were fired.

In July 1999, Carly Fiorina was chosen as the first outside president and chief executive of HP.[35] On May 3, 2002, she won a hard-fought battle to merge HP with Compaq Computers to create the second largest computer company. The merger has resulted in eliminating more than 15,000 people from the combined workforce.[36] Layoffs of that magnitude appear to fly in the face of the HP Way. As Fiorina continues to bring change to HP, it will be interesting to see what those changes will be and how they will impact the firm and the venerable HP Way of doing business.

Johnson & Johnson

Johnson & Johnson was founded in 1887 in New Brunswick, New Jersey.[37] It has become one of the world's largest manufacturers of health care products with major business interests in consumer, professional, and pharmaceutical products. Johnson & Johnson is a highly decentralized company with a strong organizational culture. The formation of this culture can be traced back to General Robert Wood Johnson, son of one of the founders, who became head of the firm in 1932.[38] The General set out to change Johnson & Johnson and succeeded in creating a series of independent operating companies that were diversified in both products and geography. This was contrary to the conventional wisdom that advocated centralization to achieve economies of scale. The General also bucked the trend by exhibiting a strong concern for his employees' welfare. He published a list of general principles for business success that began with this statement: "Accept attainment of a decent living for all as the fundamental goal of business." His belief in fair employee treatment, decentralization, and product quality was set forth in 1944–45 in a document entitled "An Industrial Credo."[39]

The original Credo has been revised over the years with the title changed to its current "Our Credo" in 1948.[40] In the 1950s the document was revised to clarify wording. In 1972 the Credo was featured in the annual report. Dinner meetings were held with over 4,000 of the firm's managers to strengthen their beliefs.[41] The Credo itself is a deceptively simple document to guide the operations of a major firm. It is less than one page in length! It is written in plain language that relates to the everyday concerns of the manager. The current Credo is shown in Figure 7.1.

During the mid-1970s, the media carried numerous stories of improper political payments being made by firms. Corporate codes were being offered as an answer to such behavior. When the issue was raised at Johnson & Johnson, management saw no need to develop a code. They already had their Credo. However, the discovery of several incidents of improper payments being made in their foreign operations, with records being altered to protect the company, raised a red flag. The Credo was not being supported to the extent thought. Thus, the president, James Burke, decided to hold a series of meetings with top management to determine if the Credo was still a valid document. These meetings, subsequently known as the Credo challenge meetings, took place between 1975 and 1978 and involved more than 1,200 managers.[42] The sessions, consisting of no more than 25 managers each, took place over two days and were headed by either Burke or David Clare, who succeeded Burke. The main issues addressed were whether the Credo was still applicable, whether any changes should be made, and how it should be implemented in the management of the Johnson & Johnson companies. The meetings uncovered a strong belief in the principles contained in the Credo and a general agreement that it was very difficult to balance the responsibilities derived from it. The meetings had another beneficial effect. When a manager would question whether the company would really support one tenet of the Credo, a manager from a different area

FIGURE 7.1   Johnson & Johnson Credo

Our Credo

We believe our first responsibility is to the doctors, nurses and patients,
to mothers and fathers and all others who use our products and services.
In meeting their needs everything we do must be of high quality.
We must constantly strive to reduce our costs
in order to maintain reasonable prices.
Customers' orders must be serviced promptly and accurately.
Our suppliers and distributors must have an opportunity
to make a fair profit.

We are responsible to our employees,
the men and women who work with us throughout the world.
Everyone must be considered as an individual.
We must respect their dignity and recognize their merit.
They must have a sense of security in their jobs.
Compensation must be fair and adequate,
and working conditions clean, orderly and safe.
We must be mindful of ways to help our employees fulfill
their family responsibilities.
Employees must feel free to make suggestions and complaints.
There must be equal opportunity for employment, development
and advancement for those qualified.
We must provide competent management,
and their actions must be just and ethical.

We are responsible to the communities in which we live and work
and to the world community as well.
We must be good citizens — support good works and charities
and bear our fair share of taxes.
We must encourage civic improvements and better health and education.
We must maintain in good order
the property we are privileged to use,
protecting the environment and natural resources.

Our final responsibility is to our stockholders.
Business must make a sound profit.
We must experiment with new ideas.
Research must be carried on, innovative programs developed
and mistakes paid for.
New equipment must be purchased, new facilities provided
and new products launched.
Reserves must be created to provide for adverse times.
When we operate according to these principles,
the stockholders should realize a fair return.

Johnson & Johnson

139

would often provide an example of such support. The value of the meetings can be shown by the comments of a president of one of Johnson & Johnson's companies:

> At the Credo challenge meetings you discover, listening to your peers, that it [the Credo] has crept into everyone's value system. Finding that out is really beneficial. You come away with a healthy respect for the document and what it says, and you pass that on in your own company.[43]

Some say that the Credo describes a way of doing business. James Burke asserts that "It tells us what our business is about."[44] The Credo challenge meetings have become a regular event held twice a year for new top managers. Company presidents are also encouraged to hold their own Credo challenge meetings for their top management. In 1979, the Credo underwent another revision to keep it current with changing company and social conditions. The revised Credo was introduced in a World Wide Managers Meeting in New York.[45] The fact that top managers are rarely all brought together emphasizes the importance the firm places on the Credo.

In 1986 Johnson & Johnson began a Credo survey. The purpose was to determine how the employees view Johnson & Johnson's Credo performance. The survey, along with quality audits, safety performance records, and reports of consumer/customer complaints, is taken very seriously by the firm's executive committee. When the reports are reviewed by the committee, company presidents are in attendance and must be prepared to talk about the reports for their organizations. The company does not look kindly on violations of the Credo. For example, some very senior executives were discovered to have expense-account improprieties. The transgressions involved use of frequent-flyer coupons, personal expenses listed on company expense accounts, expenses from an outside business venture charged to the company, and changing previously approved personal benefits. Although the amounts were not large, the executives were fired immediately. A letter was sent to all senior management indicating that senior management had committed the offenses, the exact nature of the offenses, and that such actions were in violations of the Credo.[46]

While Johnson & Johnson runs a very decentralized company, it fosters a strong culture to guide management's actions via the Credo, which serves as the compass for managers. This was evident in the Tylenol crisis referred to in Chapter 1. Larry Foster, vice president for public relations, said they had no choice but to pull Tylenol from the market. Not to do so would have been a violation of the Credo. "It would have been hypocrisy at its best or worst."[47]

On January 11, 1995, Johnson & Johnson pleaded guilty to charges of obstructing justice in federal court in Newark, New Jersey.[48] The company agreed to pay a $5 million fine plus $2.5 million in court costs. The penalty resulted from the dermatology and public-relations divisions of Johnson & Johnson's Ortho Pharmaceutical unit destroying files relating to the firm's promotion of Retin-A, an acne drug. The federal government was investigating the promotion of the drug as a wrinkle-reducing product, a use not yet approved by the Food and Drug Administration. In 1992, Johnson & Johnson notified the U.S. Justice Department that it had discovered that files relevant to the case were destroyed a year earlier. As a result, three senior employees were fired.

The Batting Average

Each of these three major companies—Boeing, HP, and Johnson & Johnson—has a history of exemplary ethical behavior. They were selected to represent a cross-section of business activity. Yet each has and continues to experience ethical transgressions. Boeing is having a particularly difficult time as it blends a number of different organizational cultures into the Boeing culture. Hopefully, they can make the transition successfully. As a firm becomes large, it employs a large number of people. In that firm, many thousands of significant decisions are made each year by many different people. Just as you and I have made decisions that we are not particularly proud of, so have companies. The important thing is how the results of the bad decisions are handled and the ratio of the good to the bad. In effect, we are talking about a batting average. Even the best people experience poor judgment at times. The important question is how they handle the results and what action they take to prevent repetitions.

It should be noted that the firms just described are a small sample of the ethical companies operating in the world. They do not usually make headlines for doing what they do right. It is expected! Instead, we hear about their negative actions with no mention of their positive acts, which would provide a more accurate picture of the organization. Boeing is a current case in point.

The Ethics of Actions

Bribery

AB Bofors is one of Sweden's oldest companies. It was purchased in 1880 by Alfred Nobel, who is better known for the Nobel prize and the invention of dynamite.[49] Bofors's main business is to produce arms for the Swedish army. Although not a large arms supplier according to world standards, just making the top 50, it has been manufacturing howitzer cannons since 1936.[50] Swedish weapons are considered to be of high quality and users report a high level of satisfaction.[51]

Sweden has long been a neutral country following a policy of "armed neutrality." The country has preferred to rely on its own arms suppliers— a practice that has led to an expansion of its domestic weapons industry. Although accounting for an average of 50 percent of Bofors's business, Swedish military orders have fluctuated widely. In some years, they have accounted for as much as 75 percent of the business, while in other years they have dropped to as little as 30 percent.[52] Swedish law prohibits the sale of arms outside its borders. However, in order to survive, the firm must have outside customers. The government has decided that to maintain a domestic weapons industry, it must make exceptions and issue export licenses to countries it considers outside "areas of conflict."[53]

Bofors had a recent history of financial difficulties. In 1983, Bofors laid off hundreds of workers from its Karlskoga plant when missile orders from Sweden's armed forces ran out. In addition, orders from its explosives subsidiary, Nobel Kemi, had to be canceled when undercover smuggling was discovered. Bofors and Karlskoga were both concerned about their survival.

Imagine the joy the people of Karlskoga felt on April 1, 1986, when Martin Ardbo, then head of Bofors, announced that Bofors had signed a contract with the Indian army for $1.3 billion worth of artillery.[54] It was the largest export contract in Bofors's history. Four hundred 155mm howitzers were to be shipped at the rate of 14 per month.[55] This order guaranteed employment for the company's 5,000 workers for at least the coming four years.

Olof Palme, prime minister of Sweden at the time, was known for his pursuit of peace and nuclear disarmament. He spent a great deal of time building bridges with the third world. However, he apparently was talking more than peace and disarmament in talks with his friend Rajiv Gandhi, prime minister of India, in a series of meetings that took place in early 1986 prior to the signing of the Bofors's contract. Palme was offering India significant state export credits to buy the Bofors's cannons rather than competing French artillery.[56] In the past, Sweden had prohibited the use of export credits in arms deals. Palme was attempting to create jobs for Karlskoga which was in danger of going under. He was also trying to save a defense firm that was considered important to Sweden.

One other incentive was provided in the arms deal, although it did not come to light until later. Apparently, Bofors transferred 188 million Swedish kronor ($26 million U.S. in 1986) to a coded Swiss bank account.[57] The beneficiary of the account was a Panama-registered company known as Svenska. When the Swedish central bank questioned the transfers, Bofors replied that Svenska was "an Indian who has been an agent for Bofors for 10–15 years."[58] The final recipients of the funds are unknown.

The sale of the howitzers was sealed with state concessions of export credits and large hidden payments to unknown Indian officials. The question is: Given the conditions, was the decision to sell the cannons to India an ethical act? The decision support model discussed in Chapter 6 will help answer this question.

You will remember that the first step in the model is to collect information. This includes identifying the relevant stakeholders and determining the positive and negative impacts on the stakeholders. The stakeholders affected by the sale to India include Bofors's employees; Bofors's stockholders; the town of Karlskoga; the Swedish government; the Indian army; the Indian government; Svenska; and the French weapons supplier's employees, community, and stockholders.

The sale would create business and thus create work for Bofors's employees. It would, in turn, create profits or reduce losses for Bofors's stockholders. Karlskoga would benefit from the employment of its citizens, who would bring money into the community and provide additional tax revenues. The sale would help the Swedish government meet its goals of maintaining a viable defense industry and minimizing unemployment as well as increasing tax revenues. The Indian army would neither gain nor lose, assuming that the French guns performed as well as the Swedish cannons. The Indian government would gain only if the Swedish export credits made the deal more attractive than the French offer. If this were the case, there would have been no reason to make the secret payment. However, someone in India gained 188 million Swedish kronor! The negative consequence would be that the French manufacturer would lose the business from the contract. This in turn would result in fewer jobs for the French employees, lower profits for the French stockholders, and put less money in the French local community. The French government would lose tax revenue and unemployment would be higher.

There would be no significant reaction from any stakeholder as long as the payment was kept secret. However, if the payment came to light, the Swedish government would likely prosecute and the Swedish people could be expected to react negatively, which could have political consequences. The Indian government would also probably prosecute those who accepted payment and the Indian people might react negatively, which could have political consequences. Although the French stakeholders would probably be upset, they would not have much leverage to take any action.

Now that we know the stakeholders and how they are affected by the decision, we must determine whether the decision to sell the weapons using the hidden payment (bribe) violated ethical norms. Historically, bribery cases in all three countries have resulted in public condemnation; thus, the moral values of the cultures do not support bribery. We can assume community norms prohibit the paying of bribes. Given consistent support by norms in all three countries, the Bofors's payment is clearly unethical.

It is instructive to examine why the three countries condemn bribes. Bribery raises questions of fairness, which invoke principles of justice. Justice requires fair treatment; it applies to competition by requiring honest representation and dealing. The payment made by Bofors was kept secret and thus the French were not given a chance to compete. This provided an unfair advantage to Bofors and thus violated the principles of justice.

The payment apparently was made to influence government officials. The officials receiving the payments were benefiting only because they were responsible for making the weapons decision. The state paid the officials to make the decision, yet the officials were gaining additional benefits not available to their peers who were performing other equally necessary government business. Thus, the payment created an unfair situation in which some officials received extra rewards for doing their job that were not available to others doing equally important work. This is a violation of the principles of justice. In addition, the payment created a conflict of interest for the government employees. Although they were employed to represent the interests of the Indian government, the payment indebted them to represent Bofors's interests. Thus, the payment of the 188 million Swedish kronor must be judged as unacceptable. This seems to be the position taken by both the Indian and Swedish people.[59]

The payment of a bribe to influence government officials is considered unethical by most cultures of the world and thus may be a hypernorm. Apparently the bribe was paid to keep Bofors from failing. Bofors was in financial difficulty because the country's weapons needs could not support a defense contractor its size. That raises the question of whether Bofors was really needed. One solution might be to downsize Bofors so it could be profitable meeting the country's weapons needs. However, downsizing does not take care of the wide swings in demand. If the Swedish government believes that it needs to maintain Bofors as a domestic weapons contractor, it has the obligation to subsidize the firm to guarantee its financial solvency. Otherwise, Bofors should be allowed to compete on the open market and fail if it cannot compete.

Apparently, top management was aware of the bribe being offered. If it was not, it is incompetent. Top management has only two choices if it wants to encourage ethical behavior. It must convince the government to provide subsidies to make up for the business revenue its military does not provide, or it must obtain approval to compete on the world market. A third alternative is to dissolve the firm.

Coercion

Maxine Munford was hired as assistant collections manager for the James T. Barnes Company on January 28, 1976, and reported to work the following day. During the morning, her new boss, Glenn Harris, asked her to go with him to the 25th floor to get office supplies. On the way, Harris made overt sexual suggestions to Munford. She immediately rejected his proposition. Harris then threatened her with the loss of her job if she did not submit to his demands.[60]

During the next few days, Harris made numerous sexual suggestions and propositions to Munford, both verbal and written. He harassed her by leaving sexually oriented cartoons on her desk. She repeatedly told him that she was not interested in any relationship with him. Finally, she told him that she had had enough and that if he did not stop, she was going to report his behavior to his boss, Robert Zulcosky. Harris said that if she reported him, she would only succeed in getting herself fired because Zulcosky was his friend.[61]

On February 12, 1976, Harris called Munford to his office. He told her that she was to go with him on an overnight business trip to Grand Rapids, Michigan, where he would book a motel room for the two of them. After they had finished work the first day, they would spend the night together in the room and have sexual relations. Munford agreed to accompany him on the trip, but said she would not stay in the same room or have sexual intercourse with him.[62] Harris repeated his demands the following day, but Munford held her ground. Harris then fired her.

Munford immediately went to Zulcosky, told him what had happened, and asked for her job back. Zulcosky backed Harris and told Munford that she no longer had a job. Not willing to drop the matter, Munford arranged a meeting with Harris, Zulcosky, company owner James T. Barnes, and attorneys representing the various parties. The company made no effort to come to her aid.[63]

The stakeholders in this case are Munford, Harris, and the James T. Barnes Company. The decision by Harris to pursue a sexual liaison with Munford created a potential benefit for Harris at the expense of Munford. Harris could gain sexual satisfaction, but Munford would be used as an object and not as a person of value; she would lose her personal dignity. The Barnes company could experience a deterioration in work performance due to Harris's actions. The time Harris spent harassing Munford was certainly not productive for the firm. If Harris was successful, Munford would likely be less productive due to her decline in self-esteem. If Munford decided to pursue the case in court, both Harris and the company would be exposed to significant financial damages. In fact, that is what happened.

Coercion raises questions of human rights. It violates the core human right of personal freedom, a hypernorm supported by the United Nations Universal Declaration of Human Rights (see Appendix B). In order to keep her job, Munford would have to submit to Harris's sexual advances. This action violates her right to life and safety, for, if she submits to Harris, she becomes a sex slave. She loses her freedom, and she is also in danger from potential abuse and/or disease. Thus, Harris's coercive acts are clearly un-ethical as well as illegal. His behavior is unacceptable.

Harris is not fulfilling the requirements of his job. He is acting unpro-fessionally and is using company time in an attempt to obtain personal benefits. The firm apparently has no clear policy on relationships among employees. One suspects that Harris may have overstepped his bounds before without any consequences. The responsibility to resolve the prob-lem lies with company owner James T. Barnes. He must establish a clear policy that prohibits sexual harassment and coercion in the workplace. To do less indicates incompetent management. Harris may have to become the first casualty of the policy. Munford should be rehired.

Deception

Volvo was incorporated as a ball-bearing manufacturer in 1915.[64] The com-pany began exporting automobiles in volume to the U.S. market in 1957. It built its reputation on safety and reliability. Volvo pioneered the laminated windshield in the 1950s, introduced the first three-point seat belts in 1959, and incorporated front disk brakes in the 1960s. In 1966 the Volvo 140 se-ries automobile was introduced with standard safety features that in-cluded a dual braking system, energy-absorbing front and rear ends, a di-vided steering shaft, and safety locks.[65] Volvo was promoting safety long before it was popular among car buyers. Volvo cars rank very high in crash tests performed by the National Highway Traffic Safety Administration, and the accident statistics published by the Insurance Institute for Highway Safety support these findings.

In November 1988, the Arthritis Foundation of Vermont held a monster truck event as a fund-raiser.[66] A number of different automobiles were parked in a line and the monster truck was driven over the automobiles. All of the cars were crushed except a Volvo station wagon, which came through the ordeal in relatively good shape. An account executive at Scali, McCabe, and Sloves, Volvo Cars of North America's advertising agency for the past 23 years, heard about the event. Subsequent discussion in the agency resulted in the idea to shoot a commercial re-creating the scene.[67]

The shooting took place on June 12, 1990, in Austin, Texas. A local res-ident, Dan White, went to the Texas Exposition & Heritage Center that day hoping to pick up a Volvo for parts. As he walked around the area, he discovered a man cutting the roof support pillars from all the cars except the Volvos. Later in the day, he discovered a Volvo wagon being rein-forced with steel C-channel supports welded inside the car. He also dis-covered another Volvo with a 2-by-4 wood framework support inside the car.[68] White took pictures of what he saw and alerted the Texas attorney general's office. The first ad showing the doctored re-creation appeared in *Forbes* in late September and began to run on cable TV on October 8 (see Figure 7.2). Volvo was notified on October 24 that the state of Texas

FIGURE 7.2 Volvo Advertisement

planned to file a suit.[69] State law requires that a notice of intent to file must be given five days prior to the actual filing of a suit. Both print and TV spots were voluntarily discontinued on October 31. Volvo reached a settlement with the state of Texas on November 5. They admitted no wrongdoing but agreed to run corrective ads in the state of Texas and pay the state $316,250 in investigative costs.[70] The firm asked to appear with the Texas attorney general at his press conference announcing the settlement. In addition, Volvo decided to run the corrective ads in the *Wall Street Journal.*

The question of who decided to doctor the cars is still unanswered. Volvo Cars of North America's president and chief executive, Joseph L. Nicolato, apologized in national newspaper ads, stating that Volvo first learned of the alterations to the automobiles on October 30, 1990.[71] The company insisted that the ads were supposed to re-create faithfully the actual event as it happened. Scali's Chairman-CEO Marvin Sloves stated that the ad agency did not authorize any alterations of vehicles at the shooting location.[72] Both Volvo and Scali had representatives at the shooting site in Austin. The actual filming was done by Perretti Productions, a New York production studio.

AB Volvo, the parent Swedish company, took control of the internal investigation. Perretti was accused of being uncooperative in their investigation. Pehr Gyllenhammar, AB Volvo chairman, called the ads ". . . an offense against our company and what we represent and an insult to all Volvo owners."[73] Both Volvo and Scali agreed to a proposed consent agreement with the Federal Trade Commission (FTC). The agreement required each firm to pay a $150,000 fine and to abide by the FTC truth-in-advertising standards without admitting any violation of the law.[74] Scali resigned from the $40 million Volvo account.

The Volvo case provides an interesting case of deception. A questionable act was committed, but we do not know who was responsible. Volvo already had a reputation for safe automobiles and thus did not need to use deception to gain an advantage. Scali had been having a bad year, but it was in no danger of losing its largest account, Volvo.[75]

Let's assume that Perretti Productions made the decision to alter the automobiles and that it was strictly a production decision. They were simulating an event that actually happened. Making a commercial is a time-consuming event with many retakes. One may want to re-create the Vermont scene, but running the monster truck over a line of automobiles would be difficult to repeat a number of times trying to get the right shot. Maybe the automobiles would not collapse the first, second, or third time like they did in Vermont, or maybe the Volvo would collapse. It would be very expensive to shoot a number of crushings until the right combination worked because many automobiles would have to be destroyed. Perhaps someone wanted to help it along a little to make sure the right effect was obtained the first time. How? By weakening the other cars and strengthening the Volvo, one would decrease the time and cost of filming the commercial while faithfully reproducing the original result.

The stakeholders involved include Volvo of North America and AB Volvo, Scali et al., Perretti Productions, and potential Volvo buyers. How are the stakeholders affected? Perretti would probably gain the most by alterations that would significantly reduce the time and cost of filming the commercial. Scali would be unaffected because their contract with Volvo called for production costs to be passed through to Volvo with no markup. Potential customers are unlikely to be affected because the car's reputation for safety is well known. Volvo and its parent company would benefit about the same as they would from any other ad. Thus, nobody would lose, assuming that the ad replicated an actual event and knowledge of the tampering did not become public. However, local resident Dan White got the word out, and his information raised suspicions that the ad did not represent an actual event. Volvo's reputation became tarnished when potential buyers as well as current owners questioned the integrity of the firm.

Deception raises the issue of an individual's right to truth. If this is not a hypernorm, it is likely to be a community norm in most local communities. Based on our assumption that the ad was re-creating an actual event, the commercial is portraying the truth. Whether it was filmed the first time using doctored cars or the 25th time using unaltered cars, the communication effect is the same. Thus, while we may be a little uncomfortable with the alterations and judge the action to be marginally acceptable, it is not violating any rights. The other cars were actually crushed in the event; they are not being misrepresented.

To increase our comfort level with the decision, we will apply two other ethics principles. Focusing on the commercial, we conclude that nothing is being done unfairly. The event is portrayed exactly as it happened. The details of how the portrayal was created do not match the event, but that is not the issue. Thus, justice principles do not appear to be violated. From a utilitarian standpoint, the fact that the alterations resulted in more efficient production argues for doctoring the cars. Fewer resources are required for the same output. Thus, there does not appear to be anything unethical about the alterations. The cost savings probably move the alternative from marginal to an acceptable level.

However, there is one important point in this case: While the alterations are not unethical, they may be illegal under U.S. law. In a communication with Volvo, the company pointed out that such deception has not been ruled illegal in proven case law. Volvo elected not to resolve the issue in the courts. The company stated it had not desired nor intended for the ad to be produced in such a manner and accepted full responsibility. The firm voluntarily withdrew the ad and offered to settle with the authorities. Volvo stated, "The ad as it was executed violated *our* principles." Thus, Volvo and Scali paid fines and Scali lost a major customer.

Theft

The Low family acquired controlling interest in Ka Wah Bank of Hong Kong in 1974. Family members were previously employed in banks in Malaysia and Singapore. Low Chung Song became chief executive; his brother Low Chun Seng was executive director; and a third brother, Low Chang Hian, was a director.[76] In 1980 Chang Ming-thien, chairman of the Overseas Trust Bank, sold his interest in Ka Wah. In late 1984, Ka Wah Bank announced that it was expanding into the U.S. market with branches in New York and Los Angeles.[77] An advertisement for the bank claimed that it was using state-of-the-art computers and communications in its modern management style. It claimed to have avoided the many property financing pitfalls that befell numerous financial institutions in Southeast Asia over the last few years.[78]

In June 1985, Chang Ming-thien's Overseas Trust Bank failed due to massive fraud by management and had to be rescued by the Hong Kong government.[79] The bank failure caused a significant drop in the stock market. The resulting loss of confidence in the financial community led to a run on the Ka Wah Bank. The government, concerned about the financial stability of the British colony, secretly arranged to guarantee a $128 million emergency line of credit from the British-owned Hong Kong & Shanghai Banking Corporation and the Communist-owned Bank of China.[80] The Hong Kong banking commissioner stressed that there was "no management problem at the bank."[81]

In January 1986, Ka Wah Bank was rescued from the verge of collapse by the Chinese government's International Trust & Investment Corporation.[82] Although the Hong Kong government may have to provide from $130 to $260 million to cover bad loans, it maintained that the failure was due to circumstances beyond the bank's control. It claimed that the bank was solidly managed.[83]

Let's examine an indicator of that management. In November 1983, Ka Wah Bank loaned Compact Investment & Finance Ltd. of Hong Kong $10.8 million. The firm's paid-up capital at the time was $1.9 million.[84] Compact provided as collateral shares of the Taiwan Hotel Company, a firm building a hotel in Taipei, Taiwan. The fact was that the Taiwan Hotel shares were worthless and Ka Wah Bank knew it! The company had been dissolved two years earlier by its shareholders' meeting in the Ka Wah Bank building. According to public records, the three Low brothers and three other members of Ka Wah Bank management were stockholders of the Taiwan Hotel as of 1981. Most of them were at the meeting that dissolved the Taiwan Hotel.[85] Two directors of the Taiwan Hotel were Malaysian associates of the Lows. On July 1, 1985, when Ka Wah was in financial difficulty, Ka Wah's management renewed the loan. Compact was dissolved in July 1986 by a Hong Kong High Court order, leaving Ka Wah little chance of recovering any of its funds.

The stakeholders involved were the bank management, the bank depositors, the Hong Kong government, and Compact. Compact can be discounted because it was only a shell. The bank management, specifically the Lows and their associates, gained millions of dollars at the expense of the depositors. In an effort to protect the depositors, the Hong Kong government lost millions of dollars; the exact amount is still unknown.

This is an obvious case of theft, the taking of private property without the owner's consent. The right to property ownership is a hypernorm that has obviously been violated. Private property, depositors' funds, was given to the Lows and their accomplices to protect and put to productive use. Instead, management substituted shares of a worthless company and took the money for its use and its associates' use. Property of no value, shares of a worthless company, were substituted for property of value, deposits. This action violates the depositors' right to own private property and is clearly unethical behavior. It is an unacceptable act. It is also unethical under the utilitarian principle—private gain at the expense of public good—and it violates the justice principle of equals being treated equally.

The documentation on this and many other fraudulent acts by the bank management lead us to believe that acquiring Ka Wah Bank was part of a plan to bilk depositors out of millions of dollars. The bank management was able to gain control of Ka Wah Bank because of lax banking regulations. This type of theft can only be controlled by government's exercising closer control over banks. Top management *is* the problem and would have no reason to solve it. In fact, the culprits quickly left the country after the failure, apparently having accomplished their mission. Several governments have cooperated in arresting many of the bank officials and extraditing them back to Hong Kong.

Unfair Discrimination

Mr. Barber worked for Guardian Royal Exchange Assurance Group of England, which provides comprehensive investment services in the United Kingdom and throughout the world. With the exception of industrial life, all principal classes of insurance are offered, as are investments in stocks, shares, loans, and property. In addition, Guardian is in the property-development and fund-management business.

Guardian contracts with an outside vendor to maintain and administer a pension plan for its employees. The pension is wholly funded by Guardian. Under the terms of the plan, employees in Mr. Barber's employment category could retire and begin receiving pension payments at age 62 for males and 57 for females.[86] That was more generous than the state social security system that began making payments at 65 for males and 60 for females. Special provisions were made for employees who were laid off. Under the section of the pension contract entitled "GRE Guide to Severance Terms," an employee who was laid off prior to retirement was entitled to immediate pension payments if he or she had reached an age of 55 for males and 50 for females.[87]

Mr. Barber was "made redundant with effect from December 31, 1980, when he was aged 52," the British wording for laid off.[88] He was given the cash payments required under the severance terms, the statutory payment required for being laid off, and an *ex gratia* payment. He also was entitled to begin receiving a pension when he reached age 62. If he were a woman, he would have been immediately eligible to begin receiving pension payments. Believing that the difference in the age requirements discriminated unfairly against him, Mr. Barber took his case to an industrial tribunal.[89]

The stakeholders of interest in this case are Mr. Barber, Guardian Royal Exchange Assurance Group, the company that is handling the pension fund, and the current female and male employees of Guardian. Mr. Barber and the current male employees are obtaining fewer pension benefits by being forced to work to an older age before beginning to collect their pensions. This has a double impact because males tend to have shorter life spans than females. The pension company is unlikely to be affected because it is simply administering the fund. Guardian has to pay less money into the fund for males because men become eligible for benefits five years later than women.

There appears to be a community norm operating that provides benefits at an earlier age to females than to males. Thus, from an Integrative Social Contracts Theory perspective, the payments decision is ethical. The community norm does not violate a hypernorm, and males are free to leave the community if they don't want to be bound by its norms. However, Barber has the right to attempt to alter the community norm, which is what he seeks to do. Consider the arguments he might use.

The issue seems to be one of fairness: Are equals being treated as equals? Guardian created the pension to replace the state system for its employees. The pension age clearly favors women over men; thus, it violates the distributive justice principle and so does the country's social security system. Although the plan discriminates in favor of women, it does allow employees to begin drawing a pension at an earlier age.

However, unfair discrimination did take place, which is the major argument to be used in attempting to change the norm. This, in fact, is the argument Mr. Barber used, although it took a series of appeals before he won his case.[90]

Summary

This chapter began with a discussion of several companies that have earned a reputation for ethical behavior. They were chosen to represent a variety of types of business: project management, high technology, and consumer products. Even among these companies, lapses do occur. Controlling such lapses appears to be more difficult during times of company expansion through mergers and acquisitions. Merging cultures of organizations is one of the most difficult challenges faced by management. Maintaining continuity across a succession of top managers is also a difficult process.

Modern corporations are very complex organizations oftentimes employing thousands of people. Because humans are not perfect, one would expect that mistakes will be made. One would only hope that they will not be frequent and will be minor rather than major. The important point is how a firm handles the mistakes. We would like to see the batting average highly in favor of ethical behavior with the errors being of small magnitude.

The chapter closed with an examination of actual ethical dilemmas encountered by five firms. They were chosen to represent the five types of ethical issues on which this book is based: bribery, coercion, deception, theft, and unfair discrimination. Each dilemma was examined using the decision support model described in Chapter 6. These examples are provided to assist the reader in applying the model to help resolve ethical dilemmas in his/her work environment in a positive manner.

Final Comments

Even highly ethical companies from time to time find employees engaging in unethical behavior. Such behavior is relatively isolated and quickly corrected. These companies' cultural values permeate their firms and create an environment where ethical behavior is expected. It is the norm, not the exception. Unethical behavior may be more likely when a merger or acquisition takes place and the new employees have not fully assimilated into the culture of their new employer. Worse yet, there is a danger that the culture of the former employer(s) may modify the culture of the acquiring firm in the wrong direction.

We hope that by examining real ethical issues that occurred in different types of firms in different countries, you have developed an understanding of how to approach decisions that contain ethical dimensions. The model in Chapter 6 provides a framework with which to structure your thinking about the issues. You also have a set of tools to use when examining the ethical dimension of a decision. The decisions are now yours.

Throughout this book, we have argued that ethics is important, that ethical behavior makes business more productive and certainly more pleasant. We do not discount the importance of business strategy and tactics.

However, we believe, as we hope you now do, that ethics is a necessary but not a sufficient condition for business success.

Discussion Questions

1. What is meant by an ethical batting average?
2. Why do the decisions of some companies tend to be more ethical than the decisions of others? What is different?
3. If you were recently appointed CEO of a firm, what steps would you take to promote a high level of ethical performance within the organization?
4. How is it possible for firms operating ethically in one country to take actions that firms operating in another country consider unethical? Does the Barber case provide an example?
5. How can you tell a hypernorm from a community norm?
6. Why might it sometimes be difficult to determine the priority rules that pertain to a decision involving community norms?
7. Would employees at Hewlett-Packard or General Motors tend to be more upset with the firm bringing in dogs to search for drugs? Why?
8. Which of the five ethical issues—bribery, coercion, deception, theft, or unfair discrimination—do you consider to be the most important? Why?
9. What community norms would you like to see changed in your country? Industry? Company?

End Notes

1. All three firms are cited in "Corporate Ethics: A Prime Business Asset," James Keogh, ed. (New York: The Business Roundtable, 1988), and Thomas J. Peters and Robert H. Waterman, Jr., *In Search of Excellence: Lessons from America's Best-Run Companies* (New York: Harper & Row, Publishers, 1982). The latter two are cited in Robert Levering, Milton Moskowitz, and Michael Katz, *The 100 Best Companies to Work for in America* (Reading, MA: Addison-Wesley Publishing Company, 1984); and Milton Moskowitz and Carol Townsend, "100 Best Companies for Working Mothers," *Working Mother,* October 1993, pp. 27–69.
2. Harold Mansfield, *Vision: A Saga of the Sky* (New York: Madison Publishing Associates, 1986).
3. Keogh, "Corporate Ethics A Prime Business Asset."
4. Ibid.
5. Ibid.
6. Ibid.
7. Ibid.
8. Ibid.
9. "Business Conduct Policy and Guidelines," The Boeing Company, 1998.
10. Letter to Boeing employees from President Frank A. Shrontz, June 2, 1986.

It's Your Turn

Your firm has fallen on hard times and there is talk that half of the people working on the line will be laid off. You are a successful salesperson with a couple of prospects that could bring in enough work to get your firm back on track. The prospects are interested in a new model your firm is bringing out that is scheduled to be available the first of the year. However, you happen to know that development work has fallen behind schedule, and the new model will not be available until May.

Your two prospects are eager to obtain the new model because they believe it will give them a significant edge over their competition. You could tell them about the delay and hope that they would be willing to wait instead of going to a competitor. However, one of your competitors is working on a new model scheduled to be available in March that will match the performance of your new model.

You can make the sale based upon the expected January delivery date. You believe you can string your prospects along until May, given that they have made their commitment. But they may lose the competitive advantage they are counting on if they have to wait. Would you try to make the sale based upon the January delivery date? Why or why not? What are the risks involved in making or not making the sale? Who gets hurt?

11. Boeing Internet website: www.boeing.com/companyoffices/aboutus/ethics/index.htm.
12. "Former Boeing Supervisor Indicted," *Seattle Post-Intelligencer* 129, no. 145 (June 17, 1992), p. B5.
13. Steve Miletich, "Former Execs of Plane-parts Firm Guilty," *Seattle Post-Intelligencer* 129, no. 145 (June 17, 1992), p. B5.
14. "Former Boeing Supervisor Indicted."
15. Bill Virgin, "Boeing May Not Practice the Ethics It Preaches," *Seattle Post-Intelligencer,* July 31, 2003, p. C1.
16. Anne Marie Squeo and Andy Pasztor, "Space Case: U.S. Probes Whether Boeing Misused a Rival's Documents—At Issue in the Investigations: A Rocket Scientist Hired Away from Lockheed—Mr. Branch's 43 Business Trips," *Wall Street Journal,* May 5, 2003, p. A1.
17. Renae Merle, "U.S. Strips Boeing of Launches; $1 Billion Sanction over Data Stolen from Rival," *Washington Post,* July 25, 2003, p. A1.
18. Ibid.
19. Andy Pasztor and Anne Marie Squeo, "Leading the News: Boeing Ex-Employee's Suit Adds to Strife on Lockheed Documents," July 18, 2003, p. A3.
20. "Boeing Acts Fast to Repair Damage," *Satellite News,* Potomac, August 4, 2003, p. 1.
21. Annual Report, The Boeing Company, 1996.
22. Annual Report, The Boeing Company, 1997.
23. Annual Report, The Boeing Company, 2000.
24. Annual Report, Hewlett-Packard, 2001.

25. "Communicating the HP Way," Hewlett-Packard, 1989.

26. "Corporate Objectives," Hewlett-Packard, 1989.

27. "HP Corporate Objectives," Hewlett-Packard website, 2003.

28. Business Ethics," Hewlett-Packard website, 2003.

29. "Social and Environmental Responsibility Report," Hewlett-Packard website, 2003.

30. "HP Supplier Code of Conduct," Hewlett-Packard website, 2003.

31. "Communicating the HP Way," Hewlett-Packard, 1989.

32. Ibid.

33. "Standards of Business Conduct," Hewlett-Packard, 1989.

34. David Sylvester, "H-P Cracks Down on Drug Use, Searches Office," *San Jose Mercury News,* September 19, 1987, NewsBank EMP 88:G11, microfiche.

35. John Markoff, "Hewlett-Packard Picks Rising Star at Lucent as Its Chief Executive," *New York Times,* July 20, 1999, p. C1.

36. "HP Says Merger May Cause More Job Cuts, Layoffs," *San Jose Mercury News,* October 2, 2001, p. 1C.

37. Katz, *The 100 Best Companies to Work for in America,* p. 161.

38. "Corporate Ethics: A Prime Business Asset."

39. Ibid.

40. Ibid.

41. Ibid.

42. Ibid.

43. Ibid.

44. Ibid.

45. Ibid.

46. Ibid.

47. "Business Ethics," Arthur Andersen video.

48. Elyse Tanouye, "J & J to Admit to Shredding Retin-A Papers," *Wall Street Journal* 132, no. 7 (January 11, 1995), pp. B1, B5.

49. Karen DeYoung, "Swedish Arms Scandals Mar Peacemaking Image," *Washington Post* 110, no. 274 (September 5, 1987), pp. A1, A30.

50. "Bofors: Hoist by Its Own Petard," *The Economist* 304, no. 7516 (September 19, 1987), p. 82.

51. "The Gun That Can Kill at Four Years' Range," *The Economist* 313, no. 7619 (September 9, 1989), pp. 35–36.

52. "Bofors: Hoist by Its Own Petard."

53. DeYoung, "Swedish Arms Scandals Mar Peacemaking Image."

54. "Bofors: Hoist by Its Own Petard."

55. Pranay Gute, "Rhetoric and Reality in the Iranian Arms Trade," *Forbes* 140, no. 8 (October 19, 1987), pp. 32–35.

56. Ibid.

57. "In the Soup over Bofors," *The Economist* 313, no. 7624 (October 14, 1989), pp. 37–38.
58. Ibid.
59. "The Gun That Can Kill"; DeYoung, "Swedish Arms Scandals Mar Peacemaking Image."
60. *Maxine Munford* v. *James T. Barnes Co., Glenn D, Harris,* 441 F. Supp. 459 (1977).
61. Ibid.
62. Ibid.
63. Ibid.
64. "Volvo: A Company on a Fast Roll Upward," *Automotive News* 5099 (October 30, 1985), p. 404.
65. Ibid.
66. Raymond Serafin and Gary Levin, "Ad Industry Suffers Crushing Blow," *Advertising Age* 61, no. 47 (November 12, 1990), pp. 1, 76.
67. Raymond Serafin and Jennifer Lawrence, "Volvo Parent Seizes Control of Inquiry," *Advertising Age* 61, no. 48 (November 19, 1990), pp. 1, 54.
68. "How Volvo's Bogus Advertisements Were Discovered," *Automotive News* 5367 (November 19, 1990), pp. 3, 11.
69. Ibid.
70. Jennifer Lawrence, "How Volvo's Ad Collided with the Truth," *Advertising Age* 61, no. 47 (November 12, 1990), p. 76.
71. Jim Henry, "Volvo Stained by Monster Truck Ad Flap," *Automotive News* 5366 (November 12, 1990), pp. 1, 41.
72. Serafin and Lawrence, "Ad Industry Suffers Crushing Blow."
73. Jim Henry, "Volvo Digs into Ad Fiasco," *Automotive News* 5367 (November 19, 1990), p. 3.
74. "Volvo Agrees to $150,000 Penalty for 'Monster Truck' Ads," *Automotive News* 5408 (August 26, 1991), p. 35.
75. Gary Levin, "Volvo Loss Worsens Tailspin at Scali," *Advertising Age* 61, no. 48 (November 19, 1990), pp. 2, 54.
76. Cheah Cheng Hye, "Records Indicate Abuse by Management Pushed a Hong Kong Bank to the Brink," *Wall Street Journal* 209, no. 4 (January 7, 1987), p. 24.
77. "Expansion Plans by Ka Wah Bank," *New York Times* 134, no. 46219 (November 5, 1984), p. D8.
78. Ibid.
79. Francine C. Brevetti, "British, Peking-Owned Banks Join in a Hong Kong Rescue," *American Banker* 150, no. 119 (June 19, 1985), pp. 2, 11.
80. Ibid.
81. Ibid.
82. "China Acts to Rescue Ailing Hong Kong Bank," *Journal of Commerce* 367, no. 26140 (January 10, 1986), pp. 1A, 5A.

83. Ibid.
84. Ibid.
85. "Records Indicate Abuse by Management Pushed a Hong Kong Bank to the Brink."
86. "Contracted-out Pensions Fall within EC Sex Equality Provision," *Times* (London), 63, no. 709 (May 18, 1990), p. 42.
87. Ibid.
88. Ibid.
89. *Barber* v. *Guardian Royal Exchange Group* (Case C-262/88).
90. Ibid.

United States Bill of Rights: (First 10 amendments to the U.S. Constitution, 1791)

Amendment I

Congress shall make no law respecting an establishment of religion, or prohibiting the free exercise thereof; or abridging the freedom of speech, or of the press; or the right of the people peaceably to assemble, and to petition the Government for redress of grievances.

Amendment II

A well-regulated militia, being necessary to the security of a free state, the right of the people to keep and bear arms, shall not be infringed.

Amendment III

No soldier shall, in time of peace be quartered in any house, without the consent of the owner, nor in time of war, but in a manner to be prescribed by law.

Amendment IV

The right of the people to be secure in their persons, houses, papers, and effects, against unreasonable searches and seizures, shall not be violated, and no warrants shall issue, but upon probable cause, supported by oath or affirmation, and particularly describing the place to be searched, and the persons or things to be seized.

Amendment V

No person shall be held to answer for a capital, or otherwise infamous crime, unless on a presentment or indictment of a Grand Jury, except in cases arising in the land or naval forces, or in the militia, when in actual service in time of war or public danger; nor shall any person be subject for the same offense to be twice put in jeopardy of life or limb; nor shall be compelled in any criminal case to be a witness against himself, nor be deprived of life, liberty, or property, without due process of law; nor shall private property be taken for public use, without just compensation.

Article VI

In all criminal prosecutions, the accused shall enjoy the right to a speedy and public trial, by an impartial jury of the State and district wherein the crime shall have been committed, which district shall have been previously ascertained by law, and to be informed of the nature and cause of the accusation; to be confronted with the witnesses against him; to have compulsory process for obtaining witnesses in his favor, and to have the assistance of counsel for his defense.

Article VII

In suits at common law, where the value in controversy shall exceed twenty dollars, the right of trial by jury shall be preserved, and no fact tried by a jury shall be otherwise reexamined in any court of the United States, than according to the rules of the common law.

Article VIII

Excessive bail shall not be required, nor excessive fines imposed, nor cruel and unusual punishment inflicted.

Article IX

The enumeration in the Constitution, of certain rights, shall not be construed to deny or disparage others retained by the people.

Article X

The powers not delegated to the United States by the Constitution, nor prohibited by it to the States, are reserved to the States respectively, or to the people.

Appendix  B

Universal Declaration of Human Rights

On December 10, 1948, the General Assembly of the United Nations adopted and proclaimed the Universal Declaration of Human Rights, the full text of which appears in the following pages. Following this historic act the Assembly called upon all Member countries to publicize the text of the Declaration and "to cause it to be disseminated, displayed, read and expounded principally in schools and other educational institutions, without distinction based on the political status of countries or territories."

Preamble

Whereas recognition of the inherent dignity and of the equal and inalienable rights of all members of the human family is the foundation of freedom, justice and peace in the world,

Whereas disregard and contempt for human rights have resulted in barbarous acts which have outraged the conscience of mankind, and the advent of a world in which human beings shall enjoy freedom of speech and belief and freedom from fear and want has been proclaimed as the highest aspiration of the common people,

Whereas it is essential, if man is not to be compelled to have recourse, as a last resort, to rebellion against tyranny and oppression, that human rights should be protected by the rule of law,

Whereas it is essential to promote the development of friendly relations between nations,

Whereas the peoples of the United Nations have in the Charter reaffirmed their faith in fundamental human rights, in the dignity and worth of the human person and in the equal rights of men and women and have determined to promote social progress and better standards of life in larger freedom,

Whereas   Member States have pledged themselves to achieve, in co-operation with the United Nations, the promotion of universal respect for and observance of human rights and fundamental freedoms,

Whereas   a common understanding of these rights and freedoms is of the greatest importance for the full realization of this pledge,

Now, therefore, the General Assembly proclaims this Universal Declaration of Human Rights as a common standard of achievement for all peoples and all nations, to the end that every individual and every organ of society, keeping this Declaration constantly in mind, shall strive by teaching and education to promote respect for these rights and freedoms and by progressive measures, national and international, to secure their universal and effective recognition and observance, both among the peoples of Member States themselves and among the peoples of territories under their jurisdiction.

Article 1

All human beings are born free and equal in dignity and rights. They are endowed with reason and conscience and should act towards one another in a spirit of brotherhood.

Article 2

Everyone is entitled to all the rights and freedoms set forth in this Declaration, without distinction of any kind, such as race, colour, sex, language, religion, political or other opinion, national or social origin, property, birth or other status.

Furthermore, no distinction shall be made on the basis of the political, jurisdictional or international status of the country or territory to which a person belongs, whether it be independent, trust, non-selfgoverning or under any other limitation of sovereignty.

Article 3

Everyone has the right to life, liberty, and security of person.

Article 4

No one shall be held in slavery or servitude; slavery and the slave trade shall be prohibited in all their forms.

Article 5

No one shall be subjected to torture or to cruel, inhuman or degrading treatment or punishment.

Article 6

Everyone has the right to recognition everywhere as a person before the law.

Article 7

All are equal before the law and are entitled without any discrimination to equal protection of the law. All are entitled to equal protection against any discrimination in violation of this Declaration and against any incitement to such discrimination.

Article 8

Everyone has the right to an effective remedy by the competent national tribunals for acts violating the fundamental rights granted him by the constitution or by law.

Article 9

No one shall be subjected to arbitrary arrest, detention or exile.

Article 10

Everyone is entitled in full equality to a fair and public hearing by an independent and impartial tribunal, in the determination of his rights and obligations and of any criminal charge against him.

Article 11

(1) Everyone charged with a penal offence has the right to be presumed innocent until proved guilty according to law in a public trial at which he has had all the guarantees necessary for his defence.

(2) No one shall be held guilty of any penal offence on account of any act or omission which did not constitute a penal offence, under national or international law, at the time when it is committed. Nor shall a heavier penalty be imposed than the one that was applicable at the time the penal offence was committed.

Article 12

No one shall be subjected to arbitrary interference with his privacy, family, home or correspondence, nor to attacks upon his honour and reputation. Everyone has the right to the protection of the law against such interference or attacks.

Article 13

(1) Everyone has the right to freedom of movement and residence within the borders of each State.

(2) Everyone has the right to leave any country, including his own, and to return to his country.

Article 14

(1) Everyone has the right to seek and to enjoy in other countries asylum from persecution.

(2) This right may not be invoked in the case of prosecutions genuinely arising from non-political crimes or other acts contrary to the purposes and principles of the United Nations.

Article 15

(1) Everyone has the right to a nationality.
(2) No one shall be arbitrarily deprived of his nationality nor denied the right to change his nationality.

Article 16

(1) Men and women of full age, without any limitation due to race, nationality or religion, have the right to marry and to found a family. They are entitled to equal rights as to marriage, during marriage and at its dissolution.
(2) Marriage shall be entered into only with the free and full consent of the intending spouses.
(3) The family is the natural and fundamental group unit of society and is entitled to protection by society and the State.

Article 17

(1) Everyone has the right to own property alone as well as in association with others.
(2) No one shall be arbitrarily deprived of his property.

Article 18

Everyone has the right to freedom of thought, conscience and religion; this right includes freedom to change his religion or belief, and freedom, either alone or in community with others and in public or private, to manifest his religion or belief in teaching, practice, worship and observance.

Article 19

Everyone has the right to freedom of opinion and expression; this right includes freedom to hold opinions without interference and to seek, receive and impart information and ideas through any media and regardless of frontiers.

Article 20

(1) Everyone has the right to freedom of peaceful assembly and association.
(2) No one may be compelled to belong to an association.

Article 21

(1) Everyone has the right to take part in the government of his country, directly or through freely chosen representatives.

(2) Everyone has the right of equal access to public service in his country.

(3) The will of the people shall be the basis of the authority of government; this will shall be expressed in periodic and genuine elections which shall be by universal and equal suffrage and shall be held by secret vote or by equivalent free voting procedures.

Article 22

Everyone, as a member of society, has the right to social security and is entitled to realization, through national effort and international co-operation and in accordance with the organization and resources of each State, of the economic, social and cultural rights indispensable for his dignity and the free development of his personality.

Article 23

(1) Everyone has the right to work, to free choice of employment, to just and favorable conditions of work and to protection against unemployment.

(2) Everyone, without any discrimination, has the right to equal pay for equal work.

(3) Everyone who works has the right to just and favourable remuneration ensuring for himself and his family an existence worthy of human dignity, and supplemented, if necessary, by other means of social protection.

(4) Everyone has the right to form and to join trade unions for the protection of his interests.

Article 24

Everyone has the right to rest and leisure, including reasonable limitation of working hours and periodic holidays with pay.

Article 25

(1) Everyone has the right to a standard of living adequate for the health and well-being of himself and of his family, including food, clothing, housing and medical care and necessary social services, and the right to security in the event of unemployment, sickness, disability, widowhood, old age or other lack of livelihood in circumstances beyond his control.

(2) Motherhood and childhood are entitled to special care and assistance. All children, whether born in or out of wedlock, shall enjoy the same social protection.

Article 26

(1) Everyone has the right to education. Education shall be free, at least in the elementary and fundamental stages. Elementary education

shall be compulsory. Technical and professional education shall be made generally available and higher education shall be equally accessible to all on the basis of merit.

(2) Education shall be directed to the full development of the human personality and to the strengthening of respect for human rights and fundamental freedoms. It shall promote understanding, tolerance and friendship among all nations, racial or religious groups, and shall further the activities of the United Nations for the maintenance of peace.

(3) Parents have a prior right to choose the kind of education that shall be given to their children.

Article 27

(1) Everyone has the right freely to participate in the cultural life of the community, to enjoy the arts and to share in scientific advancement and its benefits.

(2) Everyone has the right to the protection of the moral and material interests resulting from any scientific, literary or artistic production of which he is the author.

Article 28

Everyone is entitled to a social and international order in which the rights and freedoms set forth in this Declaration can be fully realized.

Article 29

(1) Everyone has duties to the community in which alone the free and full development of his personality is possible.

(2) In the exercise of his rights and freedoms, everyone shall be subject only to such limitations as are determined by law solely for the purpose of securing due recognition and respect for the rights and freedoms of others and of meeting the just requirements of morality, public order and the general welfare in a democratic society.

(3) These rights and freedoms may in no case be exercised contrary to the purposes and principles of the United Nations.

Article 30

Nothing in this Declaration may be interpreted as implying for any State, group or person any right to engage in any activity or to perform any act aimed at the destruction of any of the rights and freedoms set forth herein.

[1]Source: Official World Wide Web Pages of the United Nations.
<http://www.un.org/Overview/rights.html>.

Case 1

Aer Lingus Holidays

Aer Lingus Holidays (ALH) was created in late 1983 in Dublin, Ireland, by parent company Aer Lingus. Five foreign holiday companies owned by Aer Lingus—Sunbound, Blueskies, Cara, Enterprise, and Stephen's Green Travel—were merged into one large company to form ALH. The objective of the merger was to reduce operating costs, improve bargaining power with suppliers through increased scale of operations, and favorably position the new firm for future growth.

Tour operators such as ALH charter aircraft and prebook accommodations in foreign holiday resorts. The transportation and lodging commitments are crafted into tour packages that are offered to potential customers. The demand for specific holiday destinations must be estimated six months in advance because lodging and seat commitments need to be booked well in advance of the actual trip. Forecasting is difficult and mistakes are costly. Tour operators pay significant deposits up-front and heavy penalties are levied for cancellations.

Competition in the Irish tour-operation industry was intense in the 1970s and 1980s. Although consumers benefited from low prices, tour-operator failures were common. By the end of 1989, eight tour operators and 19 travel agents had gone under. These included well-known operations such as Carousel, Topflight, and Hickson Holidays. Most remaining tour operators were experiencing difficulties. Profits in the industry were marginal.

Throughout the 1980s, ALH maintained its position as one of the top three tour operators, claiming 25 percent of the market. It reported profitable operations or, at worst, broke even each year. During this time, ALH chartered about 20 percent of its aircraft from its parent, Aer Lingus. In the summer of 1989, ALH informed Aer Lingus that it was unable to pay for the aircraft it had chartered. Given the profitable operations ALH had been reporting, Aer Lingus began to suspect something was wrong.

Aer Lingus decided to hire the accounting firm of Conroy O'Neil to audit ALH books for 1989. During their first week of investigation, the firm discovered significant irregularities in the firm's accounts. Further investigation showed that the accounts had been systematically falsified. Costs were underreported and earnings were inflated.

Aer Lingus then hired the Craig Gardner accounting firm to conduct a full investigation of ALH operations. They found that the books had been falsified to cover £7.3 million in operating losses over the past five years. Invoices and bills of accounts due were falsified. False documentation of foreign agents' dealings with the company was created. Large sums of money were borrowed to purchase property but were never shown on the books. However, much of the borrowed money was used to pay normal operating costs with neither the costs nor the payments being recorded. This allowed the firm to report artificially high profits or lower-than-realized losses.

In addition, £2.1 million in losses on property deals were concealed. The losses resulted from the purchase of 70 apartments in the La Penita/ Las Vegas complex in Lanzarote, Spain, for £2.9 million and 50 apartments in the Ecuador block of apartments in Malaga, Spain, for £2.3 million. Neither the borrowing of the funds to buy the apartments nor their purchase was recorded in the ALH books. When the bubble burst, the market had declined and the properties were worth £1.3 million and £1.8 million, respectively. However, £1.2 million of the £2.1 million loss cannot be attributed to the decline in property values. ALH had simply purchased the properties at above-market value.

During the investigation, the Minister for Transport and Tourism became aware of the problem. He directed the accountants to present their report to him rather than to Aer Lingus. After examining the reports, he ordered Aer Lingus to withdraw from the tour business and to improve its accounting, control, and reporting procedures to prevent future irregularities from occurring. He also ordered the firm to take appropriate disciplinary and civil legal action where necessary.

1. Who are the stakeholders in the case?
2. What priority rank do you give to each stakeholder?
3. Were any ethical norms or principles violated or were the violations limited to accounting standards?
4. What was the purpose of falsifying the ALH books?
5. Who benefited from the deception?
6. Were any stakeholders harmed by this deception?
7. What was Aer Lingus's responsibility in the case?
8. Did the intensity of the competition force ALH to falsify its accounts?
9. What went wrong to create this type of deception?

Sources: "£10m in Losses Concealed in Falsified Sets of Accounts," *The Irish Times* (March 16, 1991), Section 13 Business & Finance; "Borrowings to Buy Spanish Property Not Recorded in Accounts," *The Irish Times* (March 16, 1991),Section 13 Business & Finance; "Gardai Uncover Evidence for Fraud Charges," *The Irish Times,* (March 16, 1991), Section 13 Business & Finance.

Case 2

American Therapeutics Inc.

American Therapeutics Inc. is a manufacturer of generic drugs based in Bohemia, New York. The firm's president is Raju V. Vegesna. Generic drugs are less expensive versions of brand-name products. When exclusive marketing patents on brand-name drugs expire, generic manufacturers can legally copy and sell the brand-name products under their generic label. However, the generic brand must be approved by the Food and Drug Administration (FDA) prior to its being sold on the market.

Timing is critical to generic drug manufacturers. Being first on the market with a new generic drug can significantly enhance market share. Thus, there is great pressure to develop the production capability and obtain FDA approval for a new generic drug before one's competitor does. As Mead Johnson Company's patent for Desyrel, an antidepressant, was expiring in the mid 1980s, American Therapeutic was developing a generic version of the drug, Trazodone Hydrochloride.

In 1987, Charles Y. Chang was the top FDA generic drug review chemist. American Therapeutic decided to give Chang $13,000 in furniture and computer equipment. The firm also paid $1,688 in shipping and other costs owed by Chang. Under Vegesna's orders, documents related to the expenditures were disguised to appear to be employee relocation expenses that could not be traced to Chang.

In a further effort to accelerate the approval process, the firm gained inside information from Jan T. Sturm, an FDA consumer safety officer. Sturm told Vegesna that key FDA officials were "sitting on" the approval of his drug. Sturm made numerous calls to Vegesna warning him of problems throughout the approval process. One key piece of information he provided Vegesna was that the FDA disapproved the outside laboratory American Therapeutics had selected to test the raw materials for Trazodone Hydrochloride. On hearing this, Vegesna immediately left New York for Jessup, Maryland, where he gave Sturm a letter indicating the laboratory had been eliminated. Sturm filed the letter with the FDA the same day and Trazodone was approved nine days later.

Three weeks later, Vegesna met Sturm at a District of Columbia Holiday Inn and handed him an envelope containing $20,000. The money was to cover the cost of a car Vegesna had previously offered to buy for him.

1. Who are the stakeholders in the case?
2. What priority rank do you give to each stakeholder?
3. Were any ethical norms or principles violated by Vegesna? By Chang? By Sturm?
4. Who were the winners and who were the losers in the case?
5. What decision dimensions might Vegesna have used when considering the development of Trazodone Hydrochloride?
6. Does this type of action put the generic drug industry at risk?
7. What liability is associated with Vegesna's actions?
8. Did Vegesna have any other alternatives that could obtain FDA approval as quickly?
9. What actions can be taken to prevent future payments from being made?

Sources: Paul W. Valentine, "Drug Firm Admits Payoffs to FDA Regulators," *The Washington Post* 113, 116 (March 31, 1990), p. A15; Paul W. Valentine, "N.Y. Man Gets Two-Year Sentence for Bribing FDA over Generic Drug," *The Washington Post* 113, 234 (July 27, 1990), p. A7; Paul W. Valentine, "$1 Million Fine Levied in Generic Drug Fraud," *The Washington Post* 113, 318 (October 19, 1990), p. A3.

Case 3

Barings PLC

Barings Bank was founded in 1762 by John and Francis Baring, sons of wool merchant Johann Baring who had immigrated to England from Bremem, Germany, in 1717. The bank financed the U.S. purchase of the Louisiana Territory from France in 1803. It also helped finance Britain's wars against Napoleon. The bank was acquired by the Barings Foundation, a charitable foundation, in 1970. Barings PLC, Britain's oldest and most prestigious merchant bank, counted Queen Elizabeth II as a customer.

Barings PLC consisted of Barings Brothers & Co., the firm's banking, capital markets, and corporate finance arm; Barings Asset Management Ltd., its asset-management company; and Barings Securities Ltd., which handled the banks international equities business. Barings was known as a client-driven firm, making money on trades for clients while doing little trading using its own money to not compete with its clients.

In 1992, Australian Ron Baker was hired to build a global fixed-income derivatives operation. The unit, based in London, opened offices in New York and Asia. Within 18 months, it had grown to 150 people. In early 1992, Baker sent Nicholas W. Leeson, a settlements clerk in the back office in London, to Singapore to resolve some backroom problems with the apparent understanding that he would report directly to the derivatives unit in London. On March 25, 1992, James Bax, head of securities operations in Singapore, sent a letter to Andrew Fraser, head of the equities department in London, cautioning the London office against allowing Leeson to develop the futures operations single-handedly. Bax also argued that Leeson should report directly to his office, not to London.

Soon after arriving in Singapore, Leeson began setting up a settlements system for Barings Futures. Within a year, Leeson became a member of Barings trading team on the floor of the Singapore International Monetary Exchange (Simex) and went on to become the firm's chief trader. He headed Barings Futures Singapore Pte Ltd., but still reported to London.

Leeson's primary job was to arbitrage Nikkei futures contracts in Singapore and Osaka, Japan. He would make relatively small amounts of money by buying contracts for his clients in one market and then selling similar contracts for a higher price in the other. He became so successful that in 1994 the firm decided to let him trade for his own account, enabling the bank to profit directly from his arbitrage abilities. Leeson was instructed to exploit the differences in contract prices but not to take risk positions. He earned more than $1 million in bonuses that year.

A report issued in July 1994 by an internal audit team from Barings Brothers & Co. warned of loose controls in Singapore. It indicated that the chief trader, Leeson, was in charge of both trading and settlement operations and recommended that separate individuals be assigned to these two functions for control purposes. Barings Securities agreed to the recommendation but never implemented it because executives in the unit did not like the other side of the house telling them what to do.

There apparently was considerable tension between the bankers and securities units within Barings due to cultural differences and personal rivalries. The banking unit was a blue-blooded United Kingdom merchant bank with strong establishment connections. Thus, it was a conservative, low-risk operation. The securities unit had developed into a major international trading power in the past decade with operations in Asia and Latin America. It was a very high-risk business concentrated on highly esoteric emerging markets.

Sometime in the late fall of 1994, Leeson began taking risk positions for the bank, switching from an arbitrager to a speculator. He bought contracts without hedging them by selling corresponding contracts. The size of his position increased dramatically as 1995 began. Apparently he was counting on selling the contracts at even higher prices in the future based on the belief that the destruction from the recent Kobe earthquake would stimulate the economy and thus drive up the Nikkei stock index. However, in the meantime, he left the bank uncovered using account 88888 as a claimed client account to cover inquiries. It should be noted that during January and February 1995, Barings in London transferred approximately $900 million to Singapore to cover margin requirements.

The Osaka stock market did not cooperate, so Leeson sold put and call options to raise cash to meet margin calls. The market continued to decline. Leeson finally left his office and never came back. He celebrated his 28th birthday two days later. Leeson faxed a letter of resignation to Barings from Malaysia. On his way back to England, Leeson was detained in Frankfurt. He fought extradition to Singapore, preferring to be sent to England to stand trial in an English court. However, the German government decided to extradite him to Singapore. A Singapore court found him guilty and sentenced him to six-and-a-half years in prison.

On February 26, 1995, Barings PLC was forced into administration, a legal proceeding similar to Chapter 11 in the United States. It had incurred loses in excess of $1 billion from Leeson's speculations. Fortunately, Barings's clients were in no danger because the losses involved Barings's own trading accounts. The Dutch bank Internationale Nederlanden Groep NV subsequently purchased Barings.

1. Who are the stakeholders in the case?
2. What priority rank do you give to each stakeholder?
3. What role could the political struggle within Barings have played in its failure?
4. Were any ethical norms or principles violated?
5. Who were the winners?
6. Who were the losers?

7. Would the outcome have been different if the Japanese stock market had not fallen?

8. What actions could Barings have taken to prevent its failure?

Sources: BBC, "Nick Leeson and Barings Bank," *http://www.bbc.co.uk/crime/caseclosed/ nickleeson.shtml;* Marcus W. Brauchli, Nicholas Bray, and Michael R. Sesit, "Barings PLC Officials May Have Been Aware of Traders Position," *The Wall Street Journal* 132, 44 (March 6, 1995), pp. A1, A6; Nicholas Bray and Michael R. Sesit, "Barings Was Warned Controls Were Lax but Didn't Make Reforms in Singapore," *The Wall Street Journal* 132, 42 (March 2, 1995), p. A3; Paula Dwyer, William Glasgall, Dean Foust, and Greg Burns, "The Lessons from Barings' Straits," *Business Week,* 3415 (March 13, 1995), pp. 30–33; Alexander MacLeod, "Youthful Trader Sinks Britain's Oldest Bank," *The Christian Science Monitor* 87, 64 (February 28, 1995), pp. 1, 8; Jeremy Mark, Michael R. Sesit, and Laura Jereski, "Losses at Barings Grow to $1.24 Billion; Authorities Begin Sale of 'Good' Assets: Trader Sent to Clean Up Backroom Woes Left a Globe-Rattling Mess," *The Wall Street Journal* 132, 40 (February 28, 1995), p. A3; Sara Wed, Michael R. Sesit, Nicholas Bray, and Robert Steiner, "Britain's Barings PLC Bets on Derivatives—and the Cost is Dear," *The Wall Street Journal* 132, 39 (February 27, 1995), pp. A1, A6; Richard W. Stevenson, "Germany Orders Leeson Extradited to Singapore; Ex-Barings Trader Prefers Trial in Britain," *The New York Times* 145 (October 5, 1995), p. C5; Michael R. Sesit and Laura Jereski, "Barings Trader Forged Document to Obtain Funds, Singapore Alleges," *The Wall Street Journal* 132, 45 (March 7, 1995), p. A17.

Case 4

Chrysler—Disconnected Odometers

On June 24, 1987, the U.S. Government issued a 16-count indictment against Chrysler Corporation and two high-level executives, charging that the odometers on selected new cars and trucks were disconnected prior to turning the vehicles over to Chrysler executives for up to six weeks of personal use. When the vehicles were returned, the odometers were reconnected and the vehicles were then shipped to dealers as new vehicles. The government claimed that the practice had been going on for the past 38 years; some of the vehicles had been driven up to 400 miles. It was further claimed that some of the vehicles had been involved in accidents and then repaired with no notice of the accident provided to the new owner.

The government asserted that at least 60,000 vehicles had been involved in this practice between July 1985 and December 1986. Chrysler vice president Baron Bates refuted the charge that vehicles were given to company executives for extensive personal use. He defended the practice of testing cars with odometers disconnected as part of a quality-assurance program that involved randomly selected vehicles. Bates stated that the vehicles were driven home overnight for the purpose of isolating potential quality or safety defects. The vehicles were driven an average of 40 miles, with a few driven more than 65 miles. Chrysler further stated that fewer than 40 cars had been involved in accidents in the last 10 years, and those cars had been fully repaired prior to being handed over to dealers for sale.

When the government began its investigation of Chrysler in October 1986, Chrysler stopped disconnecting odometers and limited the test drives to 65 miles. They also placed notices in the glove compartments of the test vehicles, advising buyers that the car had been involved in the testing program.

On July 1, 1987, Chrysler president Lee Iacocca defended the legality of Chrysler's actions, stating: "The only law we broke was the law of common sense." He went on to express that the practice may have caused buyers to lose faith in Chrysler, faith that had been carefully nurtured since the government bailout. "We asked [customers] to trust us, and they did. Now they've been given reason to question that trust. Simply stated, that's unforgivable." Referencing the odometer disconnecting, Iacocca stated: "Did we screw up? You bet we did. I'm damned sorry it happened and you can bet it won't happen again, and that's a promise."

Iacocca announced that Chrysler was extending the current five-year or 50,000-mile engine and power-train warranty on all vehicles involved in the testing program to seven years or 70,000 miles. In addition, the warranty was expanded to cover additional major systems including air-conditioning and brakes. Owners of all cars involved in the program were offered a free inspection. Owners of vehicles that were damaged during testing and then repaired prior to shipment were offered a brand new car or truck of comparable value at no additional cost. Chrysler ran ads on television and in newspapers (see Figure A.1) apologizing for disconnecting odometers on test cars and outlining its compensation program. Iacocca was careful to note that the program was not considered a legal settlement by stating: "This is not a product recall. The only thing we're recalling here is our integrity."

1. Who are the stakeholders in the case?
2. What priority rank do you give to each stakeholder?
3. Were any ethical norms or principles violated by Chrysler?
4. How effective was Iacocca's response?
5. If you had been Iacocca, what would you have done differently?
6. What decision dimensions did Chrysler use to implement the testing?
7. What decision dimensions did Iacocca use in responding to the charges?
8. What could have been done to prevent this practice from occurring?

Sources: Paul A. Eisenstein, "Chrysler Denies It Falsified Auto Mileage," *The Christian Science Monitor* 79, 148 (June 26, 1987), p. 11; John Bussey, "Lee Iacocca Calls Odometer Policy 'Dumb,' " *The Wall Street Journal* 117, p. 2 (July 2, 1987), p. 2; Paul A. Eisenstein, "Chrysler Chairman Tries to Make Amends—and Boost Image," *The Christian Science Monitor* 79, 153 (July 3, 1987), p. 11.

FIGURE A.1 Chrysler Ad Regarding Testing Cars with Odometers Disconnected

"Testing cars is a good idea. That's a mistake we won't make again at Chrysler. Period."

Disconnecting odometers is a lousy idea.

Lee Iacocca

LET ME SET THE RECORD STRAIGHT.

1. For years, spot checking and road testing new cars and trucks that come off the assembly line with the odometers disengaged was standard industry practice. In our case, the average test mileage was 40 miles.

2. Even though the practice wasn't illegal, some companies began connecting their odometers. We didn't. In retrospect, that was dumb. Since October 1986, however, the odometer of every car and truck we've built has been connected, including those in the test program.

3. A few cars–and I mean a few–were damaged in testing badly enough that they should not have been fixed and sold as new. That was a mistake in an otherwise valid quality assurance program. And now we have to make it right.

WHAT WE'RE DOING TO MAKE THINGS RIGHT.

1. In all instances where our records show a vehicle was damaged in the test program and repaired and sold, *we will offer to replace that vehicle* with a brand new 1987 Chrysler Corporation model of comparable value. No ifs ands or buts.

2. We are sending letters to everyone our records show bought a vehicle that was in the test program and offering a free inspection. If anything is wrong because of a product deficiency, we will make it right.

3. Along with the free inspection, we are extending their present 5 year or 50,000 mile protection plan on engine and powertrain to 7 years or 70,000 miles.

4. And to put their minds completely at ease, we are extending the 7 year or 70,000 mile protection to *all major systems:* brakes, suspension, air conditioning, electrical and steering.

    The quality testing program is a good program. But there were mistakes and we were too slow in stopping them. Now they're stopped. Done. Finished. Over.

    Personally, I'm proud of our products. Proud of the quality improvements we've made. So we're going to keep right on testing. Because without it we couldn't have given America 5 year 50,000 mile protection five years ahead of everyone else. Or maintained our warranty leadership with 7 year 70,000 mile protection. I'm proud, too, of our leadership in safety-related recalls.

    But I'm not proud of this episode. Not at all.

    As Harry Truman once said, "The buck stops here." It just stopped. Period.

CHRYSLER · PLYMOUTH · DODGE CARS · DODGE TRUCKS

Case 5

ConAgra Inc.

Millions of bushels of grain and soybeans are shipped from U.S. ports each year. Prior to being stored and/or transported, the grain and soybeans are dried to prevent spoilage. Unfortunately, dry grain is accompanied by dust. When this dust reaches a critical concentration level in the air, it becomes explosive, with very dangerous consequences for humans and buildings. In 1977, 65 lives were lost in 20 grain-dust explosions in the United States.

One governmentally approved method of reducing the dust is to wet down the grain. A U.S. Department of Agriculture report released in 1982 indicated that dust could be cut 80 percent by raising the moisture level in corn 0.3 percent. Some grain terminals began installing watering systems in the 1980s to suppress the dust that causes the explosions. Enough water must be added to suppress the dust without adding too much to adulterate the grain. However, no standards have been set specifying the maximum amount of water allowed.

Grain is measured by weight with a specific number of pounds representing a bushel. The actual weight per bushel depends on the grain being measured. Adding water to the grain increases its weight and thus increases the number of bushels by weight with no change in the actual volume of grain. Grain elevators earn a penny or two per bushel of grain handled. For a bushel of soybeans, the earnings could be increased another three cents by simply increasing its weight by half a percentage point. Thus, there is a strong incentive to add a little extra water to a shipment.

ConAgra controls dust levels at its Peavey unit's grain terminal in Myrtle Grove, Louisiana, by using water. James L. Swanson, a vice president of the Peavey unit, believes the terminal is much safer with its watering system. A Digital Equipment Corporation computer controls the amount of water flowing through the nozzles of a sprayer over a conveyor belt that carries soybeans to ocean-going vessels. The water is carefully controlled to add no more than 0.29 percent to the weight of the soybeans. The beans absorb the water with no change in appearance. However, the shipment will be 177.5 metric tons heavier, and the soybean buyer will pay $37,000 for the water added to the shipment.

Because moisture causes spoilage in grain and soybeans, limits are set on the amount of moisture they can contain. For soybeans the limit is 13.5 percent. However, a dealer who owns soybeans that contain 13 percent moisture is not allowed to spray the beans with water to increase the moisture level to 13.5 percent if the intent is to boost the shipment's weight to increase profits. Even though the beans would be kept within acceptable moisture limits, such an act would be considered adulteration. The dealer can, however, add water for the purpose of suppressing dust and pocket the additional profits earned from the added weight of the water. This is exactly what ConAgra says it is doing at its Myrtle Grove plant to prevent an explosion that would endanger the lives of its employees.

Interestingly, South Africa has told the United States that it will not import grain from three ports where water is used. Some trading firms in Japan, the largest importer of U.S. grains, have quietly informed the U.S. government of their concern over the watering of grain. Several individual buyers have specified that water not be added to their shipments. If water is added, the exporter must note the addition on the shipment's documentation. This requirement does not apply to water added at elevators prior to the shipment arriving at the ocean terminal.

1. Who are the stakeholders in the case?
2. What priority rank do you give to each stakeholder?
3. Were any ethical norms or principles violated?
4. Do some stakeholders' claims compete with other stakeholders' claims? If so, what claims should take priority?
5. What alternative dust-suppression methods should be considered?
6. If water is the method of choice to suppress dust, what controls should be implemented to control the amount of water used?
7. How much water should be used?

Sources: Scott Kilman, "Grain-Handling Firms Will Be Ordered to Stop Dousing Crops with Water," *The Wall Street Journal* 131, 74 (October 14, 1994), p. A12; Scott Kilman, "Some Dealers in Grain Water It, Making It Weigh and Cost More," *The Wall Street Journal* 129, 1 (July 1, 1995), pp. A1, A6; Scott Kilman, "U.S. Widens Inquiry into Possible Use of Water to Boost Weight, Price of Grain," *The Wall Street Journal* 222, 50 (September 10, 1993), p. A5.

Case 6

The Pesticide DDT

In 1939 Paul Muller, a Swiss chemist working for J. R. Geigy, was looking for a way to protect woolens against moths. His quest led him to a white crystalline powder called dichloro diphenyl trichloroethane that had a devastating effect on flies. The powder, subsequently known as DDT, would become the first modern synthetic pesticide and earn Muller the 1948 Nobel prize for chemistry. In 1942 Geigy sent some of the powder to its New York office. Victor Froelicher, a Geigy chemist in the New York office, translated the document describing the powder and its amazing attributes into English and gave a sample of the powder to the Department of Agriculture.

The U.S. Army had tasked the Department of Agriculture with finding a way to protect its soldiers from insect-borne diseases. In some of the military units, up to 80 percent of the soldiers were out sick with malaria. After testing thousands of compounds, the Department's research station in Orlando, Florida, found DDT to be most effective. It was subsequently used by the armed forces in Europe and Asia to battle typhus, malaria, and other diseases that held the potential to devastatate the allied fighting forces. It proved extremely effective and is credited with shortening the war.

At that time malaria was common in Asia, the Caribbean, Europe, and the southern part of the United States. Millions of people died from malaria each year. With the effectiveness of the pesticide proven in the war years, DDT became the insecticide of choice around the world. It was effective on a wide range of insect pests, it did not break down rapidly so it did not have to be reapplied often, and it was not water soluble and thus was not washed off when it rained. Farmers and homeowners used DDT to protect crops and kill nuisance insects and pests that spread disease. Countries used it to protect their populations. In 1931–32 more than 22,000 people died from malaria in South Africa's KwaZulu-Natal province. By 1973 the deaths had dropped to 331 for the whole country and by 1977 there was only one death from malaria in South Africa.

Chemical manufacturers were turning out DDT in record volumes. Montrose Chemical Corporation in Montrose, California, was one of the largest, beginning production in 1942. However, clouds had been building on the horizon. In 1962 Rachel Carson published a book entitled *Silent Spring* that exposed a link between the mass use of DDT and the death of birds and fish. DDT was found to be toxic to fish and indirectly toxic to birds due to its persistence in the environment. It tended to accumulate in fatty tissue, and it became more concentrated as it moved up the food chain. Birds of prey started failing to reproduce due to their egg shells becoming so thin they could not survive the incubation period. DDT began showing up in human breast milk. Some sources claimed DDT causes cancer, but there is disagreement regarding that claim among the experts.

Concern about the effects of DDT grew until it was banned for use in the United States at the end of 1972 by the Environmental Protection Agency, 10 years after the publication of *Silent Spring.* However, DDT could still be produced and sold abroad. Montrose continued to export DDT to Africa, India, and other countries until 1982. DDT was banned in Cuba in 1970, in Poland in 1976, in Canada and Chile in 1985, and in Korea, Liechtenstein, and Switzerland in 1986. The product has also been banned in the European Union, Mexico, Panama, Sri Lanka, Sweden, and Togo, among other countries. The persistence of the chemical is evidenced by traces of it still being found in the Great Lakes 30 years after application stopped.

1. Who are the stakeholders in the case?
2. What priority rank do you give to each stakeholder?
3. What is the relative priority of each stakeholder?
4. Were any ethical norms or principles violated by the Montrose Chemical Corporation by manufacturing and selling DDT to the public?

5. Was it ethical to manufacture and sell DDT to other countries after the Environmental Protection Agency banned its use in the United States due to its harmful effects?

6. Did the Environmental Protection Agency make the right decision when it banned DDT?

7. Should Muller's Nobel prize be taken away now that DDT has been found to be harmful?

Sources: Dan Chapman, "A Father & Son Story: Dusting Off DDT's Image/Long-maligned Pesticide May Be Regaining Favor as Mosquito Menace Grows," *The Atlanta Journal-Constitition* (September 9, 2001), p. D1; Malcolm Gladwell, *The New Yorker 77*, 17 (July 2, 2001), p. 42; P. S. Thampi, "India among Top DDT Users; Need Early Ban," *The Indian Express* (August 10, 1998); Edmund P. Russell III, "The Strange Career of DDT: Experts, Federal Capacity, and Environmentalism in World War II," *Technology and Culture* 40, 4 (October 1999), pp. 770–796; Michael Satchell and Don L. Boroughs, "Rocks and Hard Places DDT: Dangerous Scourge or Last Resort; South Africa," *U.S. News & World Report* 129, 23 (December 11, 2000), p. 64; Deborah Schoch, "Regional Report SOUTH BAY Chemical Reaction Discovery of DDT in the Back Yards of Two Local Homes Has Rekindled Concern and Fear," *The Los Angeles Times* (June 9, 1994), p. 22.

Case 7

First American Bank of Georgia

In 1977, Bert Lance, federal budget director for the Carter administration, sold the National Bank of Georgia (NBG) to Ghaith Pharaon, a Saudi businessman. In October 1981, Asif Mujtaba, a Pakistani native, left the Bank of Credit and Commerce International (BCCI) to head the National Bank of Georgia's Panama office and work at its currency trading desk. Tariq Jamil and Mehdi Raza, also former BCCI employees, joined NBG in the early 1980s.

Mujtaba was promoted to manager of First American's main Atlanta branch and then to vice president of corporate accounts in Buckhead and north Fulton County. In 1986, he was suddenly demoted to a business development officer.

The First National Bank of Georgia was purchased by First American Bankshares of Washington, D.C., in 1987. Bankshares, a holding company, was headed by Clark Clifford, former secretary of defense under President Carter. When the acquisition was made, according to the *Atlanta Business Chronicle,* Clifford maintained that the bank "would be run by Americans." He stated: "We had the understanding with [the investors] at the very beginning that this would be an American operation. It would be run by Americans, the policy would be set by Americans, and our personnel would be American. We have no foreign nationals on any of our boards or in any of the top positions in our banks."

The NBG was renamed First American Bank of Georgia (FABG) following its purchase by Bankshares. Shortly after the acquisition, Mujtaba's salary was cut from $80,000 to $50,000. On May 4, 1990, his loan authority was revoked. Don Tate, chief credit officer of the bank, said he took the action "because of loan charge-offs and for failure to document loans properly." Mujtaba states that his supervisor, Richard Harrell, "told me I should resign because the management of the bank did not have confidence in my business development ability."

At the close of 1991, Mujtaba, now a U.S. citizen employed as a private banking officer with the bank, filed an employment discrimination suit in U.S. District Court. He charged that NBG and its successor, FABG, were so concerned about appearing to be run by Pakistani nationals that they tried to force a Pakistani-born senior vice president to resign.

On September 17, 1992, Ghaith Pharaon, Tariq Jamil, and William Batastini, a former senior vice president and comptroller of NBG, were charged with fraud and other crimes in the BCCI case. The previous month Clark Clifford had been indicted on charges that he had lied to bank regulators about the ownership of First American Bankshares. Apparently, it was illegally owned by BCCI.

1. Who are the stakeholders in the case?
2. What priority rank do you give to each stakeholder?
3. What ethical issues are raised?
4. Clark Clifford stated that only Americans would be running the bank. Who is an American?
5. Why did NBG demote Mujtaba?
6. Can you justify the demotion?
7. Who were the winners and who were the losers?
8. Can you ethically limit jobs to the citizens of a country? To certain ethnic groups?

Sources: Edward DeMarco, "Foreign Fears at First Am?" *Atlanta Business Chronicle* 14, (December 2, 1991) p. 27; "South Trust to Acquire B.C.C.I. Unit," *The New York Times* 141 (January 21, 1992), p. D4; Sharon Walsh, "Ga. Grand Jury Indicts 4 in BCCI Scandal," *The Washington Post* 115 (September 18, 1992), p. F1.

Case 8
Friedrich Flick Industrieverwaltung KGaA

Friedrich Flick Industrieverwaltung KGaA, based in Dusseldorf, Germany, employs nearly 45,000 people. The firm is organized into three major groups. The Buderus Group focuses on new technologies for the conservation of energy. The Dynamit Nobel Group manufactures thermal insulating building products. The Feldmuehle Group makes paper, paperboard, cellulose, and home products.

German industry has a history of funding the country's three main political parties, the Christian Democratic Union (CDU), the Social Democratic

Party (SPD), and the Free Democratic Party (FDP). While restrictive laws governing contributions to political parties are on the books, German authorities often overlook under-the-counter payments. Party leaders claim that money to run the parties must be raised so that the democracy can function, and German industrialists are willing to contribute money without making specific policy demands.

During the 1970s, Flick deputy chairman Eberhard von Brauchitsch conveyed DM135,000 ($45,000) to Count Otto Lambsdorff, treasurer of the FDP in North Rhine-Westphalia, West Germany's most populous state. Lambsdorff served as the intellectual leader of the Party's free-enterprise-oriented right wing. He was known for promoting industrial policy favorable to Flick. Lambsdorff became economics minister of the federal government in October 1977 and resigned as FDP treasurer two months later. Flick had contributed DM375,000 ($125,000) to Lambsdorff's predecessor as economics minister, Hans Friderichs, when he was treasurer of the FDP. Friderichs later assumed the chairmanship of Dresdner Bank.

The money was not used personally by either man but went into the coffers of their beleaguered FDP, which was the poorest and smallest of the three veteran parties in the Bundestag. Brauchitsch routed the contributions to the party through foreign countries and/or through nonprofit policy-research foundations in order to evade taxes. Flick's total contributions to the three major political parties and private individuals may have reached DM20 million.

In 1975, Flick sold its 29 percent share of Daimler-Benz for a profit of DM1.9 billion. Most of the proceeds were reinvested in W. R. Grace and Company of New York and United States Filter Corporation. Flick requested that the government waive its 56 percent tax claim of some DM800 million on the capital gains from the sale. In 1976, Economics Minister Hans Friderichs granted a tax waiver on the purchase of 12 percent of Grace. Economics Minister Otto Lambsdorff approved a second waiver in 1978 when Flick increased its Grace holdings to 25 percent. However, a third waiver for the purchase of 30 percent of United States Filter Corporation was rejected.

The justification for the waivers was that the economy would be stimulated by Flick's investment of the profits. Lambsdorff maintained that it was more important for the money to create jobs rather than be gathered into the public purse.

1. Who are the stakeholders in the case?
2. What priority rank do you give to each stakeholder?
3. Were any ethical norms or principles violated by Flick? By Friderichs and Lambsdorff?
4. Who gained by the payments? Who lost?
5. Was the government in essence making an investment by letting Flick keep the tax money?

6. Is there a danger in letting industry finance political parties?
7. Why did Flick contribute to the FDP?
8. What decision dimensions might Flick have considered when deciding to make the payments?

Sources: James M. Markham, "Bonn Cabinet Minister Denies Corruption Charge," *The New York Times* 133, 45879 (December 1, 1983), p. A8; *Moody's Industrial Manual* 1 (New York, NY: Moody's Investors Service, Inc., 1984), p. 1386; Elizabeth Pond, "Big Business's Role in Politics Is Key Issue in 'Flick Affair' Trial," *The Christian Science Monitor* 77, 196 (August 30, 1985), p. 13; John Tagiabue, "Flick Tax Deal under Scrutiny," *The New York Times* 132, 45506 (November 23, 1982), D8; "The Count against the Count," *The Economist* 289, 7318 (December 3, 1983), p. 44.

Case 9

Ing. C. Olivetti & Co S.p.A.

Ing. C. Olivetti & Company S.p.A. was founded in Italy in 1932. It has become one of the major producers of computers and office machines in Europe. The company markets its products worldwide with two-thirds of its sales being made overseas.

In the early 1980s, Italian politicians informed Olivetti that it must begin making political payments if it expected to obtain contracts from state agencies. Although government contracts represented a minor portion of the firm's business, major overseas customers would shy away from a company that failed to obtain orders from its own government. Thus, if Olivetti refused to pay, it risked losing important foreign customers such as the Dutch Post Office and Swiss Railways. Olivetti began making general contributions not linked to specific contracts.

In the mid 1980s, the pressure to make payments for specific contracts increased dramatically. When Olivetti did not ante up, its share of contracts fell off and nearly disappeared by 1987. The firm's sales representatives weren't even received by the Ministry of Posts and Telecommunications. Postal minister Giuseppe Parrella told Olivetti that everyone else paid, so they would have to pay in order to receive a contract.

Olivetti began to make payments in 1988. The Ministry of Posts and Telecommunications received 1.2 billion lire from the company in 1988 and awarded 204 billion lire in contracts to the firm. Payments continued until 1991 when Olivetti stopped making payments. In 1992, contracts from the postal ministry dropped to 73 billion lire. Total payments by the firm to Italy's political parties amounted to just over 10 billion lire. In exchange, it received contracts worth approximately 500 billion lire.

Olivetti Chairman Carlo De Benedetti argued that he had to make payments to get public-works contracts in Italy in the 1980s because those were the rules of the game. In voluntary testimony before the Milan magistrates, he stated: "Those who have made pay-offs, and I am certain there are many, can, I believe, be divided briefly into three categories: those who have set up or acquired a company with the objective of corruption; those who have made profits through the pay-off system; and those who have decided to give in to blackmail from certain parties as a necessity to defend their company." He indicated that his company fell into the third category. Asked whether he would make the payments if he had it to do over again, De Benedetti stated: "And I'd do it with the same disgust I did then."

De Benedetti disclosed that the payments were carried on Olivetti's balance sheet as undocumented expenditures. He claimed that it would have been impossible to stay in business without making the payments. He told the Milan magistrates that since the early 1980s, "pressures of an increasing parasitic nature from both political parties and their representatives in public positions have grown alarmingly. It has involved threats, blackmail, and a manner which we would be entirely justified in referring to as a racket."

1. Who are the stakeholders in the case?
2. What priority rank do you give to each stakeholder?
3. Were any moral norms or principles violated?
4. Does the argument that payments had to be made to stay in business provide moral justification for the payments?
5. Who would have been harmed if the payments had not been made?
6. Were community norms or hypernorms violated in making the payments?
7. How could Olivetti combat the coercive forces of the government?

Sources: "Carlos Goes to Confession," *The Economist* 327, 7812 (May 22, 1993), p. 81; Lisa Bannon, "De Benedetti Says Olivetti Kickbacks Date Back to 1983," *The Wall Street Journal* 221, 96 (May 18, 1993), p. A15; Lisa Bannon, "De Benedetti Says Political Bribes Were Commonplace in the 1980s", *The Wall Street Journal* 128, 98 (May 20, 1993), p. A13; Peter Semler and Andrew Lorenz, "Olivetti Chief Lifts Lid on Bribes Racket," *The Sunday Times,* (London), No. 8805 (May 23, 1993), Section 10 Business, p. 3.

Case 10

Kader Industrial (Thailand) Company

Kader Industrial (Thailand) Company is located near Bangkok, Thailand. It is a joint venture owned 40 percent by Kader Holdings Co. of Hong Kong, 40 percent by a firm linked to Thailand's Chareon Pokphand Group, and the remaining 20 percent by Taiwan investors. The plant employs 3,000 workers, mostly young women, who make toy dolls for export. The toys include Big Bird, Bart Simpson, and the Muppets for Fisher-Price, Inc. Toys "R" Us, and Kenner Products. The company provides much-needed employment for a number of families.

The manufacturing plant consists of four large connected four-story buildings. As in many developing countries, theft is a major problem.

Therefore, it was common practice to keep the doors locked between the buildings to prevent pilferage. In addition, once a shift started, the doors to the plant were locked so that people would not sneak out or steal. Workers at the plant were paid between $120 and $160 per month.

On Monday, May 10, 1993, a fire started in materials stored next to an electrical transformer in the cloth-cutting area on the ground floor of one of the buildings. The first building, in which 800 people were working, collapsed in flames within 10 minutes. The flames quickly spread to two of the other buildings, which also were destroyed. No alarm was sounded since the plant did not have alarms nor did it have fire escapes. The security guards who had previously locked the doors at the beginning of the shift claimed that they did not have time to unlock them.

Many people jumped out of upper-story windows. Hundreds of people were trapped behind the locked doors. Many bodies were found piled up behind the doors and under stairways leading to the doors that collapsed under the weight of the workers as they tried to escape. The building had disintegrated quickly due to shoddy construction and steel beams that failed early. Nearly 200 people died, with an additional 469 injured, many of these from jumping out windows.

The company claims it had proper fire-prevention equipment and exits. It defended its safety policies on TV, stating that it had complied with all government regulations. The firm has stated that it will take care of the injured workers and compensate the families of those who died. It has offered each injured worker $200 and each family of a deceased worker $4,000.

Chaiyuth Chavalitnitikul, a government ministry labor expert, stated that the company was cited for fire safety violations on February 15 by a government inspector. The inspector ordered the company to train employees in firefighting, conduct fire drills, and to submit evacuation plans. The company failed to comply. Government spokesman Abhisit Vejjajiva admits that the government needs to take a stronger position on worker safety. There are only 50 inspectors to enforce fire regulations at 90,000 factories and businesses. Many inspectors do not seriously enforce the law. He also states that "Clearly bribery is part of this problem." He promised more vigorous enforcement in the future.

The Kader fire is an example of lax regulations sometimes coupled with corruption that exposes workers to workplace hazards in Asia's fast-growing economies. The accident growth rate is extremely high in the region. The Malaysian Trade Union Congress claims that from 1985 to 1990 the number of industrial accidents in that country nearly doubled, from 61,724 to 121,104. The Kader fire is the worst factory fire in history. The record was previously held by the Triangle Shirtwaist Factory fire on March 25, 1911, when 146 women garment workers were locked in a factory loft in New York City.

1. Who are the stakeholders in the case?
2. What priority rank do you give to each stakeholder?

3. What ethical norms were violated?
4. What decisions were made that put the workers at risk?
5. Whose responsibility is it to protect the workers against this type of catastrophe?
6. What decision dimension appears to have taken priority in the decision process?
7. What type of corporate culture do you think Kader has?
8. What responsibility do Kader's customers have to make sure Kader's employees are protected?

Sources: Associated Press, A Fire Toll Points to Lax Safety in Thai Factories, *Chicago Tribune* (May 13, 1991), p. 10; Reese Erlich, "Report Will Say Thai Government Culpable in Fatal Factory Fire," *The Christian Science Monitor* 85, 155 (July 8, 1993), p. 9; "Thai Factory Fire's 200 Victims Were Locked Inside, Guards Say," *The New York Times* 142, 49329 (May 12, 1993), p. A2; "Thailand Fire Shows Region Cuts Corners on Safety to Boost Profits," *The Wall Street Journal* 221, 93 (May 13, 1993), p. A11.

Case 11

Muebles Fino Buenos

David Finegood opened a furniture manufacturing plant with 10 employees in Bell, California, in 1956. By the mid-1980s, the firm had grown to 700 employees making bedroom sets in the Good Bedrooms plant in Compton and making tables in the Good Tables factory in Carson, as well as operating the firm's distribution center.

During this time, environmental awareness in the United States and particularly in California had been growing. This led to the development of wide-ranging environmental standards. Although Finegood had invested in new technology, his firm started running afoul of the South Coast Air Quality Management District (AQMD). AQMD levied fines of $17,500 for exceeding solvent emission limits and $400 for exceeding sawdust emission limits in 1988. In 1989, a $2,350 fine was paid for improperly preparing solvent-soaked rags in mismarked drums and a cleanup cost of $10,730 was levied. Neighbors' complaints of odors and dust brought a $1,000 fine in 1990. The firm, along with its competitors, faced the costly prospect of meeting AQMD Rule 1136, which required furniture manufacturers to switch from solvent-based coatings to water-based coatings by 1996.

Firms began to leave the state. According to a UCLA survey, 15 percent of the furniture industry workforce left California between 1987 and 1989. Finegood decided to join the exodus, believing that it was no longer economically feasible to operate a furniture plant in the state. Complying with increasing environmental regulations made operations too costly. He shut down the Compton plant in February 1990 and closed the Carson plant in March 1990, laying off a total of 600 employees. Only the Carson distribution center remained open. He replaced both plants with Muebles Fino Buenos (Fine Good Furniture) in the heart of La Cienega, a working-class district in Tijuana, Mexico.

The new plant provides jobs for 600 Mexican nationals. It contains a shower room for employees and a physician to attend to their medical needs. The company cafeteria provides lunches for 75 cents with unlimited tortillas. The plant has its own water reservoir and electric generating substation. The firm appears to be abiding by existing Mexican laws. Each week the employees are paid in cash. The average wage is $43 per week compared to $330 in the United States. Workers' compensation expenses are minimal, and there are no air-quality inspectors and emission monitors.

The Muebles Fino Buenos plant emits more pollution than did the two former U.S. plants. It operates longer hours and, as a result, more gases flow from its stacks. When pressed, neighbors complain of strong odors, dizziness, headaches, and nausea. Fine dust coats of lacquer accumulate on vehicles. However, the neighbors do not complain, except among themselves. The emissions are considered part of progress. There is no law limiting air pollution from furniture factories.

1. Who are the stakeholders in the case?
2. What priority rank do you give to each stakeholder?
3. Did Finegood violate any ethical norms or principles?
4. What trade-off would you be willing to make between jobs and pollution?
5. What decision dimensions might Finegood have used in arriving at his decision to move to Mexico?
6. Would you have made the same decisions Finegood made? Why or why not?
7. What responsibility does the Mexican government have in the case?

Sources: Judy Pasternak, "Firms Find a Haven from U.S. Environmental Rules," *The Los Angeles Times* 110 (November 19, 1991), pp. A1, A24.

Case 12

Optifast

Sandoz Nutrition Corporation is a subsidiary of the Swiss pharmaceutical giant, Sandoz Ltd. Sandoz, based in Minneapolis, Minnesota, began manufacturing Optifast 70, a liquid meal-replacement weight-loss program in 1976. The six-month program is designed for people who are at least 30 percent or 50 pounds over their ideal weight. Health problems often acompany excessive weight. Optifast provides an opportunity to get rid of the weight fast.

The Optifast program is only available through doctors, hospitals, and medical clinics; a prescription is required to purchase the products. The

Optifast program typically begins with the patient being placed on a 420 to 800-calorie-per-day diet of liquid protein for 12 to 16 weeks. Calorie intake is then increased to 1,000 or 1,200 calories per day for the remainder of the program. The total cost is between $1,400 and $2,800.

Optifast sales grew slowly following its introduction as the medical community and consumers became aware of the program. Sales continued to build slowly until mid-November 1988. Then Oprah Winfrey announced on her TV talk show that she had lost 67 pounds using Optifast. She appeared on the program in size-10 jeans to prove her point. Here was a celebrity endorsing Optifast without being asked or paid! Within hours, Sandoz received more than 200,000 phone inquires about the Optifast diet program. The firm does not publish sales figures, but they forecasted a sales increase of from 25 to 30 percent during the six weeks following Oprah's announcement.

In 1989, Sandoz launched a print advertising program mostly in professional journals. Its promotional brochure and ad claims included: (1) "The one that's clinically proven safe and effective" and (2) "You can call the Optifast program today, and have all you need to control your weight for the rest of your life."

Unfortunately for Oprah, she regained 17 pounds during the first year after she had completed the Optifast program. Studies at the University of Pennsylvania suggested that people who undertake quick weight-loss programs such as liquid diets are likely to experience weight rebounds. Studies at the University of Michigan indicated that as many as 90 percent of dieters regain weight within five years after losing it. Liquid diets have also been linked with dizziness, headaches, nausea, gallbladder problems, and irregular heartbeat. Thus, there appears to be some difference between claims and use experience.

1. Who are the stakeholders in the case?
2. What priority rank do you give to each stakeholder?
3. Were any ethical norms or principles violated by Sandoz?
4. What are the benefits of using liquid-diet products? What are the hazards?
5. Are liquid-diet products ethical products?
6. What decision dimensions might Sandoz have considered when developing its promotion messages?
7. What moral responsibility does Sandoz have to its customers following completion of their program?

Sources: Denise Gellene, "3 Diet Firms Told to Trim Fat Claims," *The Los Angeles Times* 110 (October 17, 1991), p. D1; David S. Hilzenrath, "Liquid-Diet Firms Must Back Claims," *The Washington Post* 114, 316 (October 17, 1991), pp. A1, A49; "How Oprah Lost It," *Time* 132, 22 (November 28, 1988), p. 77; "3 Liquid Diet Marketers Told to Alter Ad Claims," *The New York Times* 41, 48756 (October 17, 1991), p. D2; Patricia Winters, "Oprah's Loss . . . ," *Advertising Age* 59, 53 (December 12, 1988), p. 62.

Case 13

Pepsi-Cola Products Philippines Inc.

Pepsi-Cola Products Philippines Inc. is the Pepsi-Cola bottler in the Philippines. The U.S. company PepsiCo Inc. owns 19 percent of the company via its overseas beverage unit, Pepsi-Cola International. The Philippines is the 12th-largest market for soft drinks in the world, and it accounts for approximately 2 percent of Pepsi's overseas sales.

Pepsi's sales had been running a distant second to Coca-Cola with a market share of 20 percent compared to Coke's 78 percent. In an attempt to take sales from Coke, the Pepsi bottler launched a "Number Fever" promotion campaign in February 1992. Numbers were printed on the underside of Pepsi bottle caps, and winning numbers were announced each day. Prizes were awarded to people who brought in caps containing winning numbers. The campaign was trumpeted in ads in newspapers, on the radio, and on TV, proclaiming "Today, you could be a millionaire."

Prizes ranged from 100 pesos to 1 million pesos (approximately $40,000 U.S.). The promotion was a huge success, with Pepsi's market share climbing to nearly 40 percent. Buoyed with the campaign's success, the company extended the campaign for five more weeks for a total of 12 weeks. As the campaign wore on, more than 51,000 winners came forward. Most won 100 pesos; however, 17 people won the 1 million pesos prize. The big winners were incorporated into Pepsi's advertising campaign.

Victoria Angelo, an unemployed mother of five, lives with her family in a tin-roofed shack in a squalid Manila slum. Her husband Juanito earns about $4 a day carrying people in his three-wheeled pedicab. As a result of the campaign, they began drinking Pepsi with every meal and snack. Each morning they prayed that they would get a cap with a winning number. Every evening they gathered with their neighbors around a small television set to see if their prayers had been heard.

On May 25, 1992, the number 349 flashed on the screen as the winner. Victoria Angelo searched through her caps, spreading them out on a table, and suddenly screamed "We are a millionaires (sic)." She turned excitedly to her family: "I tell my children you can finish school and go to college. I tell my husband he can buy a [passenger jeep]. I tell myself we can buy a real house. Can you imagine? It is a dream come true!"

Unfortunately, the number 349 appeared on between 500,000 and 800,000 bottle caps. Pepsi quickly realized the mistake when thousands of people began demanding payment. Knowing that billions of dollars could be at stake, the company refused to pay. Riots broke out and Pepsi delivery trucks were stoned, torched, or overturned. Molotov cocktails and homemade bombs were thrown at Pepsi plants and offices. In one incident, a fragmentation grenade was tossed at a parked Pepsi truck. It bounced off the truck and killed a five-year-old girl and a schoolteacher and wounded six other people. Pepsi executives received many death threats.

The violence frightened company officials, who quickly decided to offer 500 ($18.50 U.S.) pesos to each winner. More than 480,000 winners have come forward. The original promotion was budgeted at $2 million for prizes. Pepsi has paid over $10 million in prizes. The cost would have been more than $18 billion if the 1 million pesos per winner had been paid as promised.

The violence resulted in more than 30 burned delivery trucks. Approximately 6,000 people have filed civil suits for damages. At least 5,000 criminal suits charging fraud have been started. All of this is a result of what Pepsi Philippines' officials call a computer error.

1. Who are the stakeholders in the case?
2. What priority rank do you give to each stakeholder?
3. Were any ethical norms or principles violated?
4. If ethical norms or principles were violated, who violated them?
5. Was Pepsi justified in not paying the full 1-million-pesos prize?
6. What should Pepsi have done differently? When?
7. Would the response of the people have been different in Europe? South America? Asia? Africa?

Sources: Bob Drogin, "Bottle Cap Flap Riles the Masses," *The Los Angeles Times* 112 (July 26, 1993), pp. A1, A8, A9, A10; Michael J. McCarthy, "PepsiCo Is Facing Mounting Lawsuits from Botched Promotion in Philippines," *The Wall Street Journal* 129, 19 (July 28, 1993), p. B6; "Pepsi Loses Big in Philippine Sales Gamble," *The Christian Science Monitor* 85, 184 (August 18, 1993), p. 2.

Case 14

Phar-Mor Inc.

Phar-Mor Inc., a closely held dry goods retailer headquartered in Youngstown, Ohio, was founded in 1982 by David Shapira and Michael I. Monus. (See Table A.1 for a list of stockholders.) Monus assumed the presidency of Phar-Mor and was heavily involved in its operation. Shapira, CEO of the Giant Eagle supermarket chain, Phar-Mor's largest stockholder, became chief executive officer. The company grew rapidly from one store in 1982 to over 300 stores and $3 billion in sales in 10 years. Phar-Mor stores are characterized by high stacks of deeply discounted merchandise in warehouse-size stores. The merchandise ranges from videotapes to prescription drugs.

In the 1980s, Youngstown was reeling from a restructuring of the steel industry. Nearly 50,000 jobs were lost and many businesses left the down-

TABLE A.1   **Phar-Mor Stock Ownership, August 17, 1992**

% Shares	Company
38.3	Giant Eagle
15.8	Corporate Partners
5.6	Shapira Family
5.0	DeBartolo family, Associates & Affiliates
3.2	Sears, Roebuck & Co.
2.9	Monus Family & Associates
2.0	Westinghouse Electric
1.3	Robinson Family of Pittsburgh & Associates

town area. Under Monus, Phar-Mor became one of Youngstown's largest employers and supporters. Monus began by taking over two of the vacant downtown buildings, opening the first Phar-Mor store in one and converting the other, a vacant department store, into Phar-Mor headquarters. The headquarters became the focal point for many downtown events. Monus also supported the city fireworks display and Camp Tuff Enuff, a program for "at risk" inner-city children. He served as a trustee at Youngstown State University, where his family endowed a business chair.

An avid sports enthusiast, Monus persuaded the Ladies Professional Golf Association to hold its championships in Youngstown. He bought an interest in the Denver Rockies after failing to persuade Major League baseball to award Youngstown a franchise. In 1987, he started the World Basketball League, which fielded 10 teams in midsize cities.

Note: *Much of the information provided below is taken from news reports based on a report prepared by court-appointed examiner Jay Alix.*

Phar-Mor began to lose money in 1987. The losses were hidden from view by Monus and several subordinates who inflated inventory levels and other assets and understated liabilities and other expenses to cover shrinking profit margins. Two sets of books were kept, an official ledger that contained the false entries and a hidden ledger in which they kept records of the false entries. These actions disguised the losses and enabled them to claim performance bonuses as well as maintain access to capital and credit markets.

The false financial statements were used to obtain $1 billion in credit as well as additional capital from investors, including Sears, Roebuck & Co.; Westinghouse Electric Corp.; mall developer Edward DeBartolo Sr.; and Corporate Partners, an affiliate of Lazare Freres. As the firm's finances deteriorated, they relied on supplier payments to hide losses. Suppliers such as Coca-Cola Enterprises Inc, Fuji Photo Co., and Gibson Greetings Inc. paid $138 million between 1988 and 1992 in exchange for Phar-Mor's promise not to carry competing brands.

Phar-Mor purchased goods from dozens of suppliers with which Phar-Mor executives or directors had connections. For example, the firm leased phone equipment from a firm partly owned by Monus. It sold sports clothes from the World Basketball League. Costume jewelry was purchased from Jewelry 90, a Youngstown company that purchased the jewelry from a New York wholesaler. Jewelry 90 was owned by David Karzmer, a business associate of Monus. Michael Monus's father, a director of Phar-Mor, served as a paid consultant for Jewelry 90. His fees were $354,754 for six months' work in 1992. If Phar-Mor had bought directly from the wholesaler in New York, it would have saved $2.1 million.

During the summer of 1992, a Youngstown travel agent told Edward DeBartolo, an outside shareholder, that a Phar-Mor unit had made an $80,000 payment to settle a delinquent World Basketball League account. DeBartolo passed the information to Shapira, prompting an internal investigation of Phar-Mor. The investigation disclosed that DeBartolo had seen only the tip of the iceberg. Over the course of several years, Monus had funneled approximately $10 million to the World Basketball League. As the league's general partner, he owned controlling interest in at least 60 percent of each team. Thus, he was responsible for the major portion of the league's expenses. Team owners said that whenever they needed money, they would contact Phar-Mor's chief financial officer or a contact in the small-business division and the money would be forthcoming. Monus had also siphoned off a sizable amount of money for his personal use, including $180,000 for a new 18,000-square-foot mansion he was building, complete with basketball court. Numerous other officers and directors had benefited at the expense of Phar-Mor.

Phar-Mor Inc. filed for Chapter 11 bankruptcy in August 1992. Losses from internal fraud amounted to approximately $1 billion. The subsequent reorganization cut the number of Phar-Mor stores in half, with a corresponding loss of employees.

1. Who are the stakeholders in the case?
2. What priority rank do you give to each stakeholder?
3. What ethical norms or principles were violated?
4. What stakeholders were harmed by the fraud?
5. How could the fraud have been prevented?
6. What role did conflict of interest play in Phar-Mor's decline?
7. Is a conflict of interest unethical?
8. Would an outside audit by an accounting firm have exposed the fraud?

Sources: Michael Schroeder, Zachary Schiller, and Sandra Atchison, "A Scandal Waiting to Happen," *Business Week* 3280 (August 24, 1992), pp. 32, 33, 36; Gabriella Stern, "One Messy Store: Chicanery at Phar-Mor Ran Deep, Close Look at Discounter Shows," *The Wall Street Journal* 223, 14 (January 20, 1994), pp. A1, A6; Gabriella Stern and Clare Ansberry, "Fouling Out: A Founder Embezzled Millions for Basketball, Phar-Mor Chain Says," *The Wall Street Journal* 220, 26 (August 5, 1992), pp. A1, A5.

Case 15

Pico Korea, Ltd.

Pico Products Inc. manufactures cable TV equipment in Liverpool, New York. The firm decided to open a plant in Buchun City, South Korea, in 1985, to take advantage of the prevailing low-wage rates. Pico Korea employed 300 workers, mostly middle-aged women with families, paying them about 80 cents an hour. The low labor costs provided a significant production cost advantage for Pico Products.

The Korean workers formed a union in 1988. By November, the union had reached a collective-bargaining agreement with Pico Korea management. The agreement called for a minimum wage of $6.85 per day effective at the beginning of 1989. This was the first minimum-wage agreement negotiated in South Korea. The contract also contained an agreement to pay $350,000 in layoff payments in the event the plant was closed.

On March 3, 1989, the workers arrived for a scheduled meeting with top management. Management did not appear. After a long wait, the employees decided to go back to work. They continued to work until supplies ran low several days later. There was still no sign of top management and bills were beginning to pile up. The workers decided to ask the U.S. Chamber of Commerce in Seoul to help them find their boss. The Chamber staff learned of the women's intentions and left the building prior to the Pico Korea employees' arrival. When the union members entered the building, they were unable to find anyone to help them. They decided to stage a sit-down strike. Police were called and they dragged the women off into buses.

The Pico Korea employees never saw their top management again. Management had, in effect, closed Pico Korea, Ltd.'s doors and returned to America. The $350,000 in layoff payments were never paid. Pico Products Inc. apparently avoided those payments by simply walking away from their Korean operation.

1. Who are the stakeholders in this case?
2. What priority rank do you give to each stakeholder?
3. Were any ethical norms or principles violated when Pico decided to locate a plant in Korea to take advantage of low wages?
4. Did Pico Products violate any ethical norms or principles when they closed their Korean plant?
5. Did Pico Korea owe the workers wages for production after top management left?
6. What decision dimensions might Pico Products have used when they decided to close their Korean plant?
7. If you had been top management, what would you have done differently? Why?

8. Did the Pico Korea employees violate any ethical principles with their sit-down strike?

Sources: Rachel Thompson, "Korean Women Pin Down U.S. Boss," *The Progressive* 55, 4 (April 1991), p. 15; Charles W. Thurston, "Korea Union's Plant-Closing Suit Goes to Trial," *Journal of Commerce and Commercial* 390, 27595 (October 31, 1991), pp. 1A, 3A.

Case 16

Reindeer and Game Ltd.: *(Poro ja Riista Oy)*

Reindeer inhabit the far northern reaches of America, Asia, and Europe. Both sexes have antlers and are semidomesticated by the indigenous people of the regions. In Finland, the reindeer belong to the Laplanders living in the northern part of the country. They regularly harvest the reindeer herds and sell the meat to northern Europeans.

The Chernobyl disaster in the Ukraine in 1986 contaminated the Finnish reindeer herds. The radiation level of the animals' meat rose significantly. This led to a sharp decline in the number of reindeer slaughtered. Fortunately, by 1988, the radiation levels had fallen to within the limits set by the European Community (EC), allowing normal harvesting to resume. In the interim, the herds had significantly increased in size.

Reindeer and Game Ltd. was a major reindeer meat processor located in Rovaniemi, Finnish Lapland. In the mid 1980s, it held 60 percent of the reindeer meat products market with the remaining 40 percent divided among three other companies. In 1988 it employed 70 people. Its largest stockholder was the Reindeer Association's Union comprised of three local reindeer-breeding associations. Its capital stock amounted to 1.3 million Finnish marks (approximately $300,000 U.S.). Reindeer and Game Ltd. was governed by a 14-member supervisory board selected by the shareholders who oversaw the four-member board of directors and the CEO, Risto Sarala. (Finnish law allows firms whose capital stock exceeds 1 million Finnish marks, approximately $250,000 U.S., to establish a supervisory board.) The supervisory board was comprised primarily of reindeer owners. The firm had a weak financial position due to excessive liabilities.

With Finnish reindeer meat again meeting EC standards, a large reindeer harvest was planned for the fall of 1988. Reindeer and Game Ltd.'s owners, supported by the supervisory board, pressed the firm to increase significantly its purchase of reindeer carcasses. The firm agreed and began to increase the size of its factory to meet the projections.

During the winter, reindeer are caught and slaughtered on the tundra. With the area's extremely cold temperatures, it is common for some of the carcasses to be stored there for a few days. As long as the temperature stays several degrees below zero, the meat is protected from harmful bacteria.

The plant expansion at Reindeer and Game Ltd. fell behind schedule and was not ready for operation as planned. Thus, the firm was not able to process carcasses as fast as it had originally intended. In addition, the winter was milder than usual, with temperatures in November and December fluctuating between 0 and −30° C. Carcasses stored on the tundra longer than originally planned due to the delay in production capacity expansion thawed and refroze more than once, resulting in a buildup of harmful bacteria. In December, work on the plant expansion required Reindeer's refrigeration machinery to be turned off. Four hundred carcasses in cold storage decayed due to excessively high temperatures.

In January 1989, 17 butchers from Reindeer and Game Ltd. told the local newspaper that the company was butchering decaying carcasses. Inspectors discovered that reindeer meat from Reindeer and Game Ltd. contained 900 times the allowable level of bacteria. Although they ordered the meat destroyed, the CEO, Sarala, decided to save the best parts for processing. A few days later, an inspection by a county veterinarian found sound and decayed reindeer carcasses mixed together in Reindeer's warehouse. Further investigation by health authorities resulted in 6,000 whole reindeer carcasses, 32,000 disjointed carcasses, and 200,000 kilos of processed meat being declared unfit for human use. Total value of the condemned meat was 18 million marks (approximately $4 million U.S.). In addition, spoiled reindeer meat products were found on sale in Southern and Eastern Finland.

Nearly 10 days after the meat was condemned, butchers told the press that decayed meat was no longer being processed, but decayed meat was still being cut and mixed with sound meat under Sarala's orders. Later they revealed that meat known to be decayed had occasionally been sold over the past three years.

Reindeer and Game Ltd. was a major player in the reindeer meat-packing industry. It decided to expand to take advantage of a supply bulge in reindeer even though its financial position was shaky. Things began to fall apart when the expansion was delayed and the supply of carcasses began to exceed processing capacity. Unfortunately, cold storage was not adequate to protect the oversupply of carcasses. The CEO was faced with the prospect of processing and selling decayed meat or destroying meat valued at more than the capitalization of the firm.

1. Who are the stakeholders in the case?
2. What priority rank do you give to each stakeholder?
3. Did Reindeer and Game Ltd. violate any ethical norms or principles?
4. What decision dimensions did Reindeer use in deciding to sell the contaminated meat?
5. What would you have done differently, given that you already own the contaminated meat? (Remember all your stakeholders.)
6. What is the root cause of Reindeer's problems? How would you avoid this dilemma?

Sources: Minna Halme and Juha Nasi, "Stakeholder Pressure against Immoral Management: A Case Study of a Company's Destruction," International Association for

Business & Society. *1992 Proceedings,* Sandra A. Waddock, ed., 3rd Annual Conference, Leuven, Belgium, June 13–20, 1992, pp. 276–284; Minna Halme and Juha Nasi, "Stakeholder Pressure against Immoral Management: A Case Study of a Company's Destruction," *Business and Society in a Changing World,* Dean C. Ludwig, ed., Lewiston, NY: The Edwin Mellen Press (1993), pp. 77–99.

Case 17

Tateho Chemical Industries Ltd.

Tateho Chemical Industries Ltd. is a Japanese industrial chemicals manufacturer. Its major products are electro-fused magnesia, calcia, and zilconia. It also produces magnesium chemical products. The firm's primary customers are Japanese steel companies. Tateho has been quite successful, benefiting from the good fortunes of the steel companies.

Business activity tends to ebb and flow over time. Fluctuations result from changes in demand that at times are caused by price shifts due to changes in currency values. In the mid-1980s, the Japanese yen (¥) began to appreciate. Its rise caused a significant drop in earnings for Japanese industrial companies as Japanese exports became more expensive. The increase in steel prices significantly dampened overseas demand. As a result, the steel companies sharply curtailed orders placed with Tateho Chemical. They also applied strong pressure to reduce profit margins for the orders that were awarded.

To offset decreased earnings, many Japanese companies began to practice *zaitech,* or financial engineering. This consists of replacing earnings from selling products with earnings from speculating in the financial markets. As sales of chemical products declined, Tateho Chemical turned to *zaitech* to maintain net profits at around ¥950 million. This worked fine as long as the markets in Tokyo continued to climb.

In the fiscal year ending March 31, 1985, Tateho's operating profit was ¥100 billion. By March 31, 1987, its operating income had dropped to ¥186 million. To offset this loss, Tateho relied on *zaitech* to bolster its sagging profits. In fiscal year 1987, 82 percent of Tateho's profits were from *zaitech,* with the remainder coming from product sales. During the spring of 1987, Tateho invested heavily in the Tokyo futures cash market for Japanese government bonds. At least ¥100 billion was committed when the bonds were yielding approximately 2½ percent. As the market started to collapse in late May, Tateho tried to recover by buying bond futures, a highly speculative maneuver. By the beginning of August, bond yields had risen to 5 percent.

Hanshin Sogo Bank of Osaka was a major credit source for Tateho. Hanshin also owned a large block of Tateho stock. On September 2, 1987, Hanshin decided to sell its large holding of Tateho Chemical's stock. The stock price at the end of August was ¥1840 per share. On September 3,

1987, Tateho announced publicly that it had incurred losses of about ¥20 billion on its ¥100 billion investment in the cash futures market. The company's net worth was ¥17 billion at the time. Tateho had previously informed Hanshin of its loss, and Hanshin's sale was perfectly legal. Tateho's stock price plummeted. By the end of September, its stock was selling at ¥577 per share.

1. Who are the stakeholders in the case?
2. What priority rank do you give to each stakeholder?
3. Who were the winners and who were the losers?
4. Were any ethical norms or principles violated by Hanshin Sogo Bank's sale of Tateho Chemical's stock prior to the public announcement of the loss?
5. What would have happened if Hanshin Sogo Bank were based in your country?
6. The sale was legal in Japan. Was it ethical?
7. Is this case an example of a micro social contract in which such a sale is ethical in Japan but perhaps not in your country?
8. What do you think would have happened if Tateho had not informed Hanshin of its loss prior to public announcement?

Sources: Barbara Buell, "Japan Writes a New Definition of *Zaitech:* 'Investor Beware,' " *Business Week* 3017 (September 21, 1987), p. 45; "Burnt by Bonds," *The Economist* 304 (September 5, 1987), p. 78; Lee A. Daniels, "Japanese Loss in Bonds Stirs Fear," *The New York Times* 136, 47251 (September 3, 1987), pp. D1, D5; Tetsuo Jimbo, "Japan's Inside-Trading 'Tradition' under Attack," *The Christian Science Monitor* 80, 202 (September 13, 1988), p. 12.

Case 18

WFI Corporation

Montserrat is a British-dependent island in the eastern Caribbean. During the 1980s, the British, eager to reduce their grant-in-aid payments, encouraged the island leaders to develop an offshore banking industry. The venture was launched by selling banking licenses for $10,000 each. Three hundred forty-one licenses were sold, providing many opportunities for banking with a minimum of regulation and a maximum of secrecy.

WFI Corporation, a bank charter wholesaler, purchased approximately 200 of the licenses. It then sold the banks to individuals for $20,000 to $30,000. The new banks were given names similar to well-known existing institutions, such as Chase Overseas Bank Ltd; Deutsche Bank Ltd; Fidelity Development Bank Ltd; Manufacturers Overseas Bank Ltd; Prudential Bank and Trust Ltd; and so on. WFI also purchased bank charters in the

Marshall Islands for $350 each that it then sold for $20,000 per charter. The purchaser of each bank received an impressive leather binder containing corporate memoranda, preprinted certificates of deposit, and letters of credit.

Jerome N. Schneider, president of WFI, claimed that his company carefully checked out potential buyers. It obtained references from banks, lawyers, or CPAs. Credit checks were made and personal data were collected using individual questionnaires. However, after a bank was sold, little or no further contact was maintained.

Bank purchasers included J. David Dominelli, who started J. David Banking as an intermediary for foreign-exchange currency transactions to funnel legitimate investment dollars into the United States. In fact, most of the money handled by J. David Banking was funneled into Dominelli's pocket, resulting in investors being bilked out of $80 million. A California chiropractor used two of the offshore banks to try to sell phony certificates of deposit to residents of the state of Oregon. Another bank charged eight people nearly $450,000 in loan-origination fees for more than $55 million in loans that were never made. One of the victims, a Chicago union official, invested his life savings, hoping that his union could use the loan to buy the failing railroad that employed its members.

WFI used sales seminars as its primary marketing tool. Promotional literature read: "Owning your own Private International Bank may enable you to obtain hard-to-get loans, privileged credit information, free product samples, and access to political leaders and other VIPs!" Up to 300 people paid $385 apiece to attend a seminar. A postseminar cocktail party where individual interests could be discussed was held for promising candidates. The sales agreement buyers signed cautioned them to seek professional advice from an attorney or certified public accountant before doing business in the United States or elsewhere.

WFI purchased a number of corporate registrations in Grenada with the word *bank* in their names. It sold the corporations as offshore financial institutions, although Grenada officials claimed that they had not registered any legitimate offshore banking operations on the island. Daisy Johnson Butler used one of the registrations, the Grenada European Overseas Bank Ltd., to bilk nearly $1 million in up-front fees for fraudulent loans. As with most of the other Grenada banks, hers was a shell company with no assets and no valid banking license.

While large banks and some large corporations and investment houses have legitimate uses for offshore banks, individuals who purchase offshore banks frequently use them for money laundering, investment scams, tax evasion, and other illegal activities. However, WFI's operations have been entirely legal according to British and U.S. authorities.

1. Who are the stakeholders in the case?
2. What priority rank do you give to each stakeholder?

3. Who were the winners and who were the losers?

4. Did WFI violate any ethical norms or principles by selling the offshore banks?

5. Does the large difference between the price WFI paid for the corporations and what it sold them for have any ethical implications?

6. Do you believe WFI knew what the banks would be used for when it sold them? If so, does this alter the moral responsibility of WFI?

7. Were the seminars designed to draw clients with motives that were ethically questionable?

8. What moral responsibility does a company have for the way customers use its products?

9. WFI's actions were legal. Were they moral?

Sources: James Bates, "Company That Set Up Offshore Banks to Fold," *The Los Angeles Times* 111 (December 4, 1991), p. D2; Gail DeGeorge, "PSST, Wanna Buy a Bank? How about a Few Dozen?" *Business Week* 3232 (September 23, 1991), pp. 88–89; Douglas Frantz, "Island Bank King Profits as Industry Faces Scrutiny," *The Los Angeles Times* 108, Section 4 (April 16, 1989), p. 1; "Oh, My Brass Plate in the Sun," *The Economist* 318, 7698 (March 16, 1991), p. 84.

Case 19

WorldCom's Creative Accounting

In 1996 Betty Vinson landed a mid-level accounting position at WorldCom, a small long-distance telephone company in Jackson, Mississippi. During the next few years, the company grew very rapidly via acquisitions of companies such as Brooks Fiber, a high-speed telecom services company; MCI, the number-two long-distance carrier; Skytel, a leading paging firm; and UUNet, a major owner of Internet backbone. Two years after joining WorldCom, Vinson was promoted to a senior manager in the firm's corporate accounting division reporting to Buford Yates, Director of General Accounting. She and her staff of 10 compiled quarterly reports and analyzed company operating expenses and loss reserves. The reserves were set aside to cover specific kinds of expenses.

WorldCom's profits grew rapidly until the middle of 2000 when the telecommunications industry entered a protracted slump. The company's line costs, lease fees paid to other telephone companies to use portions of their networks, began to increase as a percentage of the firm's revenue. This ratio was closely watched by Wall Street as an indicator of the firm's health. The company's CEO, Bernard Ebbers, and CFO, Scott Sullivan, warned Wall Street that earnings for the second half of the year would fall below expectations. During the third quarter, due to the failure of some of its small customers, WorldCom was saddled with $685 million in unpaid bills.

Vinson, Yates, and Troy Normand, the accountant in charge of monitoring the firm's fixed expenses, searched for ways to cover the shortfall in preparation of the release of the third quarter report. They were able to locate $50 million that could be applied to the unpaid bills, but that was a far cry from $685 million. In October Yates met with Vinson and Normand and told them that Sullivan and David Myers, the firm's controller, directed him to take $828 million out of the reserve account designated to cover line costs and other items for the telecommunications unit and use it to cover other expenses. That would reduce reported expenses and increase earnings.

Vinson, Normand, and Yates were concerned that the adjustment was not an approved accounting transaction. Accounting rules state that reserves can be established only if there is an expectation that a loss will occur in the unit where the reserve is established. The reserve can be depleted only if there is a good business reason for doing so. Because no business reason existed for dipping into the reserve account, Vinson and Normand told Yates that doing so was not following good accounting practices. Yates replied that he was not pleased with the action, but he was assured that this was a one-time transaction and would never happen again; thus, he had agreed to go along with the transfer. On that basis Vinson and Normand agreed to make the transfer.

The company's third-quarter results were reported on October 26. On that day, Vinson told Yates that she was planning to resign. Normand expressed similar inclinations. Ebbers got wind of the unrest in the accounting department and told Myers that the accountants would never again be placed in such an untenable position. Myers and Sullivan met with Vinson and Normand several days later. Sullivan explained that he was working on the firm's financial problems. He appealed to them to stay until he was able to get things under control and then they could leave if they wanted to, but he needed them to right the ship.

Normand stated that he was concerned that he would be held liable for making the accounting changes. Sullivan told the two that nothing they had done was illegal and that he would assume all responsibility for their actions. He further stated that the profit projections for the coming quarter had been cut in half and an accounting manipulation would not be needed. Following the meeting, Vinson's resolve to find another position weakened. She told her husband about the meeting and her concerns over the accounting irregularities, and he urged her to quit. But she was the chief breadwinner of the family earning more than her husband's $40,000 a year, and her job provided the family health insurance. She was also worried about finding a new position because she was a middle-aged woman.

Vinson rationalized that because Sullivan was considered one of the top CFOs in the country and had approved the transaction, it must be all right. After talking with Normand about how difficult it would be to find another job, both decided to stay. During the first quarter of 2001, things got worse. There were no reserves to tap and the funds gap was $771 million. Sullivan ordered that the amount of line costs be transferred from an operating expense account to a capital expense account. That moved them from a direct expense against income to a depreciatable expense, thus increasing short-term "profitability." Vinson was shocked with this directive. She knew that line costs were operating costs that could not legally be counted as a capital expense.

In fact, Yates had balked at the plan when Myers had told him about it, and Myers had told Sullivan that the transfer could not be justified when he was given the order. However, Sullivan told Myers that the transfer was WorldCom's only way out of its financial troubles. Vinson felt trapped. The threat to resign had already been used and she was afraid to quit her job before she had another one. Vinson, Normand, and Yates met to discuss the order but did not resolve the issue. Vinson decided to update her résumé and begin looking for another job.

Vinson, Normand, and Yates finally went along with the order to transfer the expenses. To do so, they had to decide which of five capital expense accounts to transfer the expenses to. Meyers met with them during this process and they all expressed how unhappy they were with the transaction. But they felt they had to do it to save the company. Vinson executed the entries to transfer the $771 million, changing dates of numerous transactions in the computer. The same process took place during the following three quarters: $560 million for the second quarter, $743 million for the third quarter, and $941 million for the fourth quarter. Early the next year, Vinson was promoted from senior manager to Director of Management Reporting, and Normand was promoted to Director of Legal Entity Accounting.

1. Who are the stakeholders in the case?
2. What priority rank do you give to each stakeholder?
3. Were any ethical principles or norms violated? If so, by whom?
4. Should Vinson have refused to release the reserves?
5. Should Vinson have refused to transfer the expenses?
6. What actions should Vinson have taken and when? What prevented her from taking such actions?
7. What actions should Vinson's colleagues have taken?
8. Who is ultimately responsible for the accounting irregularities?
9. Who is legally responsible for the irregularities?
10. Who is morally responsible for the irregularities?

Sources: Michael E. Kanell, "Ebbers Building a WorldCom Empire Fearless: CEO Not Expected to Let Up on Acquisitions, A Key to Firm's Stunning Success," *The Atlanta Journal-Constitution,* (May 21, 2000), p. G1; Susan Pulliam, "A Staffer Ordered to Commit Fraud Balked, Then Caved," *The Wall Street Journal* 141, 121 (June 23, 2003), pp. A1, A6; *Securities and Exchange Commission* v. *Betty L. Vinson and Troy M. Normand,* 02 CV 8083 (JSR) Complaint (Securities Fraud). United States District Court for the Southern District of New York.

Case 20

Zurich Insurance Company

Zurich Insurance Company, based in Toronto, Canada, is the country's fifth largest auto insurer. Zurich's insurance premiums are based on the industry standard rate classification system used by all auto insurance companies in the country. The rate classification system places individuals under 25 into a higher risk category than those over 25. Males under 25 are placed in a still higher risk category. Higher yet are unmarried males under 25.

In 1983, Michael Bates of Islington, Ontario, applied for auto insurance with Zurich. He was quoted a rate of $1,002 per year to insure his 1976 Chevrolet Camaro. A woman claiming to be his twin sister who possessed a similar driving record was quoted a rate of $522. The difference was justified on the basis that Michael Bates was in a much higher risk category than his "sister." Bates was not satisfied with that explanation and decided to appeal the issue in court.

Zurich argued that the rates were based on statistical experience with drivers in both categories. The higher rate for unmarried adult males under 25 was necessary to cover the higher losses that had to be paid for that group. In 1979, the Insurance Bureau of Canada estimated that eliminating the age classification would result in 84 percent of the driving public paying 12 percent more for insurance. Herb Phillips, chief actuary for the Insurers Advisory Organization of Canada, the advisory body for insurance ratings, has argued that doing away with age, sex, and marital classifications would actually result in unfair discrimination.

On the other hand, Bates argued that his rate should be based on his driving record. It is unfair simply to classify him as part of a large group and set rates accordingly. His rate should be set according to his own individual performance.

1. Who are the stakeholders in the case?
2. What priority rank do you give to each stakeholder?
3. Has Zurich Insurance Company violated any ethical norms or principles?
4. What is the basic rationale for insurance?
5. What decision dimensions may have been used in establishing the insurance rating system?
6. If you were making the decision, what type of rating system would you devise?

Sources: Gordon S. Findlay, "A Landmark Decision on Discrimination," *Best's Review: Property/Casualty Insurance Edition* 86, 6 (October 1985), pp. 116–117.

Acknowledgments

Page 6, Figure 1.1, Courtesy of Sears, Roebuck and Co.

Page 33, Figure 2.2, Reprinted with permission of Intel Corporation.

Page 75, Figure 4.4, The Boeing Company.

Page 130, Figure 7.1, Johnson & Johnson.

Page 139, Figure 7.2, Courtesy of Volvo.

Page 167–168, Figure C5.1, Reprinted with permission of Chrysler Corp.

Index